DreamMakers

To Vivienne

May all your
beautiful Dreams
come true!

Michele Hunt
Sept 23, 1999

DreamMakers

Putting Vision and Values to Work

Michele Hunt

Davies-Black Publishing
Palo Alto, California

Published by Davies-Black Publishing, an imprint of Consulting
Psychologists Press, Inc., 3803 East Bayshore Road, Palo Alto, CA
94303; 800-624-1765.

Special discounts on bulk quantities of Davies-Black books are
available to corporations, professional associations, and other
organizations. For details, contact the Director of Book Sales at
Davies-Black Publishing, an imprint of Consulting Psychologists Press, Inc., 3803 East Bayshore Road, Palo Alto, CA 94303;
650-691-9123; Fax 650-988-0673.

02 01 00 99 98   10 9 8 7 6 5 4 3 2
Printed in the United States of America

Library of Congress Cataloging-in-Publication Data
Hunt, Michele
    DreamMakers: putting vision and values to work /
Michele Hunt.—1st ed.
       p.   cm.
    Includes bibliographical references.
    ISBN 0-89106-108-8
    1. Social values—United States.   2. Social problems—
United States.   3. Community leadership—United
States.   4. Community power—United States.   5. United
States— Social conditions—1980–
I. Title.
HN59.2.H86 1998
303.3′72—dc21
                                                    97–46350
                                                    CIP

FIRST EDITION
First printing 1998

To Nicole Hunt Levey

This book is dedicated to my daughter,
my greatest teacher and closest friend.
Thank you for your love and patience, and for giving me
the time and space for DreamMakers.

CONTENTS

FOREWORD

"They closed the jail several years ago."

How could one fail to read the rest of the story? Over and over in *DreamMakers,* I read the stories our families and students and children yearn to hear. Stories we hope that our leaders will take seriously. Stories of people who have defined and created for themselves an ethical space within which they have reached toward their potential and produced amazing results. One of the folks who closed the jail in Surry County, Virginia, says, "I think if there is one sentiment that comes out of our experiences, it is the fact that people are your treasure." What a wonderful prospect to think of working alongside a person like that!

In another of this book's powerful stories, Rita Cleary says that she has committed herself to the work of "opening hearts in our world." Such a commitment makes me want our adult grandchildren to look her up and apply for a job.

DreamMakers is not about theory but about achievement—in many cases, amazing achievement. It's not about the success of ego but about serving others—not so much about reaching goals as about approaching potential.

Stories about people tell us both who we are and who we might become. Stories map the paths toward potential and unity. The stories in *DreamMakers* are honest, real stories. Not everything works. Not everything is easy. Ann Denison writes, "We had to call the police, and they arrested him." Leadership and service are demanding.

The people in these stories are not embarrassed to tell us what they believe and how they arrived at those beliefs. If you sometimes feel hopeless, read Sharlonda Gillis's story. If you sometimes despair about our children's education, listen to the school board member who says, "I don't like to hire teachers who don't want a kid to touch them." If you wonder at the selfishness and greed in the corporate world, think about the courage of a company whose leaders say in this book, "We wish to become one of the best companies in the world, by any measure." I would like to spend an evening talking to people like these.

As you read this book, some of these people sound like heroes. If they are, they became so not by holding up hero status as a goal, but by trying hard to become the right person and do the right thing. They have learned the distinction between goals and results. They understand that service to a common good can move people and organizations and communities beyond mundane success.

These stories teach us that our future lies not so much in technology, although that is important, as in discovering who we intend to be. In many of their lives, they demonstrate even a reckless antithesis to the selfish individualism, so common these days, that promises so much and delivers so little. As you will see, this book is about hope, filled with credible promises, a real innovation in a society clobbered by empty ones. The promises in *DreamMakers* are based on results, not on theories and polls. This book is about hope because it teaches us that all people, when given the right support and environment, are extraordinary. There is real power in a group that owns a shared vision. There is real power in the understanding that we are all connected and interdependent.

Michele Hunt introduces us to people of serious breadth, people from many disciplines with a variety of pursuits and strong commitments. They take moral purpose seriously. They speak about the contemporary scourge of materialism. They show us that decent behavior is rooted in good values, and they become models for parents, children, communities, and organizations. They become our teachers. They have taught me a great deal.

Max De Pree
Author of *Leadership Is an Art,* and
former chairman and CEO of Herman Miller, Inc.

DreamMakers are people who make dreams happen. They have the deep insight and long foresight necessary to perceive the consequences their actions will have. The ability to see our actions in relationship to others and to collaboratively transform ourselves and others requires special people. DreamMakers perceive the myriad of connections both among and within individuals. They have the faith and courage to hold a positive vision for the future, and the heart to love and respect what it means to be human in a world that may increasingly appear to be broken. DreamMakers have the unique ability to energize others, to tap in to the seeming chaos of our lives and find the common yearnings for something better. They have the unique ability to help others give voice to their personal vision—and to then build a common vision based on truth, good faith, and hope. In short, Dream-Makers are the leaders who are putting vision and values to work in our businesses, our communities, and the world.

This book tells twelve different stories that could not have happened without the DreamMakers involved. These DreamMakers come from all sectors of society all over the world—corporations, local and national governments, nonprofit organizations, and voluntary community groups. They also come from different economic and social backgrounds. They come from different national, cultural, ethnic, and racial backgrounds. What they share, however, is far more powerful and important than how they differ. As we shall see, each and every one demonstrates a strong sense of connectedness, a deep and abiding respect for *all* human beings, and a belief in some higher power and purpose that transcends the corporate selfishness and individual materialism that have wracked our environment and our relationships with one another. In addition, they all demonstrate a strong commitment to and love of learning, faith in themselves, and the great gift of being able to hold on to bold visions while understanding and being able to articulate current reality. Finally, all have the courage to engage others in the formulation and quest of those visions.

I went on a journey to engage these DreamMakers in the creation of this book because I felt the sense of frustration, anxiety, and even fear most of us experience living in these times of deep and rapid change and transformation. We experience firsthand, and daily hear stories about, the pain and helplessness caused by the deterioration of and diminishing trust in those institutions that carried us in the past. Our workplaces, our educational institutions, our governments, our communities, and even our personal lives seem to be in chaos. However, DreamMakers have found ways to transform that chaos into opportunities. They are not blind optimists. Rather, they use their personal struggles and the realities of the world to fuel their passion to create new, healthier, and more nourishing organizations, communities, and lives.

This is a book about hope, intended for anyone who is seeking to create a better future. It is especially for those who choose to accept leadership roles, who sense on an intuitive level that we are living in an unprecedented time in which to make a difference, and who are looking for inspiration, insights, and ideas to reshape our institutions, communities, and lives. The people I call DreamMakers are not those we read about in the headlines every day. They are not necessarily, nor would they identify themselves as, heroines, heroes, or geniuses. They have, however, discovered and tapped in to the extraordinary nature and power we all have within us. It is my hope that, from hearing these personal stories, others may discover that ability as well.

How did I find these DreamMakers? As I began sharing my idea for this book with friends and colleagues, a wonderful, almost magical thing happened: Everyone could describe a DreamMaker they knew or had heard of. They began to send me in directions I hadn't guessed at. I had assumed that the leaders I was looking for would come primarily from business—perhaps because that is where the bulk of my own experience lies. But I should have known better. I kept hearing about extraordinary leaders—in all sectors of our lives. And so this book is divided into the three main categories that emerged as I pursued interviews in Norway, Michigan, Virginia, Aruba, Maryland, California, and Massachusetts.

Chapter 1 tells more about my own perspective and the theories underlying this book. Having served as deputy warden of a state prison for male offenders, I had seen firsthand the results of a world that is broken and sadly in need of vision-led and values-based leadership. I had risen through the ranks of a reputable midwestern manufacturing firm, Herman Miller, Inc., where I drew strength and wisdom from my mentor, Max De Pree, and from the many wonderful people both inside and outside the company with whom I was fortunate to connect. I had seen, again firsthand, how a corporate entity could create a different paradigm for how it defined its community and its responsibilities toward that community. I also saw the dark side of business, and I pondered how it could be avoided. Finally, having served as director of the Federal Quality Institute under Vice President Al Gore, I had experienced the ravages of chaos in our government under the best-intentioned people. I have been searching throughout my career, through all these different situations, for the qualities that will make it all better. Perhaps we can never make it *all* better. But I have found enough good hearts, good intent, and good action out there to convince me that we have within us the capacity to make a lot of it better indeed.

Chapters 2 through 5 are grouped into the category "DreamMakers at Work." These chapters tell the stories of the following individuals:

- Ernst Volgenau, William (Bill) Brehm, Ted Legasey, Gary Nelson, and Ann Denison of SRA International, Inc., a small, dynamic high-tech firm in Washington, D.C.

- Gary and Janet Smith of The Ivy Planning Group

- Tormod Bjørk of Hydro Aluminum, in Norway

- David Cole, former president of Internet Services at America Online and chairman of Aquaterra

Each of these DreamMakers describes doing business in the world in a way that expresses responsibility to that world beyond quarterly earnings.

Chapters 6 through 9 are grouped into the category "DreamMakers Building Communities." These chapters tell the stories of the following individuals:

- Sharlonda Gillis, executive director for youth development program at the Warren Connor Development Coalition

- Marilyn King, founder of Beyond Sports

- Terry Lewis, Dr. C. P. Penn, Walter Hardy, and Thomas Hardy, all community leaders from Surry County, Virginia

- Juliet Chieuw and Joyce Bartels-Daal of the Aruba Quality Foundation

Each of these DreamMakers describes the powerful forces for change accessible through shared vision and values.

Chapters 10 through 13, grouped into the category "DreamMakers for a Better World," tell the stories of the following individuals:

- Joe Brodecki, executive director of the Campaign to Remember for the United States Holocaust Memorial Museum

- Michael Lane, deputy director of the U.S. Customs Service

- John Abbott, Education 2000

- Rita Cleary, president of Visions of a Better World Foundation

Each of these DreamMakers describes the deep sources of courage and hope that can turn the tide of world pain toward healing and inclusiveness.

Finally, Chapter 14 tells my own story in greater detail, my struggles and learnings, and offers my own vision for a better world—and ideas for how we just might get there.

ACKNOWLEDGMENTS

Thank you to my dear friends Liz Horton Strother, Bob Buda, Gerhart Blendsthrup, and Julie Reis. I truly appreciate our late-night conversations, your words of encouragement, your constructive criticism, and, most of all, your love and support.

To my editors and good friends Clark Malcolm and Linda McFadden: your contribution was a true gift.

And a very special thank you to Max De Pree, my mentor and dear friend. I hope you know how much I cherish and respect you for seeing and sensing my potential, trusting my competence and commitment, challenging me to stretch and grow, and hanging in there through my mistakes and learnings.

The last chapter of this book, "A Personal Reflection," is a tribute to my family. Thank you *all* for being who you are. The diversity, debates, and controversy, combined with the love, intimacy, and your incredible commitment to family and community, have given me the ingredients for *DreamMakers*.

Michele Hunt is the founder of Vision & Values, a firm based in Washington, D.C., where she and her colleagues serve as change catalysts, partnering with leadership teams in the transformation and renewal of people and organizations seeking to move to a new level of participation and performance. Her focus is on vision, values, and the alignment of organizational strategies, processes, and systems. She works with leaders of organizations to unleash the collective gifts and energy of their human resources. Her clients have included Hewlett-Packard, Mobil Oil, SRA International, the U.S. Food and Drug Administration, the Episcopal Divinity School at Harvard University, St. Agnus Hospital, the National Council of Teachers of English, the National Council of Negro Women, the nation of Aruba, BHP of Australia, the John Fetzer Institute, Swiss Reinsurance, Motorola, and the Boeing Company.

In June of 1993, President Bill Clinton appointed Michele to serve as executive director of the Federal Quality Institute, with a mandate to help seed the reinvention of government. Until June of 1995 she led the institute, working with Vice President Al Gore and the cabinet leadership teams on this important initiative. She brought the best thinking and practices to this effort through public-private partnerships with world-recognized leaders and organizations, including Peter Drucker, John Gardner, Max De Pree, Peter Senge, Meg Wheatley, GE, Herman Miller, Inc., Ford, Corning, and the Brookings Institution. Her primary "clients" were the U.S. Department of Education, NASA, the U.S. Department of Energy, the Export-Import Bank, and the U.S. Customs Service.

Prior to this appointment, Michele spent thirteen years with Herman Miller, Inc., a global office furniture company. As vice president for people and quality, she guided the company's organizational renewal, participative management process, human resources, and quality management initiatives. She also partnered with Petrer Senge's Organizatiional Learning Research Center at MIT in creating a learning organization at Herman Miller. Her service contributed to Herman Miller's recognition by *Fortune* magazine as one of the most admired companies in America, one of the best for women, and one of the best for which to work.

After earning her bachelor's and master's degrees in sociology from Eastern Michigan University and the University of Detroit, respectively, Michele began her career with the Michigan Department of Corrections. She was the first female probation officer to supervise adult male felons on probation in Detroit, and she later became the first female deputy warden over treatment programs in a men's prison in the state of Michigan.

Michele serves on the boards of the Society for Organizational Learning chaired by Peter Senge, the ServiceMaster Company, the Foundation for Enterprise Development, Visions of a Better World Foundation, the Studio Theater, and the Detroit-Windsor Dance Academy, and she is a member of the Society of Fellows and a facilitator for corporate programs at the Aspen Institute. An active keynote speaker and panel participant, she has worked with the following programs and groups:

- The United Nations' Vision for a Better World Dialogue

- President Clinton's Workplace for the Future

- The Conference Board's CEO Conference and Conference on Healthy Companies

- The Aspen Institute's executive seminars

- NASA's top management team

- AT&T Top 200 Managers

- The NAPA Academy

- Hewlett-Packard's 2800 Executive and Professional Women's Conference

- New York State Governor's Conference on Quality Management

- Mobil Oil's Learning Organization conference

- AT&T and Cellular One's Learning Organization program

- Secretary of Defense William Perry's Forum on Strategic Human Resources

LEADING AND LIVING ON PURPOSE

The Power of Vision and Values

Now more than ever we need to imagine our future, to see the world we want to create. This is what I call *visioning*. The sea of change we are all living in also calls us to ask some crucial questions: "What's important? What values do we need to embrace and build into our future? What kinds of organizations, institutions, communities, and lives do we want to create together?" People are struggling with these questions in all sectors of life: in our families, work, communities, and governments. Moreover, there seems to be a growing desire or need to live *on purpose*—to be deliberate about how we shape and live in our organizations and communities. A whole new level of accountability and responsibility is therefore required as we approach the new millennium.

Compelling Reasons for Change

When I was growing up in the 1950s and 1960s, I thought that everything had already been discovered or invented. I used to marvel and wonder about what it must have been like to be a pioneer—a great inventor, a great discoverer, a great explorer. Much to my surprise, I'm finding out—not by sailing into space or trekking into the wilderness, but simply by participating in and witnessing the world today as it transforms itself into something it has never been before.

1

Leadership guru Peter Drucker describes our era in his book *Post-Capitalist Society* as "The Great Divide." "Every few hundred years in Western history," he writes,

> there occurs a sharp transformation. We cross a divide. Within a few short decades, society rearranges itself; its basic views; its social and political structure; its arts; its key institutions. Fifty years later, there is a new world. And people born then cannot even imagine the world in which their grandparents lived, and into which their own parents were born. We are currently living through such a transformation.

With the acceleration of change and the explosion of technological innovations, I believe not only that our children will experience a whole new world, but that we ourselves are seeing this new world unfold before our very eyes. *How* the world unfolds will depend on how we see and think about that world; and the decisions we make now are powerfully shaping our future.

Anthropologist George Land describes our era as a "breakpoint" in his book *Breakpoint and Beyond.* Like many futurists, he believes that we're in the midst of unprecedented change and that we're going through a fundamental shift in our world. Charles Handy, business author, believes change today is so all-encompassing that he calls it "discontinuous" change that requires "upside-down thinking."

Change has become so rapid, so unpredictable, and so pervasive that many of the systems, processes, structures, policies, and behaviors of the past aren't serving us today. Every major institution is going through deep and fundamental change. We constantly hear words like "reinventing," "renewing," "changing," and "transforming." No organization, community, institution, or person can avoid having to grapple in some way with change.

Breakthroughs in science, medicine, and information technology, the new physics, and the latest brain research—all are challenging the basic assumptions by which we've built our organizations and societies. These innovations and discoveries require us to rethink how we live, how we work, how we learn, and how we grow. Something deeper is also happening—a rippling awakening across our world of our sense of spirit, and a growing desire to bring that spirit alive in our work, communities, and personal lives.

A friend of mine has described our times thusly: "It's like the past has relinquished its hold on the future." Indeed, there are no easy answers, no blueprints, no prescriptions, no gurus or great leaders to save us. We have to learn how to be in this new world together.

What Is Changing?

Organizational Life

In our institutions and organizations, no longer are the hierarchies, the internal systems and processes, the routines, and habits sufficient to sustain the individuals they employ and are meant to serve.

W. Edwards Deming, a quality leader and teacher, often claimed that "our organizations destroy people." Recently I found confirmation of that opinion from an unlikely source. On "Take Your Daughter to Work Day," I took my fifteen-year-old daughter, Nicole, into a traditional workplace, believing my home office was not representative of a real work environment. After spending about an hour there, Nicole asked as we left, "Mom, isn't going in there every day hazardous to the health of those people?"

If we take an honest look at our organizations, we see that they were built to control. They mirror what was believed and may have been appropriate for the industrial era we are rapidly leaving behind us, based on the scientific method of management proposed by Frederick Taylor *at the turn of the century!* They were not designed to support autonomy, rapid and effective decision making at the time and place where decisions are needed. They were not designed to enable people to grow and contribute, to foster creativity. Instead, they compartmentalize us and put us into boxes; they *restrict* our creativity. Organizations aren't fun; some are even unbearable.

Most of our organizations to this day are designed so that people serve structures, rather than structures serving people in their quest to create something meaningful together. Most institutions and organizations simply don't nourish very many sides of human beings. I've often been struck by the fact that we expect people to leave most of ourselves, all that makes us human, at home. Inside the workplace, we aren't supposed to show strong emotions—anger, tears, or even laughter. We shouldn't be surprised when we aren't able to do this very well, but that we can do it at all!

One day I was walking through the halls of the U.S. Office of Personnel Management, the human resource function for the federal government.

I love to laugh, and as I laughed at a comment a colleague made, a federal worker said to me, "That's not professional." I have thought about this remark often, and about the environment we've created where we expect people to be all that they can be and contribute their gifts, yet where, at the same time, laughter is considered unprofessional or inappropriate.

Not only do we need to rethink our organizational policies, structures, designs, and systems, but we need to examine our beliefs and basic assumptions about how people learn, work, and grow. Most employees, families, and communities are experiencing the stress and fear of losing jobs, or the more insidious fear that our "bosses" don't support or care about us. Many people are frustrated by an inability to grow and develop at work, and to contribute their gifts to the fullest. The greatest disappointment, however, may be that most organizations don't *engage* their people; they don't help them find meaning and purpose in their work. A corporate officer once said to me, "If God had a nonessential list, my company would be the first to be laid off." Too many of us feel this way about the companies we work for.

Our Communities

There are mammoth changes coming to our communities as well. For a variety of "big" reasons—the environment, the interconnectedness of the world's economies, a growing gap between the haves and the have-nots, and ongoing racial and ethnic tensions across neighborhoods and across nations—no one person, community, organization, or institution can function in isolation. Businesses, schools, governments, and community organizations are all connected by the same people and families; each one is part of a larger system of interdependencies. The shifting and growing population, the advances in information and communications technology, the increased mobility of people, and the rise in global corporations and organizations are all bringing the world closer together and weaving a web of interconnection and interdependence that challenges the old norms and boundaries placed by governments and nationalism. To witness how dramatic and real these changes are, one need only visit some of the growing number of "online communities." A recent online "conference" called CivicNet, held in June of 1996 to explore the effective creation of community networks, drew 350 participants from over fifteen countries around the world. There are now "virtual communities," "communities of interest," and "communities of practice" in addition to our traditional communities of place.

Letting Go

Our times are more revolutionary than the close of the eighteenth century or the middle of the nineteenth. The difference is that today the great transformations of thought are realized not through war and insurrection but through the determined actions of DreamMakers, a group whose quiet activism is described in the chapters you are about to read.

It's hard to let go of the past. In fact, to create our future we need to learn from our past. In this era where every institution is "reinventing" itself, we must certainly take the time to examine and inquire about what has worked, what needs to change, and what needs to be abandoned. Only then can we decide what we truly want our institutions and communities to be and do.

So now is the most important time for us to listen to different stories, different ways of organizing work and communities. Most people alive today feel the fundamental transformation our world is undergoing. As Albert Einstein put it, "We must learn to see the world anew." And as author Meg Wheatly says, "To be responsible inventors and discoverers, we need the courage to let go of the old world."

A friend, Debra Jones, told me a wonderful story told to her by a Hoopoe Indian elder. The Hoopoes and many native peoples across the globe have "tribal stories" and metaphors to help explain our times, which they call "the Quickening," referring to the pace and depth of change we are all experiencing. The metaphor the Hoopoes use is a river moving swiftly down a mountain: We are swept up in the current. Many of us panic and try to hold on to the side of the bank or a rock. But by holding on we are bruised and battered by the current and debris in the river. However, when we learn to let go and move with the natural flow of the river, we float buoyantly along, discovering new and wonderful sights, sounds, and experiences.

But letting go isn't easy. The confusion and ambiguity that accompany deep change is spawning anxiety, fear, and even a sense of helplessness and hopelessness. That's why I believe that having a vision of what we want in the future and clarifying our values are so important. Our vision and values become our guide to an otherwise uncharted frontier: They show us the way the future can be created.

The Power of Shared Vision

Marjorie Parker has a beautiful description of vision in her book *Creating Shared Vision:*

> Visions are powerful mental images of what you want to create in the future. They reflect what we care about most, and are harmonious with our values and sense of purpose....

> They are a product of our collective heads and hearts. Vision, although it is our desired future, is experienced in the present. It integrates the individual's and organization's mission, values, and uniqueness. It integrates and aligns the cultural and business environments.

> A vision is our deepest expression of what we want to create together.

I believe vision fuels our passion and lifts us above our fear. It is our North Star for exploring and charting our future.

Organizations and communities that will thrive in the twenty-first century understand and are consciously, deliberately, and with a sense of urgency redesigning, realigning, and reinventing themselves to be more natural, nurturing, inclusive, and enabling for human beings. They are engaging people in creating shared visions of preferred futures, and developing values that support diversity and honor the integrity of all people. They are creating learning environments that liberate people to bring all of who they are and can be to their work, and that encourage shared meaning around shared information as well as the discovery of new knowledge together.

Only by engaging the hearts and minds of people will organizations and communities—both local and global—be able to tap into the creativity of all their members to create a better quality of products, services, and life. The DreamMakers in this book understand this and have applied new and inclusive planning technologies and methodologies and new theories of learning to their work with their respective organizations, whether they are for profit or not.

Furthermore, organizational and community leaders who believe that people are extraordinary and fundamentally want to contribute and grow are those most able to help their organizations and communities build bridges to the future. They have been able to relinquish their old model of leadership, which required them—theoretically—to be all seeing, all knowing, and all powerful. In my work with leadership teams in businesses, organizations, and communities that accept these fundamental concepts, I see very exciting things happen—the stuff of which dreams are made.

For example, the ServiceMaster Company, a $3.5 billion global organization, has the courage to openly declare its corporate objectives as follows: "To Honor God in All We Do; To Develop People; To Pursue Excellence; To Grow Profitably." Everything they do is guided by this vision and these values. They understand it is all about people: employees, customers, shareholders, and communities. And despite the daunting prospect of high goals, they are committed to being leaders in the twenty-first century. They are providing the environment and "moral compass" that acknowledges the fundamental dignity of the people who serve us in our homes, hospitals, and schools, improving our grounds and serving us food. As a result, over the last twenty-five years, revenues have grown at a compounded rate of over 18 percent and net income has grown at a compounded rate of over 23 percent.

Another example: the John Fetzer Institute, a nonprofit foundation in Kalamazoo, Michigan, is a gift to our world. They have the courage to challenge our key health care and educational institutions to operate according to a holistic vision of mind, body, and spirit. This foundation has sparked the health care revolution that has resulted in the appreciation and involvement of the patient in the healing process. And they are helping to effect deep change in the teaching community by bringing their holistic values to education as well.

The DreamMakers in this book tell us of other communities of work and living that bear testimony to transformation that can be good for people, that can be uplifting, and that can inspire us to dare to hope for and work toward a better world.

Vision provides the direction and the impetus for change. From vision and values, we can change and align our structures, our processes, the rules and policies we make, our behaviors, our thinking, and our way of being with one another.

Our vision helps us negotiate the rough road. It helps us navigate through storms, troubles, and crises. It lifts us up, so that we aren't consumed by the day-to-day minutiae. It helps us and reminds us that we're living on purpose.

So vision also allows us to tap the power within us.

There are and have been many DreamMakers in the history of civilization: Nelson Mandela, Helen Keller, Jonas Salk, Steve Jobs, an inventor whose bettered inventions have changed our lives, a scientist whose quest has saved countless lives, a winning sports team, a high-performing nonprofit organization, a director who brings a great play to life, a musical group that stirs our souls. There are the DreamMakers in this book and the many more we will discover as the circle of dialogue grows. All of these DreamMakers have in common a red thread of beliefs, linked to and born from deeply held values and conviction. They also share an uncanny ability to make their vision real by engaging the hearts, minds, and gifts of others.

Shared Values of DreamMakers

Visionary leaders, or what I call DreamMakers, seem to share a mind-set or worldview. When you think of leaders who have made lives, organizations, and communities better, although they are highly diverse and unique in their own right, they also seem to embrace core values and perceptions—a way of looking at life that transcends time, culture, ethnic origins, geography, institutions, or circumstance.

How they see the world: DreamMakers share a sense of responsibility beyond their own lives. They take responsibility for the world they live in and are committed to making it better. They share a characteristic I call "practical optimism." Although they clearly perceive current reality and unflinchingly confront it, they have a deep faith that any challenge can be overcome. Their visions are large, deep, and unmuddled by cynicism.

How they treat people: DreamMakers share a deep faith in people, their capabilities and potential, and their basic goodness. Interpersonal relationships are precious to them and at the core of everything. They therefore lead their organizations with a reverence for all human relationships.

How they take in information: DreamMakers are multidimensional—deeply involved in and with their family, their community, the arts, and the environment as well as their work. They derive their knowledge and wisdom from all these sources, so their diverse experiences provide them with a rich array of choices and ideas.

How they make decisions: DreamMakers feel deeply about things. They trust their intuition. They see relationships and the consequences of various actions. They trust the knowledge and judgment of others. Their visions express emotion and compassion for people and ideas. They seem to make decisions with their hearts as well as their minds. And when their logic and their feelings are at odds, they trust their hearts more often than not.

How they build teams: DreamMakers understand that we are all flawed; nevertheless, they focus on people's talents and strengths. They build teams that fill in our weak spots, allowing us to focus on our strengths and allowing others to compliment us with theirs. They understand the value of collaboration and cooperation in accomplishing goals, getting superior results, and fulfilling our basic human desire for a sense of belonging.

How they use creativity: DreamMakers allow creativity to soar. They share a spirit of invention, believing that any breakthrough idea or product requires an environment that fosters diverse perspectives, experimentation, risk, and play.

How they act: DreamMakers are out of step with the norm, ahead of their time. They succeed not because they lead us to reconcile ourselves with reality but because they help us see we can change it. They share a sense of freedom—freedom to choose their own path—and an inability to accept conformity. As Joseph Campbell said, they "follow their bliss."

How they respond to "failure": DreamMakers are courageous and resilient. They have all faced tremendous challenges, made mistakes, and failed. They have also been able to learn from their failures and come back—quicker, stronger, and wiser. Indeed, they have used the lessons learned from mistakes and failure to fuel their visions.

How they learn and grow: DreamMakers have an insatiable appetite for new information and different perspectives. They look to everyone and every situation, diligently seeking new information and improved knowledge.

How they are anchored: DreamMakers all express their spirituality. They believe they are a part of something greater than themselves. Some call it God, some call it an "invisible wholeness," some refer to it as a "field of energy." Regardless of what they call it, they make decisions and take actions in light of their impact on the world.

Although the DreamMakers in this book are enormously different kinds of people in different organizations, cultures, and situations, strangely enough they share these values. I deeply believe that all people are extraordinary and capable of extraordinary accomplishments. Somehow, though, it takes a DreamMaker to help all of us living ordinary lives to find our extraordinary potential.

Lessons We Learned

DreamMakers express vision and values. They engage others in their vision. They work with others to build a shared vision.

DreamMakers understand that we are all connected and interdependent. They support diversity and honor the integrity and contributions of all people. They value and nurture interpersonal relationships. They tap in to the extraordinary potential in all of us.

DreamMakers question and challenge the status quo. They find unprecedented opportunities for transformation and renewal in the current climate of rapid change. They collaboratively transform and renew themselves and others. They make their dreams a reality.

DreamMakers focus on education and continual learning. They learn from their mistakes. They trust feelings, emotions, and intuition. They are both passionate and compassionate. They foster creativity and hope.

DreamMakers follow a moral compass. They believe in a higher power and purpose. They demonstrate responsibility toward a larger community. They are committed to making the world a better place.

The business leaders we meet here have chosen a different path than most of their peers. While many corporate managers are looking to reengineer, downsize, or outsource in response to challenge and change, these DreamMakers are focused on tapping all of the extraordinary capacities of human beings—their individual ability to envision new possibilities, their personal sense of *connectedness* and of what it means to be human, and their unique and collective powers of creativity and collaboration—to create preferred futures rather than accept the status quo.

CEO Ernst Volgenau's deep caring for human beings and inviolable sense of integrity seemed to propel him to create the kind of company we see in SRA International, Inc., and to enlist the leadership of William Brehm, Ted Legasey, Gary Nelson, and Ann Denison. They tell of shared experiences serving our country and how, out of that tradition, they emerged with strong convictions that they had a clear charter of service to others and to the nation. We hear Ann Denison, vice president for human resources, describe the need for and process of change as SRA experienced tremendous growth—change that honored the potential of every employee, when given appropriate support, to deal with a complex and demanding environment, develop new knowledge of capabilities, and make

Part 1

DREAMMAKERS
AT WORK

SRA INTERNATIONAL, INC.

GARY AND JANET SMITH
The Ivy Planning Group

TORMOD BJØRK
Hydro Aluminium

DAVID COLE
America Online

creative contributions to the client relationship. All these managers describe the tremendous challenges of operating a business committed to honesty, quality, and customer service, and getting good people and helping them fulfill themselves. It is perhaps this desire to help people fulfill their potential that the leaders of SRA share most pointedly with Janet and Gary Smith of The Ivy Planning Group. The leaders of SRA also share a sense of responsibility to something greater than themselves and, like David Cole, Tormod Bjørk, and the others in this book, have the ability to view themselves and their businesses holistically, as an integral partner with society and the environment.

Gary and Janet Smith founded The Ivy Planning Group when they hit the glass ceiling in corporate America. This African American couple decided to create a firm that draws its talents from others who have experienced similar frustrations. The Ivy Planning Group now consults with some of the leading companies in the world, competing with the Big Seven consulting firms and considered by their clients to be one of the best. The Smiths' achievements, like those of David Cole, would not have been possible had they not had a strong sense of personal empowerment, first tested in the corporate world of IBM and then successfully exercised in their own business, which is based on a very different kind of vision: "Our vision is to bring [people] who are traditionally underutilized into an environment that is professional, with a proven process for successful outcomes, with the right value system, to nurture personal and professional growth." The Smiths share the sense of wholeness in life and work demonstrated by all of the DreamMakers. Janet loves it "when a client meets me professionally, then sees me in my 'mom' role with my three boys, or ends up at the house when I'm making buffalo wings." And they know through personal success about the power of shared vision and values. As Janet would say, it is "real life. And it works."

From across the world, Tormod Bjørk tells the incredible story of building shared vision at Hydro Aluminum in Norway when the company was confronted with its own responsibility for a badly damaged environment. Hydro Aluminum is Europe's largest manufacturer of aluminum and the sixth largest in the world. In the late 1980s their largest plant, in Karmoy, Norway, was losing money and polluting the environment. It was unclean and unsafe, and quality and productivity were declining. Then they went on a visionary quest, galvanizing 17,000 people around a desire "to be better," using, of all things, a garden metaphor. Tormod describes his own journey in this process: his fears, the test of his values, and how much he himself learned. This man of deep integrity, who developed asthma because of the pollution in his own work environment, speaks openly of being afraid of being laughed at for devising the garden metaphor. Yet through his ultimate belief in the goodness and power of people to work together in community— a refrain we hear in so many of these stories—and through his own ability to "connect" with his workers, he was able to help Hydro Aluminum effect a complete turnaround, producing record-breaking improvements in productivity, safety, and environmental stewardship. We hear as well the often repeated theme of learning: At Hydro, continual learning became the norm.

David Cole's strongest values are an intuitive feel for the environment, acquired from his birthplace in Hawaii; a sense that justice is possible through people connecting with one another; and a deep appreciation for lasting relationships based on trust and integrity. His parents, his wife, his children, his business colleagues, and the Nature Conservancy have been his closest partners in creating a meaningful life in a broad definition of that phrase. We will hear in David's story themes that are echoed elsewhere in the book. He shares the sense of responsibility to our children we will see in Part Two, "DreamMakers Building Communities." And his sense of personal empowerment, the individual's ability to get things done that matter, is heard time and again in each of the stories that follow.

Each of the voices you will hear in this section tells a different story of what it means to practice business in a world that William Brehm fears is overly corrupted by materialism and selfishness. Those looking for a values-based model for how a business can function in the world will find it here, I believe. And that should give us all hope.

TED LEGASEY

is executive vice president and chief operating officer of SRA International, Inc., an information technology and professional services firm that designs, develops, and integrates information systems for business and government. He is a director of the Professional Services Council.

GARY NELSON

served as an economist with the Rand Corporation, the Institute for Defense Analyses, and the Congressional Budget Office before joining SRA. As SRA's vice chairman, he is responsible for corporate ventures and initiatives. Nelson is a charter member of the United States Senior Executive Service.

ERNST VOLGENAU

is founder, president, and CEO of SRA. He has thirty years of experience analyzing, designing, and developing large technological systems. During his twenty years as a U.S. Air Force officer, he developed space boosters and satellites, and conducted large-scale weapons system and command structure analyses.

WILLIAM BREHM

was vice president for corporate development at Dart Industries, and director of Computer Network Corporation. He is currently executive chairman of SRA, chairman of the board of trustees of Fuller Theological Seminary, a director of Herman Miller, Inc., and a trustee of the Center for Naval Analyses.

ANN DENISON

is vice president and director of human resources at SRA, where she oversees employee relations, compensation, and benefits; staffing and selection; training and development; and employee communications. Previously, she worked at American Management Systems in its Human Resource and Systems Center.

EXCELLENCE THROUGH SERVICE

SRA International, Inc.

William (Bill) Brehm served on the board of directors at Herman Miller, Inc., when I was vice president for people services and quality there in the late 1980s and early 1990s. I always knew him as a man of great integrity and was delighted when he invited me to help SRA through a renewal process meant to address their ongoing commitment to service and employees during a time of phenomenal growth. As I worked closely with Ann Denison, vice president for human resources, and came to know the SRA people and culture more intimately, I was struck by how different this company is from so many others I knew.

Rarely do corporate leaders have the courage and insight to aspire to be one of the best companies in the world, *by any measure.* Many leadership teams want their company or division to be the largest or the most profitable or the most innovative, but "by any measure" is a lofty goal. When I began working with the SRA leadership team in 1995, I wondered if they knew what they were getting into—if they would or could make the investment in people, time, resources, and leadership that it would take to achieve this goal.

Now, two years later, I have my answer. They have used their foundation to leap forward by just about every measure. They are aligning everything they do and how they do it around their vision and their core values. The five leaders in this interview accepted a responsibility for creating and maintaining a vision and enabling all of the people at SRA to help make it

15

a reality. They are following their own path with a belief in the potential, capabilities, and basic goodness of their people.

Let me introduce you to CEO Ernst Volgenau, chairman Bill Brehm, executive vice presidents Ted Legasey and Gary Nelson, and vice president for human resources Ann Denison.

Defining Moments

The Early Years

Ernst Volgenau: The genesis of SRA came around 1970 through an office in the Pentagon: the Office of the Assistant Secretary of Defense for Systems Analysis. In the early 1960s, Secretary of Defense Robert McNamara chose Dr. Alain Enthoven, an economist, to develop this office and recruit a bunch of very bright people, including my partner, Bill Brehm, and me, and many others—I'm not that bright, but he recruited a lot of bright people.

Remember how President Kennedy had this mission to bring the best and the brightest to government? McNamara was one of the best and the brightest, recruited around 1960. He had been a superstar at Ford Motor Company and before that had been an outstanding young officer working on analytical problems in World War II.

The Office for Systems Analysis grew out of the premise that there should be an analytical approach to tackling huge problems. The office had some very talented people, and several went on to form companies, some bigger and more successful than SRA. The Air Force had sent me to get a Ph.D. in electrical engineering, so I couldn't leave government service just yet. I was a lieutenant colonel at the time and didn't really want to leave. I wanted to serve my obligation and *then* start my own company.

As an engineer, I wanted a company that would use technology to solve societal problems—not just *be* a technology company, but take a broader approach, a systematic approach, a systems approach. The word *systems* has been used more recently to mean computer systems. But to an engineer, particularly an electrical engineer, *systems* means taking a holistic approach to a problem. I told myself that I would like to have a company that mirrors my interests—an area of business math called *operations research,* where you combine mathematics and the scientific approach to solve problems; you don't just throw computers or other technology at them. I incorporated SRA in 1976.

Then a friend of mine, an astronaut who went to the moon, convinced me to go into a government position that was a good chance to serve and was too good a position to turn down. So, even though I'd started my company, I went into the government as head of inspection and enforcement at the U.S. Nuclear Regulatory Commission. We inspected all the nuclear power plants under construction and in operation. I took a detour, fully intending to return to my company. We began operations in July of 1978. I hired Ted Legasey three weeks later.

Ted Legasey: I was a graduate of the United States Air Force Academy, and Ernst was a graduate of the United States Naval Academy, where we had both stood up and taken honor code pledges and were, frankly, indoctrinated in a way that led to our current beliefs.

Through some stroke of good luck, we [the leaders of SRA] have come together as a group of people and share the same values and principles. Obviously, this was no accident—our chairman, Bill Brehm, and our CEO, Ernst Volgenau, met each other in the early 1960s, when they were both part of a group of people known as the Whiz Kids in the Pentagon, in the early days of the Kennedy and Johnson administrations. I met Ernst Volgenau about twenty-six years ago in the Air Force, when we were both officers. While we have a working relationship with one another, we have also developed a real professional and personal respect for each other. We've now become lifelong associates and colleagues and friends. Gary Nelson, the other executive vice president, joined us through another member of that Whiz Kids crowd, who referred him to Ernst and Bill. The four of us have been together since 1982.

Bill Brehm: The notion of building something or going into business for myself goes back to the time when I was a child. In high school and college I had a dance orchestra and then a vocal trio. That's a small business. You have to get the jobs, you have to market yourselves, get everyone there on time, get the music, the stands, the lights, keep everybody happy, provide the transportation—personnel, logistics, marketing, payroll—it's all there. I enjoyed the music end of it because that's my hobby, but I also enjoyed the management side.

Eventually I got caught up in very large organizations, aerospace giants, but after a dozen or so years of that, I had a yearning for public service. I think that was part of the adventurer in me—I wanted change, I wanted to see something different, to see business from a different side. So I joined the Defense Department. But again I was part of a very large organization. When I left after my first tour, six years at the Pentagon, I joined yet another very large company, this time in the consumer products business, Dart Industries, which owned Tupperware, among several other companies. I learned a lot from Justin Dart about how to build a marketing-oriented enterprise. I learned a lot about what it takes in the way of courage and conviction, resources and drive, and not getting bogged down in the details while pursuing a vision.

Then I came back to public service. During that second tour, as assistant secretary of defense, Ernst talked to me about going into business together. It was clear he'd had an idea in his mind for a very long time, that this was something he'd wanted to do since childhood. We really had a meeting of the minds. But it turned out not to be our time yet.

After a few years—during which I turned down two very interesting and substantial job offers with large companies in the Southwest—I joined a ninety-person company in the data processing business in Washington, D.C., involved in what we used to call computer systems "time sharing." This company, COMNET, was ready to explode. It had won some major contracts, and it needed to triple in size. I was asked to come in as a director and as executive vice president and build a management team. This turned out to be a tremendous experience for me, because in a ninety-person company, everybody does everything.

Then Ernst finished his tour at the Nuclear Regulatory Commission, and he restarted SRA and asked me to be on his board. The company wasn't big enough then to hire another full-time person, but in a year or so we were ready and I joined full-time. I needed a title, and we decided on "chairman." But with only fifteen people, titles didn't have much relevance. Work and vision did.

Gary Nelson: I joined the company at the beginning of 1982. There were forty people in the company when I joined, and today there are 1,200. We did $2.5 million in sales the first year I was with the company, and this year we will do somewhere between $180 and $200 million. We have to be a very aggressive company—very aggressive in marketing and sales, and very creative and innovative when it comes to proposing solutions, tackling new business opportunities, trying to add new clients to the business. That has to distinguish us. The challenges are much bigger, because we're playing in a much broader marketplace. We have to do a lot of things differently than we've done in the past. So we have heavily focused on how we do our work and on what kind of environment we need to create.

A Time for Change and Renewal

Gary: Why did we decide to become one of the best companies in the world by any measure? There were really three reasons. The first is that we have very talented people who naturally want to do their best and who see even greater opportunities in the future. Second, we were getting into a scale of operations in excess of $100 million in business and approaching 1,000 employees. We really began to define ourselves in global terms. Third, we had gotten to the point where we couldn't run the enterprise effectively through direct personal intervention. We really needed to be able to communicate to all the SRA people and to set out our expectations for the business.

We needed to strengthen the company, both internally and in terms of how we related to the marketplace. We wanted to do this in a time of relative growth and prosperity as opposed to a time when we were doing poorly or, God forbid, declining. If you're in difficult times, then adopting new courses is invariably interpreted as a desperate act, rather than a sincere attempt to change. The time to change is when you're doing well and willing to hire people—also, at those times you typically have more money and resources to commit to change.

We had to put in place internal processes involving project leadership, investments, and ways that would enable us to do work more efficiently—training and developing people, and thereby giving ourselves the ability to perform at a higher level.

Ann Denison: I was overwhelmed by all that needed to be done, but the answers were within the people at SRA. The leadership team and I believed that and trusted it to be true. Ted got the theory, took the leadership position, and started the action teams that identified and recommended changes. As vice president for human resources, I was able to put those suggestions into action. HR had to be the place where the change occurred first, and then that would bring the rest of the company along. Because of the programs that we manage, because they affect everyone, unless we at HR changed, nothing was going to happen.

Just look at last year's growth. Between one-third and one-half of our current staff is new to the company in the past year and a half. We have almost recreated the company in the last two years, and almost everything has changed or is in the process of being changed. It seemed that there was an enormous effort to begin to move the machine. And at first, it moved only a hairline. We could barely feel the motion. Then little things began happening. Once little things began happening, then a lot of things began happening faster. The overall process seemed to take on a life of its own.

I truly think that the process of change couldn't happen until enough people—although they might be uncomfortable with change—said, "Change is good; what do we have to change?" It took a little while to get that mind-set going, before everyone knew that "We've done it this way before" was not an acceptable attitude. My role was probably part coach, part catalyst, part facilitator. The way to get this to happen was to get other people involved and make them part of the solution, as opposed to trying to give them all the answers.

Vision and Values

Bill: We set out to build an enterprise that would be of value to society and do useful things. We set out with the goal that we would never do work that was not in the national interest or society's interest; we would never do work that somebody else could do better; and we would not knowingly take on work that wasn't challenging to our people. Three very tough criteria.

We want SRA to be a firm of integrity. I once chased down a car in a parking lot that was driving away after having backed into another car. It made me furious, that lack of integrity on the part of the five grown men in that car, their failure to take responsibility for what they had done. My only weapon was an umbrella, but they returned to the scene. Our customers tell us we are a firm of integrity, and it thrills me to hear that.

Ted: The decision to codify a vision that would inspire SRA to be one of the best companies in the world was really a decision that said, "To carry out the imperatives that we need to carry out, and to have this business achieve its destiny, we need some sort of a mobilizing principle." Saying that we wanted to be one of the best companies in the world allowed us to apply virtually any measure that one can apply to a company.

If you commit to four objectives—satisfying customers, running the enterprise in an efficient way, building the business with a strategic focus while capitalizing on tactical opportunities, and providing a workplace where you can attract the best people and then get them to stay—you're going to be one of the best companies in the world. At the same time, we believe we're here for but a blink of an eye in the grand scheme of things—so let's have fun while we're doing it.

In addition, this company truly believes in service to the country. We believe in being good corporate citizens, that we have an obligation to give back to those in the community who aren't as fortunate as we are. We have a responsibility toward one another to support and help one another. It's not just that teamwork is good for business; teamwork is the way people *ought* to work together.

Ernst: We have three primary cultural attributes—honesty and service, quality work and customer satisfaction, and attracting good people and helping them fulfill themselves.

Honesty and Service

Ernst: Honesty means more than simply complying with laws. It means maintaining a high ethical framework. Laws can be defined in a court. If you violate them, presumably you get convicted. Ethics is more abstract, a little bit like beauty: It's hard to define, but you know it when you see it. We say to each of our employees that of course SRA obeys all laws, but we hold ourselves to a higher ethical framework. If you see anything that you believe is unethical, and certainly if you see anything that violates the law, as an SRA employee you have an obligation to report it. If you don't, then you're part of the problem.

Now, on the service side. The best way a company can serve is by delivering value to its customers—performing excellent work on useful contracts. We don't want work that isn't delivering value to our customers. Even if it's delivering profit to us, we don't want it.

Another thing about service. We have tried to focus on charities that make a big difference. My number one favorite is inner-city learning centers, where poor kids go to find computers and mentors who care for them. Mentors do two things: They improve their education, and they strengthen their ethical framework. We have helped start two centers, and we've supported two others. We have a budding partnership with a young man whom you've probably heard of, Darrell Green, cornerback with the Washington Redskins, an absolutely outstanding player. If I had to put my bet on somebody who can help us to develop not only ten or twenty but maybe even hundreds of these learning centers one day, it's Darrell Green.

Our number two charity is D.C. Cares, an organization that involves some businesses here. Our employees volunteer their time—serve food in a soup kitchen, take poor kids to a cultural event, clean up a riverbank, or paint a school. These things are going on every month in the D.C. metropolitan area. We probably have several hundred employees involved in D.C. Cares. We also adopted a local elementary school right over here.

The third charity we have supported is the Nature Conservancy. Two things I like about them: They not only buy up land before it gets developed and ruined, but when they become a landowner, they try to solve the local landowners' problems. If you can't solve the economic problems, you can't solve the pollution problems. They take a holistic approach, a systems approach.

Quality Work and Customer Satisfaction

Gary: There needs to be something unique about the company in terms of what we offer to the marketplace. To really be a world-class company, you can't just copy somebody else. You really have to define yourself as clearly creating value for customers in ways that others do not. You need to be innovative and entrepreneurial, and you need to exploit things that you're very good at and create special value for your customers. We're doing it today in Internet and intranet services and technology and products, but that is only one of many such value-added areas in which we can serve our clients well.

People Orientation

Ann: Ernst Volgenau cares very deeply about people. It was obvious right from the start of our company. In his heart of hearts, he wants people to be fulfilled in their work. He truly believes that our employees should be excited to come to work every morning.

While many define "people orientation" merely as hiring good people and helping them find fulfillment in their work, SRA's commitment to its employees is often manifested in the way the company deals with the employees' crises. When one of our employees experiences a family, personal, medical, or other type of crisis, we go to great lengths to help him or her through it. With people who have chemical imbalances causing mental illness, we work with the courts, the doctors, and their families to help them become productive again. After one recent episode, I received an e-mail from a doctor saying that he had never seen a company work so hard to get people on their feet again. For people in financial crisis, we have gone as far as loaning them money. If an employee doesn't work out in a particular position, we try to find another within the company that will allow him or her to succeed. The senior managers at SRA are held to a high standard. If an employee isn't working out, Ernst assumes that we have done a poor job in either hiring or managing the employee. Our success is measured by their success.

The second and more traditional way in which our orientation toward people is manifested is through our thoughtful and methodical hiring process. We take time to interview and carefully check references to ensure that a candidate is a really good fit for the company. While many companies in our business hire exclusively on a contract basis, we hire with the intention that the relationship will be long-term. We look for people who are adaptable and flexible, and who can learn quickly and be innovative in meeting our customers' needs.

Although these two characteristics are commendable and set us apart from other companies, they are not enough in an era when IT people can move from one company to the next with minimal effort. The SRA renewal effort has taught us that we have to be more intentional and conscious about providing our employees with the things that make them want to come to work. We need to ask every day, "Have we created a sense of excitement and responsibility in our employees?" We need to let go of the paternalistic view—"Don't worry, we'll take care of you"—and create an environment in which employees can be masters of their own destiny—"Here is the information, and these are the options (and there are many at SRA). Now tell us where you want to go and we'll work in partnership with you." We are investing like never before in training, conferences, and other activities that are aimed at empowering employees to build their skills. We've gotten the employees involved in helping define career paths and career development options as well as in defining the roles and responsibilities of the managers who must help along the way.

I value most that the leadership—my bosses and my colleagues—trust me to do the right things in these situations. They're reasonable about what they ask, and they know that if I say no, it's because I can't do it. And I'm reasonable in what I ask, and I know that if they say no, it's because they can't do it. Having the trust and the credibility of the company's leaders—with the understanding that we're all doing the best we can, given that we all have constraints and external forces pulling at us—is very important to me. My own value is to send people who work with me home with successes in whatever they do.

Gary: I think there has to be a first-class working environment for people. Today it's a tough recruiting market. In three or four years, it may be even tougher. I don't think we can be successful otherwise, because we are totally dependent on people working together. This company has always attempted to provide a good professional home for people and to delegate an awful lot of responsibility to the people who are here.

We want people to really be innovative and client-oriented, creative people who can look at a situation, have the experience and ability to really understand the customer's environment, and then come up with an innovative solution and an innovative way for us to provide that solution. If we want to see innovative behavior, we have to work very hard to create the right kind of environment, one that includes respect for individuals and honesty and trust in dealing with people.

We can try to inspire people to move quickly and make things happen. We can create a sense of momentum, rather than letting people sit back and say, "Gee, that's really good." I try to develop a personal rapport with the people who report to me and sort of nudge them in the directions in which I think they'll be most successful. I've tried to develop some degree of competence in counseling people in developing performance plans and determining what they need to do to be successful. Success is contagious. Congratulate people on successes and counsel people when they're not pulling their weight.

When people are trained and qualified, let them perform to their absolute maximum capability. That is the only way this model works at all.

If you try to centralize decisions, if bosses try to make all the technical decisions or review everything, this process breaks down fairly quickly. Obviously, an environment that shows that you care about people encourages them to do their best.

Ted: You must view employees as valued assets, and then you must treat them with the personal dignity and respect that they're entitled to as individuals. If you do that, it's a smart business decision. On the other hand, if you choose to treat them like chattel or like interchangeable parts, they'll contribute as if they are. For the most part, people will give you what you deserve.

Ernst: No ethical company takes advantage of its employees. Even if I can hire somebody at below the market price, I shouldn't do that. I should try to compensate them fairly, and I should make the compensation directly proportional to that person's contributions. We're not the greatest company in the world; we're not even one of the best. We haven't fulfilled our own standards for that yet, but we are on our way.

On Leadership

Ted: My philosophy on leadership encompasses five factors. The first is vision. When people can see a whole picture, when they can really see where they're headed, then they have a context for their own actions. And while they may disagree with decisions, they at least see the context in which to carry out their jobs better. Therefore, the process by which you arrive at that vision must involve as many people as possible. The job of a leader is to inspire and lead that visioning *process*—not necessarily to come up with the specific vision.

Second, I am a great believer in communicating everything, from the littlest things to the biggest things, as many times, in as many ways, by as many modes as you possibly can. There's never an excuse to say, "They don't need to know that." Never. It's a leader's job to make sure that communication is taking place, that information is being pushed through all the channels, so that stakeholders feel, in their own way, that they know what's going on. It's all pointed at getting people to participate more fully and make the contributions that they're capable of making. Communication is everyone's job.

The third factor is trust. Leaders have to show that they trust one another, and they've got to encourage trust building throughout the organization. You don't just say to someone, "I trust you." You exhibit trust. And to earn another's trust, you've got to cooperate, share information, and share power.

Which leads to the fourth point, participation. If leaders signal that people are just their employees, or if people's jobs are narrowly defined, then you're only going to get some marginal result or marginal return from that employee. You really want their full participation.

The fifth point is about learning: As leaders, we have a responsibility to understand our own strengths and weaknesses, and to work to correct our weaknesses, or avoid them whenever we can. We also have to allow people to fail gracefully when they encounter one of *their* weaknesses. Let them land soft. I'm not talking about flagrant violators; I'm talking about people who make mistakes when they lean too far forward. Similarly, we've got to learn from our corporate failures, when our enterprise leans too far forward, when we make strategic mistakes.

Moreover, we don't learn in quiet—we've got to discuss our failures openly, freely. We've got to bare our souls. Stand out there naked for everyone to see. Only if we get all opinions can we ensure we're getting the best ideas. And that's really what we're after.

Bill: I think Max De Pree [former CEO of Herman Miller, Inc.] put this in such beautiful words: "The first job of a leader is to define reality." A lot of leaders simply don't do this. They allow themselves to dodge the issues; they don't want to face up to the really tough challenges. Max has helped me to crystallize that idea.

Another principle of leadership is to maintain a sense of management discipline while at the same time giving people the freedom to make mistakes, thereby allowing them to tap in to their creativity and learn. One of the greatest feelings a manager can experience is when a subordinate comes up with something out of the box that is powerful. If we don't create the environment to allow people to do that, then we'll miss it, and finding some powerful new idea is the way businesses grow.

Another leadership principle has to do with hiring people. I think that a lot of firms just fill pigeonholes: They look for a person to fill an existing job description. When I interview a person for a job, especially when I interview people who can become key contributors, I say, "We are not hiring just to fill a vacancy. We have a need, but if you join us, you will forever change and so will we. You can expand, and in two years, you could be doing things that we haven't even thought of. You will change the company forever."

Finally, a leader should never be a monomaniac. A leader should have outside interests, because those outside interests provide different perspectives. In the entrepreneurial world, it's very easy to get totally focused on business, and that isn't healthy. Music and photography are important to me, and through my interest in them, I have entirely different views on the rest of my life and work.

Obstacles

Bill: One obstacle for a company like SRA is the ability to recruit for senior positions. We have not done very much recruiting outside the company for these positions. Relatively speaking, we have grown our own senior leaders. And I think to some degree this has slowed our growth. So why have we done this? Because the SRA culture is so incredibly strong that it isn't easy to bring a senior person in from the outside and have her or him be readily accepted. What occurs is sort of a tissue rejection, and this is the other side of the coin of having a strong culture: People feel quite protective about what they have.

Ted: You want to know my greatest obstacles? People! Get rid of all the people, and all the problems will go away, right? Of course not. We try very hard to recruit people with five basic characteristics: personal integrity, intelligence, a strong work ethic, a positive attitude, and competence. But even if you can get all five of those perfect, everybody's different from one another, and we certainly all have had different experiences. On the one hand, it's a tremendous benefit to get all the richness associated with such diversity. On the other hand, you get all sorts of different ideas about how you're going to carry out your agenda. Well-meaning people working toward the same result can really stymie one another, because they have different views about how to get there. This is a relatively small enterprise, but when you take that kind of diversity of opinion into a place of any real size, just getting everything harmonized is the biggest hindrance to moving forward. Ironically, the real obstacle to achieving success is the very thing that's going to enable you to get there—talented, diverse people.

As we sit here today, one-third of the employees in this company have been with us less than fifteen months. That ratio of newcomers magnifies the challenges of instilling leadership behaviors and communicating with people. There's very good stability in the senior management around here. But a lot of the senior people are used to running a much smaller and more stable enterprise: We haven't yet taken on all the behaviors that are appropriate and necessary to running an enterprise that's changing at the rate we are.

Gary: There are never enough really outstanding people. You've got to do what you can to attract them. You have to develop and utilize people with the skills that they have. You've got to cast your lot with people who don't have as much experience, ability, or client savvy as you'd like. But that's inevitably the case, particularly in a company like ours that sets a high standard and that really isn't ever completely satisfied with things.

And then there are some people who come into the company and don't share our values. People who don't share our values are not supporting the model, and that's always an obstacle.

Ernst: First, we've grown so fast, and we've worked so hard—we've pumped our resources into growing fast, and we haven't spent enough on training good leaders. Even though we've got some great leaders in this company and some outstanding examples of good management, we aren't uniformly good in this area. Second, we haven't developed a career management program equal to the other quality attributes of our firm. Ann Denison and her people are working on that. Third, we haven't achieved the diversity that I believe is important and necessary to our future. We don't have enough female executives, and we don't have enough minority employees. Having said that, I'll also tell you that those are really difficult goals to achieve. There simply aren't enough women and minorities entering this field.

This whole system-integration business is really only about thirty years old, and it's not a very mature industry. You've got to set up an education and training infrastructure to fulfill this emerging industry, which is growing like mad. There's a chronic shortage of people in our field. We're asking our key people to do all of this work, more than is reasonable to ask any people to do, and on top of that we're asking them to get more diversity. Moreover, SRA has imposed this on itself. We're not doing it because the government has mandated or legislated it. It's just good business sense: If you don't use half the population's minds, you're making a big mistake. Half of the people are women. If you don't use the minds of the minorities, which probably represent more than 20 percent in this country and soon will be 50 percent—maybe in our lifetimes—that's just stupid. It's economically dumb, and it's socially irresponsible.

Vision for a Better World

Bill: I am deeply offended by the way a lot of the energy in our country is expended. There is a tendency toward too much materialism. Someday we are going to conclude that materialistic growth is really not the answer. When I go to the drugstore and see the number of different kinds of shampoo available, I'm really appalled. What is it about our society that motivates companies to provide that incredibly wasteful number of choices? All of the packaging costs, the marketing costs—that's just ridiculous. We want SRA to grow because if we're larger, we can solve more problems, but we don't want to be solving problems that aren't there. We don't want to provide ten different solutions when one will do. This is kind of heretical in the American enterprise system, but I'd like to see businesspeople focus more on the values in our society, each according to his or her own background and personal faith, but all having standards that are consistent with the strong traditions—and there are many good traditions out there that have been handed down through the ages.

Society has marched down through the centuries struggling with the constant tension between liberty and equality. A lot of people think these two ideas are the same thing, but they are actually opposites. When I talk about this, I think of a highway. We have this highway, and it starts to get busy, and pretty soon people start getting hurt—they start running into each other. Someone says, "We are going to have to put a stripe down the highway. That way, everyone will have an equal amount of space." For the sake of equality, we give up half our liberty. The people who honor that compromise stay in their lanes. But there is always a selfish person with one foot in each lane, saying, "Mine, mine—I've got liberty, and it goes all the way across this highway." I believe the desire for personal liberty has gotten way out of control. Equality has taken a backseat. We have to work to get this balance back in all we do—churches, schools, communities, and businesses. Businesses can set an example. We intend to do so at SRA.

Lessons We Learned

DreamMakers express vision and values. "If you commit to four objectives—satisfying customers, running the enterprise in an efficient way, building the business with a strategic focus while capitalizing on tactical opportunities, and providing a workplace where you can attract the best people and get them to stay—you're going to be one of the best companies in the world. "We have three primary cultural attributes—honesty and service, quality work and customer satisfaction, and attracting good people and helping them fulfill themselves."

DreamMakers support diversity and honor the integrity and contributions of all people. "You must view employees as valued assets, and then you must treat them with the personal dignity and respect that they're entitled to as individuals. If you do that, it's a smart business decision. On the other hand, if you choose to treat them like chattel or like interchangeable parts, they'll contribute as if they are. For the most part, people will give you what you deserve."

DreamMakers value and nurture interpersonal relationships. "It's not just that teamwork is good for business; teamwork is the way people *ought* to work together."

DreamMakers tap in to the extraordinary potential in all of us. "I was overwhelmed by all that needed to be done, but the answers were within the people at SRA."

DreamMakers find unprecedented opportunities for transformation and renewal in the current climate of rapid change. "I truly think that the process of change couldn't happen until enough people—although they might be uncomfortable with change—said, 'Change is good; what do we have to change?'"

DreamMakers collaboratively transform and renew themselves and others. "The way to get this to happen was to get other people involved and make them part of the solution, as opposed to trying to give them all the answers."

DreamMakers focus on education and continual learning. "We are investing like never before in training, conferences, and other activities that are aimed at empowering employees to build their skills."

DreamMakers learn from their mistakes. "We don't learn in quiet—we've got to discuss our failures openly, freely. We've got to bare our souls. Stand out there naked for everyone to see. Only if we get all opinions can we ensure we're getting the best ideas."

DreamMakers foster creativity and hope. "One of the greatest feelings a manager can experience is when a subordinate comes up with something out of the box that is powerful. If we don't create the environment to allow people to do that, then we'll miss it, and finding some powerful new idea is the way businesses grow."

DreamMakers follow a moral compass. "Honesty means more than simply complying with laws. It means maintaining a high ethical framework."

DreamMakers demonstrate responsibility toward a larger community. "We believe in being good corporate citizens, that we have an obligation to give back to those in the community who aren't as fortunate as we are."

GARY AND JANET SMITH
left corporate America to found Ivy Planning Group, a management consulting firm. Building on their Ivy League backgrounds, firm family foundations, and unwavering faith, they have built a premier strategy firm. Their vision is to demonstrate that business and personal success come from valuing the differences in each individual.

GREATER TALENT THROUGH DIVERSITY

Gary and Janet Smith,

The Ivy Planning Group

I first met Gary and Janet Smith while I was leading the Federal Quality Institute. Our strategy at the institute was to ask leaders who had experience with continual transformation to share their stories and lessons learned. The people who came to the table were not affiliated with a certain political party, nor were they there for the money. In fact, everyone there made a tremendous sacrifice financially and generously gave their time to serve their country. The Ivy Planning Group was part of this team and is now part of my own collegial network.

Janet and Gary founded and built The Ivy Planning Group on their beliefs about human beings and the principles they had learned from their families, their supportive communities, and even the institutions where they had gained experience over the years. They share a strong belief that people with extraordinary talents and gifts come from many cultures, all races, and both genders. This belief drives their vision and values. They invest their faith, their commitment, and even their future in providing a corporate opportunity and a culture that knows how to get at the great potential of people who might otherwise be passed over, people who ultimately create value in their enterprise. Janet and Gary honor the wholeness of our lives, making it possible for men and women to enjoy family and work without sacrificing one for the other. Furthermore, they bring their knowledge about human potential and the value of diversity, along with model practices, to their clients, with measurable results.

The Ivy Planning Group is a successful management consulting firm with clients like IBM, Morgan Stanley, and Xerox. The Smiths have an impeccable reputation for results, integrity, and professionalism. I had never experienced a more competent management consulting firm, and I had hired and fired my share. In particular, Gary Smith partnered with the Federal Quality Institute to expand the latest thinking on transformation, whole-systems change, and quality. He was music in action, totally confident and competent to partner gracefully with high-level people.

The Smiths know what I have experienced myself: When individuals are given the opportunity to think well of themselves from their youth, to believe in themselves, to tap in to supportive families and communities, their potential to do great things is enormous. The Smiths' willingness to give back to others what they have received themselves touches me deeply.

Finally, while they don't talk about this in the interview, I know the Smiths have derived great benefit from the rich network of colleagues from those institutions Gary talks about and from their many positive encounters with those they hire and those they serve. I hear this theme often among DreamMakers and have experienced the power of networking myself. In a way, it is this that supports the dialogues we so urgently need to make this a better world.

Defining Moments

Formative Institutional Cultures

Gary Smith: I've always been affiliated with institutions—the church, the Smithsonian Institution, Yale University, and IBM Corporation. When I speak of institutions, I mean organizations that behave in a way that's bigger than what the organization actually does. People, by and large, when thinking of the term *institution,* have a negative connotation, a sense of rigidity, too much structure, which then eliminates creativity. And that's not what I'm talking about. It's actually a very positive thing. People can flourish and can be as individualistic as they like, but there are tenets that govern some of their behavior, so that creativity is in context.

When I was in the eighth grade, no one in my class wanted to volunteer as a Smithsonian intern because they weren't getting paid to do it. I said, "Who cares? I'll do it anyway." After three months, the woman who hired me said, "This is so wonderful. I'm going to find a way to pay you. You're going to be part of the Smithsonian team forever." I was at the Smithsonian through high school, until I went off to college. The director wrote one of my letters of recommendation.

There is no better place to learn how to operate a museum than at the Smithsonian. There are a lot of museums and galleries in the world. Many people own art and collect art, but institutions, using my simplistic definition, seem to define the thing being done. The Smithsonian really defines curatorship, museums—the whole concept of promoting the transformation of knowledge and learning in that environment.

The Black church falls into that same category. It is not only a place of worship; it defines religion for a lot of people. The church was an institution for me.

The next big institution in my life was Yale. Yale wasn't just another place to go to get a degree; it wasn't just another place to learn. When I talked to friends at other schools about which books they were using, their books were written by our professors at Yale. Yale made its mark on two levels: its impact on the Yale community, and its impact on education in a much broader sense.

Finally, IBM wasn't just a company that sought to manufacture and sell products. It wasn't just a company that sought to solve business problems. It was a culture. It was a group of people who created a sense of how they were going to do what they were doing. This manifested itself in many ways. Here were thousands of people all wearing white shirts and dark suits, exhibiting brutally efficient professionalism in everything they did. All of this was part of the IBM way. And it was consistent from experience to experience. An IBM customer in Omaha and one in Massachusetts had the same experience. I could land at any IBM office in the country, and it would feel the same. Some people didn't like that; they thought it was too regimented.

These four institutions helped to shape my approach, my concept of the way things were supposed to be done. I felt that an experience with Gary Smith ought to be consistent enough that I could start to replicate it and predict outcomes. I got to a point where I felt I had a success formula. I couldn't guarantee a win every time, but I could certainly minimize the likelihood of losing. So our goal with the Ivy Planning Group was to build not just a company but an institution.

Janet Smith: Ivy has a very strong culture. Gary and I talk about it a lot. There is an "Ivy Planning Group way" of doing things. It was somewhat intuitive early on, and we are now documenting it. We are third-party observers, capturing processes and approaches so that the Ivy Planning Group "way" can be taught and passed along.

Gary: Ivy as an institution does two things: It forces our clients to think—literally forces them to accept that they have problems—and it drives a desire to fix the problems. I think organizations get very good at ignoring their problems, or the way they do things now. We help organizations to think, to look in the mirror, and we challenge the way they do what they do without trading off their core, their culture, their "way" of being.

Family, Community, and Identity

Janet: When Gary and I met, it was immediately clear that we had very similar backgrounds. But people who know us think that we are very different. The institutions are similar: the Black church, Ivy League education, IBM. One critical factor that Gary did not mention, however, is family. We both come from very close, empowering families. Gary and I laugh about it now, but I truly grew up believing that I could do anything and that I was the best at everything. I don't know if my mother and father were aware of what they were doing, but they made me believe that I was perfect. Some of the realities didn't hit me until I was an adult, but by then it was too late. I had already been empowered. My senior year in high school, I already knew I'd be valedictorian and decided to apply to Ivy League schools. The counselor told me not to apply, that I'd never get in because no one from my high school ever had. (I later learned that to be untrue.) I said, "So what? If I can't get in, who can?" I grew up in an *all*-Black environment on the South Side of Chicago. It was a wonderful, middle-class life. My mom as a role model has served me well. She was always working—the ultimate multitasker. She showed me that it is possible—not easy—but doable and rewarding. My dad is an attorney, and we lived on the same street as a bus driver, a teacher, and the unemployed. It was an empowering environment.

Gary: I grew up in northeast Washington, D.C. The president of the bank lived two doors down, with teachers and laborers on the block, too. If a crime was committed, the arresting officer, the defending attorney, and perhaps even the sentencing judge were all Black. So I understood that we as a people have a capacity to span all stations in life. There were no limits to what we could be.

Janet: I was accepted at Harvard. Daddy and I flew to Cambridge for minority pre–freshman weekend during spring break. I didn't know it at the time, but this was designed to prepare us for the Ivy League culture. My father was treated poorly somewhat on campus, but particularly in Boston. He said, "You're going to Harvard, but I'll never come here again. Things have changed a lot, but Boston hasn't changed enough." My mother visited me while I was there but my father didn't come back until I graduated.

Gary: Janet's right. I don't know if our parents knew they were doing it, but they knew they had overcome a lot, and they had a faith and spirit that we would do even more.

Janet: The attitude was also supported by the church. I gave my high school valedictory address to my church. My pastor asked me to do it, and I said, "Reverend James, it doesn't have anything religious in it." He said, "You're going to give it anyway." At the time, it seemed odd, but in retrospect I realize how important it was for me, and the others who heard him say, "Janet was valedictorian and is going to Harvard."

Gary: People tell me all the time, "Gary, your IBM training really shows through. You're so comfortable in front of large audiences." I say, "You don't understand. I overcame stage fright at Florida Avenue Baptist Church." Whether I was good or not, hundreds of people were going to cheer me on and encourage me at a time when it truly mattered.

Like Janet, I was most influenced by my parents. The notion of having choices and keeping your options open came from my mom and dad. As a nurse, my mom believed that there was a specific way to do everything. My dad taught me to complete things, to not be afraid to *make* an opportunity. There's no question that, had circumstances been different when my dad was younger, he too would have a college degree and a company like IBM behind him. There is an important message in that—hopefully for everyone.

Exploring Careers

Janet: My upbringing gave me the confidence to venture into many things. During college I had a typing business. While at IBM, I started up a delivery dry cleaning business that I sold for a nice profit. I published a new magazine. As I think back, I believe I did so much outside of IBM because management didn't encourage the use of my skills and potential inside the organization— or I didn't feel comfortable displaying those skills in that environment.

Gary: Janet has a tremendous capacity to get work done. People like her can get the job done in half the time, but have nothing at work to do with the other half. Flattening organizations sometimes confuse the inability to have frequent promotions with the inability to challenge employees. With Janet, the solution would have been creating an environment where she could have channeled her entrepreneurial talents *inside* IBM.

The defining moment for me was simple. I believe that having two bad managers in a row—either two in one chain of command, or two successive bad bosses—is the kiss of death for any employee. And I had two bad managers in a row at IBM.

Janet: "Bad" meaning that they were poor people managers.

Gary: They didn't care about me. I was having success at IBM. I was a guy that "bled blue" and loved it there. I was not an entrepreneur like Janet; I didn't want to be. Entrepreneurs have to first build enough resources in order to execute what they're smart enough and/or good enough to do. Big companies have the resources; you just have to be smart enough and/or good enough to get the job done. So I was at a good company with resources, making it work for them and for me. I'd make or exceed my sales quota; they'd raise it. I'd make the new quota; they'd raise it again. At the time it was okay. I was a loyal IBMer and understood.

I didn't have problems until my manager told me that he didn't think I was "promotable." I hadn't "demonstrated the qualities" to be promoted. I had been in institutions long enough to know that when institutions no longer serve you well, you've got to go. My boss's boss said, "Well, Gary, we're not sure that your success thus far hasn't been a fluke. Give us another successful year to prove that you're as good as you think you are." Then came his fatal mistake. He mentioned that Janet and I were expecting our first child and that people like us wouldn't leave IBM because it would be stupid. I typed my resignation letter that night.

Janet: We had little Gary soon thereafter. I lay in the delivery room, and the nurse asked for the father's employer and I said, "IBM." Gary looked at me like I was crazy. I just couldn't contribute to the image of "unemployed Black fathers."

Vision and Values

Valuing Potential

Janet: The key to our vision and values is our belief that anything is possible—early on because our parents said so, now because of our own faith.

Gary: And we know we'll have significant impact.

Janet: Our vision is to bring young minorities, females, and others who are traditionally underutilized into an environment that is professional, with a proven process for successful outcomes, with the right value system, to nurture personal and professional growth. Downsizing and resource constraints have limited the number of big companies willing to do that anymore. However, The Ivy Planning Group will do it. And we are able to attract the best people! The biggest obstacle for growth in service firms is the ability to find and retain good people. Yet our network and company culture enable us to attract and retain the best.

Gary: There is an inherent advantage in acknowledging the underutilization of some people. We didn't set out to benefit from it, but we do.

Janet: I understand the challenges that top executives face. When you're busy running a large corporation, you often don't have the time to concentrate on finding different people. You're concentrating on finding good people. But someone with guts must explain to the top guy that, by definition, in order to have good people, everyone cannot be the same. If there are ten people in a room thinking about future direction and strategy for an organization, I don't want everybody to come up with the same answer.

Gary: Talent and intellectual assets are leaving organizations in droves because those organizations aren't concentrating on retaining the talent of different people. We want to help organizations think strategically about that and their core business.

On Living a "Whole" Life

Janet: Something that is often pegged as a women's issue (but isn't) is becoming comfortable with "life management." I have three little boys—ages seven, eight, and ten—a demanding husband, aging parents, and a multitude of responsibilities. How do I handle it all? I have found that it is very important to blend everything together, and not to compartmentalize my life. My appointment book is not just a business appointment book; it's all in there. I may have a pediatrician's appointment in the morning and a business meeting two hours later. It's all my life. And once there is a comfort level with seeing the pieces as part of one whole that works, it is much easier to manage all of it.

Gary: It's the same for me. It is not uncommon to see that I have a morning meeting followed by a field trip for school followed by an afternoon meeting.

Janet: And it's the same for our employees. It makes me feel good that when we're trying to schedule something, an employee will feel comfortable saying, "Well, that day is not great because I have to be at a meeting at my child's school, but let's make it in the afternoon."

Gary: But I had to mature to that point. There was a time when I would think, "How can someone be that comfortable telling me they have to interview baby-sitters in the morning so they can't make this meeting?" Those were the times I bristled. My initial response was, "This person is sharing a little too much!"

Janet: Yes, it's difficult and takes constant work. But it's damaging when people can't talk about all of the influences in their life when they're at work. It's not natural. If your parents are ill and you're trying to figure out health insurance for them, it's bugging you now, not after work. When you force people to separate their lives that way, it builds resentment and lowers performance.

Gary: Which is not to say that people don't work like dogs in our company, too. It's just that if people have made their own decisions to combine work and family, they should be allowed to.

Getting to Acceptance and Valuing Diversity

Gary: Deep down I don't believe that only certain people can be bright, or that only certain people can do certain things. We're pretty much the same. It's a matter of what you are told and shown is possible.

I am reminded of a two-day strategic thinking session I attended a few years ago, held for the senior management team of a Fortune 100 firm. Three of us participated in the session. We had actually been hired by one of the divisional presidents, someone we had known professionally for years. By design, he was not present at this meeting. He had given us free rein to support the creation of a new organizational structure, business strategy, and—this was the interesting part—to provide a perspective on the strengths and weaknesses of the executives who would participate in the session. The new organization would have 40 percent fewer managers, and everyone in the room knew that. The participants—all senior-level professionals in this multinational corporation—had received background information on our firm and knew that their boss was an Ivy Planning Group fan.

When we arrived at the conference room, it was clear that the participants certainly had no idea that we would be Black—that familiar expression of shock on their faces was a dead giveaway. We did the customary presession chitchat. As we moved to the meat of the session, aggressively debating strategies, providing perspectives on how other organizations have overcome similar challenges, and mapping out the future, the group became comfortable with us. It didn't matter that outsiders had insinuated themselves into their world. What mattered was our ability to jump in, provide some perspective, drive action, and formulate a path for meaningful change.

When Janet, who is a highly skilled facilitator, takes charge, it can be a little unsettling to some because her goal is to provide for a fair exchange of ideas. She's very savvy, but sometimes I look at the faces of these guys and I can imagine them thinking, "Who does this woman think she is, telling me,

'Please hold that thought; we don't want to miss what some other person is trying to say'? Who cares what somebody else is saying? I'm talking." The magic moment came when the participants threw their expletives at us as freely as they did at each other. After spending a few grueling days with these guys (and unfortunately, most of the time there are few women or minorities in such sessions), we had established the foundation for a long-term relationship.

Over the years it always seems to work out. We inevitably create great working relationships with the client. I should point out that what makes them great is that we are able to work on difficult issues, to disagree, and to explore new organizational opportunities while always maintaining a professional experience.

Janet: The Ivy Planning Group does as much for diversity by doing basic strategy work as we do when we are designing or executing a cultural diversity initiative. Unfortunately, there are still very few opportunities for different people to get to know each other. I love it when a client meets me professionally, then sees me in my "mom" role with my three boys, or ends up at the house when I'm making buffalo wings. I've had a Xerox vice president end up in the middle of a bid whist game at the house, with all of the associated chatter. It was real life, and it worked.

Gary: And it is important to understand all those "Janets."

Janet: Yeah, because the next time—and maybe this is too idealistic—but the next time they see a woman of color, and they know absolutely nothing about her, maybe they will assume the best, not the worst. It is probably a lot of unnecessary pressure to put on ourselves, but I think a lot of minority professionals hope to have that effect.

I speak often about an idea called "Opportunity Knocks" because I'm hoping that someone will run with it. It's about exposing minority kids to minority professionals to show them, "Oh, we do that, too." It's about exposing young girls to Wall Street to show them, "Oh, that's a good job to want." We're doing some diversity work with investment banking firms, and it's clear that many minorities and young women don't see investment banking as a possible career—mostly because they weren't aware of it early on. There are many careers and opportunities that many children simply aren't exposed to. I'd like to change that.

Gary: I can't imagine having done this solo, because at critical junctures the team cannot all be down or frustrated at the same time. Having good and true partners has been a lifesaver. I started this business with two people I incredibly and inherently trust, people about whom I knew that, no matter what happened, our relationship would not be at risk.

We should have started the business sooner. I think we waited longer than we needed to reach what we thought of as a level of comfort. Even with no safety net, we should have done it with less experience under our belts.

Janet: I tend to not see anything as a failure. I talk a lot about how good life is, and people sometimes say, "Janet, what are you talking about?" Then they'll list what's gone wrong along the way for me, as if I'm in denial or something. I say, "Yeah, I guess that's right, but you know, this and that wasn't that big a deal." I've come to realize that I don't expect things to be particularly easy anyway. So if something bad happens, you just deal with it. I truly expect to work hard and play hard. It's fun.

Gary: I grew up with the notion that asking "Why me?" is a sin because it implies that someone else was more deserving of this plight than you were.

Vision for a Better World

Gary: The ability to have an impact and change course and direction for the following generation makes me want to own something large now more than at any other time in my life. Having children has motivated me to build something more than before. I understand now how much of the race one generation can run for the next generation. If generation one covers sixteen miles of the marathon, then generation two has a very different race.

Never tell children that their dreams are impossible. They start out believing they can do anything. Sadly, they "unlearn" the possibilities from adults. Janet and I know and believe that our ship has come in right now, and we go down to the dock to receive it every day. That is our blessing as a company and as a couple. We had and will always have bold, deep, and meaningful visions.

Janet: And we are making them come true. We are making a difference. As we continue to build The Ivy Planning Group, the excitement comes from overcoming some significant challenges. We are demonstrating to big companies, Wall Street, and federal agencies that a Black-owned and -led management consulting firm really can become a world-class provider of core business and strategic thinking consulting services. We are developing methodologies that naturally link core business issues to "people issues" in a way that convinces bottom-line oriented CEOs to begin caring about issues such as cultural diversity, and that convinces successful minorities and women to become even more comfortable with their culture in the workplace, and to reach back and pull others along with them. We are demonstrating the power of difference both internally and externally. It's a slow and painful process, but it's happening. And we're having a ball!

Lessons We Learned

DreamMakers express vision and values. "Our vision is to bring young minorities, females, and others who are traditionally underutilized into an environment that is professional, with a proven process for successful outcomes, with the right value system, to nurture personal and professional growth."

DreamMakers work with others to build a shared vision. "It didn't matter that outsiders had insinuated themselves into their world. What mattered was our ability to jump in, provide some perspective, drive action, and formulate a path for meaningful change."

DreamMakers understand that we are all connected and interdependent. "It's damaging when people can't talk about all of the influences in their life when they're at work. It's not natural. If your parents are ill and you're trying to figure out health insurance for them, it's bugging you now, not after work. When you force people to separate their lives that way, it builds resentment and lowers performance."

DreamMakers support diversity and honor the integrity and contributions of all people. "Someone with guts must explain to the top guy that, by definition, in order to have good people, everyone cannot be the same. If there are ten people in a room thinking about future direction and strategy for an organization, I don't want everybody to come up with the same answer."

DreamMakers value and nurture interpersonal relationships. "We inevitably create great working relationships with the client. I should point out that what makes them great is that we are able to work on difficult issues, to disagree, and to explore new organizational opportunities while always maintaining a professional experience."

DreamMakers make their dreams a reality. "We are demonstrating to big companies, Wall Street, and federal agencies that a Black-owned and -led management consulting firm really can become a world-class provider of core business and strategic thinking consulting services."

DreamMakers are both passionate and compassionate. "Maybe this is too idealistic—but the next time they see a woman of color, and they know absolutely nothing about her, maybe they will assume the best, not the worst. It is probably a lot of unnecessary pressure to put on ourselves, but I think a lot of minority professionals hope to have that effect."

DreamMakers believe in a higher power and purpose. "The key to our vision and values is our belief that anything is possible—early on because our parents said so, now because of our own faith."

DreamMakers demonstrate responsibility toward a larger community. "The ability to have an impact and change course and direction for the following generation makes me want to own something large now more than at any other time in my life. Having children has motivated me to build something more than before. I understand now how much of the race one generation can run for the next generation. If generation one covers sixteen miles of the marathon, then generation two has a very different race."

DreamMakers are committed to making the world a better place. "I speak often about an idea called 'Opportunity Knocks' because I'm hoping that someone will run with it. It's about exposing minority kids to minority professionals to show them, "Oh, we do that, too."

TORMOD BJØRK *was trained as a metallurgist and has worked for Norway's Hydro Aluminum for twenty-eight years. He is currently senior vice president, Global Business and Project Development.*

SHARED VISION

Tormod Bjørk,

Hydro Aluminum

I hosted many benchmarking visits to Herman Miller, Inc., while I was there, but perhaps the most unusual was the visit of eighteen people from Hydro Aluminum, in Norway, representing all levels and functions in the organization. They stayed for four days and certainly taught us as much as they learned. They were serious about learning and were committed to transforming their organization into a more productive, safer, and more environmentally conscious place.

I was so impressed that I asked the consultant who had brought them halfway around the world, Randi Skaamedal, to come back and spend more time with my own team. She ended up helping Herman Miller with its own "creating shared vision" process and is a good friend and colleague to this day.

Three years after their visit to western Michigan, Hydro Aluminum invited me to come see what they had accomplished. When I got to Norway, I was astonished. I saw an aluminum plant that embraced the highest values about people, quality, and the environment. And they were profiting from these good values.

So when I decided to write this book, I knew I had to include Hydro. Tormod Bjørk, the plant manager during much of the transformation, graciously agreed to tell the story. After leaving the interview, I once again understood what makes DreamMakers. Tormod Bjørk expressed deeply held values. In the face of his doubts and fears, he went for it. He followed his intuition; he did what he thought was the right thing to do. He has an unwavering belief in people, and he truly believed they could create what they wanted together. Shared vision was his driver, and he risked everything to lift the people to a common ground.

Tormod's story is one of a gentle yet strong spirit and a combination of rock-hard commitment and genuine compassion.

Defining Moments

Tormod Bjørk: Hydro Aluminum is Europe's largest producer of aluminum and the sixth largest in the world. The Karmoy plant is its largest plant. It employs over 1,700 people. I began my career at Karmoy in 1969 as an operator, a frontline factory worker. In Norway, at that time, you had to have practice in an internship before you could become an engineer. So my practical training was at Karmoy, doing ordinary work.

I was like all the other workers: I went to meetings with the unions, I met the top management, and so on. After I completed my education, I was very lucky and got a job as an engineer, my first real job. I made gradual steps upward in the organization.

Before the 1986 Organizational Change

I highly respected the person leading the plant the three years before I did because he had almost the same values as I have—openness, trust, equality, and so on. Having the right values is the most important responsibility a leader has. That's why we had a fantastic upward curve.

Before we started changing, we had numerous problems, serious problems. Within three years, because of the change process, the employees at Karmoy improved operating profit by 100 percent, productivity increased 33 percent, accident rates were cut in half, labor-management relations moved from adversarial to a partnership, and employee suggestions increased dramatically. The plant moved from having a devastating pollution problem to producing emissions that are over 50 percent less than what the government requires. We received the Norwegian environmental award. We invested a lot to protect the external environment.

But there was no regulation inside the plant. And the people inside said that something was wrong. In fact, I got asthma because the pollution in the atmosphere inside was very bad. Yet we trusted each other, because we think that trust creates cooperation, and cooperation is a basic prerequisite for good results. At the time I was not the plant manager, but he supported me because I knew the people. He said, "You know the workers. I want you to give me advice." And I said, "The only advice I can give you is to listen to all the people." And it worked. Everyone committed to improve the situation at the plant: costs, safety, environment, everything. I was a section manager in the most polluted area of the plant when the change process began.

1986 Transformation

Then, in 1986, I was appointed plant manager, head of the whole organization. I was proud, but I was also very doubtful that I could play the role. I knew I had to be myself because the people there knew me as an operator. That was very good for me. I understood their problems and concerns. It was tough, but it was also good. When I got the job, everyone was proud of me: They finally got one of their own, someone from within the organization, to be in charge. In the past, the top manager had always come from the outside. Now they finally had someone from within. So I felt a great respect for the people. I couldn't cheat them. I also felt pressure to do a good job, not to disappoint them.

I had to continue driving this change, but I had to do it my way, being who I am.

I understood that if you want to do something, develop something, don't start with the top of the organization. Bring the operators with you. For example, we flew almost a hundred people to Japan on business class. They stayed at the best hotel in Tokyo. We treated them like managers or directors. That was one of my first significant learning experiences and perhaps the most important lesson for me: Treat people equally. They give you trust back, and they support you. I think a true leader wants everyone in the operation to share the success.

Vision and Values

I'm not a turnaround person like my predecessor. I think I am a transformation person. I hate to effect a turnaround and then stop and start on a new turnaround. It isn't healthy for the organization to do that. That's why I sought *continuous* improvement. When I became plant manager, my goal was to empower people to keep changing. I got advice from Marjie Parker and Inger Tajord, two consultants who helped me to think. I am a typical doer, very eager to get things to happen. They asked me what I wanted in my new job: "What is important for you?" I think I like decentralization, but it's so important for people to belong to a community and have an identity. Inside the fence of the plant, we have four or five different business units, and I wanted them to be one community. I told Marjie and Inger that I believed in continuous improvement. Everything outside us is continuously changing, and competition will continuously increase. I wanted a self-responsible organization. I wanted people to be willing to take responsibility and then continue to improve. That cannot be done from the top of the organization; it has to be done from inside the individual units. So I had to involve both the local management and the people and the union, because the union had to learn that there are so many different areas we are working with—a smelter, a rolling mill, an extrusion plant, an R&D center, a finished-product plant. These areas all involve totally different qualifications and totally different customers. That's why I talked about a decentralized community, but we all come in the same gate every morning. I told Marjie and Inger that I wanted to invite all the people in the whole organization to build our vision and figure out how to implement it.

I told them I wanted this place to be the best place to work in and the most competitive aluminum plant in Europe, maybe in the world, even though I didn't know too much about the world at that time. I wanted people to work on improving holistically. We should focus not only on volume; we should work on everything—safety, health, environment, quality, cost, price, just everything. To talk only about cost reduction is a very boring thing. If you work with margin instead of cost, that gives you another dimension, another responsibility. If you try only to lower cost, you are forced every day not to use money. But if you try to increase the profit margin, you also give the workers responsibility to create premiums on the products. Then you have to use money, but you get more value added.

We were lucky because we had customers inside the plants. The rolling mill and the extrusion plant are something you normally see farther down in Europe. But why don't we treat our closest customer the best way? That's why we started to think about internal customer orientation, even customers inside the individual departments. But it wasn't easy to get everyone to think in that way. Marjie really helped me. I remember we were sitting in a hotel room in Haugesund, and she was questioning me about how I saw the plant in the future. I was talking about the people, how I wanted to see them— happy, responsible, proud. "We're meeting the customers, and we don't get any negative interference from the corporate office in Oslo. We are acknowledged for being an outstanding operation."

And when it comes to the environment, we should always go beyond the regulations. We said that maybe the best way to assess our environmental impact was to have cattle and sheep grazing around the plant. Their health would immediately tell us if the environment was okay or not, whether we had a balance in nature. We were destroying the environment totally before. The sheep were losing their teeth. And we said, "Never again." Marjie forced me to think about how I would like to see this plant six years from now. Today we cannot even cut the grass in the spring because all the seagulls have their nests outside in the grass, and the cows are grazing outside the walls.

The Garden Metaphor

Then Marjie asked me, "What are your hobbies?" My only hobby is gardening. I have planted four different gardens in my life because we have moved from house to house. So we started to think about how a manufacturing plant could be like a garden. Then we started to think, "If our plant were a garden, what would it represent? The different business units? The organization? What is important for our organization? Where do we have competence? How does competence grow?"

When we first came up with the garden metaphor, I was nervous. I thought people would criticize me, especially people from the outside, like economists, lawyers, and people in our headquarters. I thought they might think it was a little frivolous to be talking about a garden. But we did it. The garden metaphor became how we defined everything.

This is how we described our decentralized community: We said that each plant in the garden represented one of the business units. We sell products at different stages. Some are flowers, some are berries. Finished products are berries. One unit was a water lily because it was offshore industry. The wintergreen plants represented the service functions: They service the flowers and the berries. That is important. Customers became the birds and the bees: They come and pick up the nectars, and some pick up the berries and fly away with them. The sales and marketing people ended up being the smell from the flowers. So the garden is the whole organization.

The leaves tell us how an organization functions. A few small leaves indicate decentralized organizations, while big leaves indicate a centralized organization. Long stems with many leaves are dangerous in the wind because they can break. That means you have too many people. When you have very strong wind, you have cold winters; and if you aren't protecting your garden, that's when the prices go up and down. Then you can destroy the whole plant.

We also said that soil is very important, so that you can grow things, and that's how you develop the people in the organization. In autumn, when the leaves fall to the soil, that represents learning. Managers are the water channel in the stem: They have to go down into the soil, be enablers. People in the organization and the products are the most important. Management provides the water and the fertilizer for the plant to grow. Instead of management saying, "Are you doing your job?" we were saying, "What can I do for you to help you do a better job?" The rest is about self-responsibility. The workers are responsible for their own health, their own safety, their own workplace, their own cost level, everything. They are responsible. As plant manager, I am here only to help and guide.

We couldn't communicate very well before I suggested this metaphor, because we didn't have a common language. A lawyer speaks a totally different language from that of an economist. Even among engineers—I'm a metallurgist—we have a totally different language compared to electrical engineers. It was very important that we create our own common language. Lots of our workers had been fishermen, some on the East Coast of America because they couldn't get a job in Norway. Some had been alone fishing up in Iceland. They are all very good people, but their differences can make communication difficult. They can take responsibility. They can make big decisions. I don't think educated people are necessarily always the best decision makers. Sometimes education can destroy creativity and vision because you so easily get boxed into models.

So our metaphor worked. It liberated us from our boxes and brought us together. I'm so grateful I had the courage to go forward with it. I had an enormous conflict about it inside myself. I thought it could be very dangerous. What if they laugh at me? I even thought, maybe I'm being influenced too much by these two ladies. Then I realized that it was my idea, and it's quite natural for me to think of myself as a water carrier, a water channel. And I love Japanese gardens. So we went with it.

I discussed it with my two closest colleagues in the management group, and I talked to the union leader. And he said, "Let's try it." So we prepared everything and went to a big off-site conference where 130 people represented all the groups at the plant—the union, the workers, and management. And that gave me a good opportunity to present the metaphor. Marjie and I were extremely nervous. I didn't sleep at all the night before. I think I was very anxious three or four days before the conference.

But she and I were very happy when we saw the painting of our metaphor—also a very interesting story. We had gone to a painter to explain the metaphor to her. She said that if we had not been interested in decentralization and the workers, she would not have made the painting for us. I explained how I saw the plant, talking about gardens, and she saw the metaphor immediately. I didn't know how her painting would turn out. But she came back after three days, and it was perfect.

We printed up 1,700 copies of the garden painting, and we gave one to each employee. I think everyone in the plant has it in a glass frame in their house. If they can talk about our philosophy, be proud because they can describe where they are, they can be even more enthusiastic. If they have their friends over for a drink on Saturday evening, they can talk about it.

So I explained my metaphor at the conference. I would either win or lose. There was no in-between. I started to talk about where we were by pointing out our place on the globe, just a spot. Then I focused on Europe— where we were, where we wanted to be, why we were there, and what we could do. I talked about all the positive things we had done in the last three or four years, as well as the very serious problems we had. People were suffering as a result of these problems. All of them were suffering, but they still believed in me. I told them, "I just want to support you and make you proud." I was very frank with them up front, so that it wouldn't make it too difficult for them to reject the garden metaphor if they didn't like it.

I think they were mystified when we started to talk about the garden. But then I started to talk about the individual units, why it was a garden, why we wanted to have a decentralized community. I told them, "Some of you will be very disappointed. The managers in the maintenance department were the big guys before, but in this metaphor you are just supporting the production people who are producing value added. We in management, the personnel department, the economists—we are all in support roles." But the funny thing was that they agreed they had been playing the wrong roles. They had been blaming the operators for destroying equipment, for having loss and pollution, for having accidents, and so on.

I had worked to build trust before doing this, and when you build trust you have to be frank, you have to tell the truth. When I stopped talking, I had a pain in my stomach I had never had before. I was very tense. And then I got applause, and they were rising from their chairs and applauding. I said to myself, "This is something!" Then we had a coffee break and asked them to break into work groups with others in their area to reflect a little on what they had been doing. I listened, and the feedback was very positive. We continued in the afternoon by giving them jobs for the individual areas. We didn't split up the different departments. They were working together— the management, union leaders, operators, representatives, middle management, and so on. They were very enthusiastic.

People went through the same phases of emotion and thought as I did— enthusiasm, doubt, fearing that something was wrong, aggressiveness, wanting to go home, disappointment, thinking that this model was impossible to implement. And then it suddenly started to come through. They were making drawings, making up songs, writing poems. They were even having fun. I got everything I needed.

The conference ended with everyone reporting back how their plans were developing. That was the biggest show I have ever seen. I was just sitting there, and I was so happy because some were playing at theater, some were singing, and what was most fascinating was that the ordinary operators were talking exactly the way the well-educated engineers and economists were. And that was the most important result—the common language. The metaphor allowed everyone to be on the same level. So we had a shared vision. I believe if you start to speak a common language, as we did with the garden, to stand on something and describe what you say, it's much easier to change.

Garden Seminars

Then we went back to the plant, and everyone was asking how we should tell the home organization what we had done. Would they believe us? Would they think we were drunk because we had been having fun? That's why we decided to have everyone—all 1,500 people—go through the same process. That meant eleven sessions. We called them Garden Seminars. I had to do exactly the same performance eleven times, starting in the morning and ending at eight o'clock in the evening, at the biggest arena we have in town. And the same thing happened every evening. At 2:30 in the afternoon, it was hell. Everyone was angry and frustrated because they didn't know how to attack the problems. And then when we had dinner at 5:30, almost nobody showed up because they were so busy preparing for their presentations. I would say that of the 1,500 people that attended, a hundred were not so positive. But the majority were very positive.

Focus on Customers and Quality

Another very important result was that everyone started focusing on the customer and not just on the production systems. They were describing how they wanted to receive the customers: how they should meet them at the airport, how they should treat them, where they should stay, what they should serve them, and what they wanted to show them in the plant. That was important. By talking about customers, they began to understand why the customer is important, and that everyone was responsible for the company's income—not just the salespeople. We have to produce quality, and if we make a mistake, we have to go and see the customer immediately, in France or Germany or wherever.

We have a rule that if there is a quality problem, the operator who has been producing that product should go to the customer, together with the quality engineer. I think this is important because the person you send out gets a little ashamed and feels responsible and learns. He comes back home, and you can be sure that he doesn't want to do that again. And he explains to his colleagues what has happened. The next time the customer comes to visit our plant, he sees the same operator again, and they can communicate. It isn't wise to have only management going out to do these things; you have to involve the people responsible for making the product. The same goes for safety: That has to be a part of everyone's thinking and everyone's responsibility. Now, this is a tough way to run a business—I was exhausted every day. But people were motivated, and they took responsibility for the future.

I want to say thanks—to all the people in the plant, to the union leaders, and to my family and friends. But a special thanks to Marjie Parker. She provoked me to think deeply about what I wanted to do, even though in many ways she was driving me crazy. I forget things very easily, but I will never forget the hours I spent with her. She helped me change.

Obstacles

When I was a young operator, I saw so many negative things from management. They weren't motivating people. I remember my first boss gave me some advice: "This summer you will get a broom in your hands. That's not an important job, but sooner or later you will have a job as a manager. Look around and see how people are reacting to the different styles of managers. Learn from that." And that was very wise advice for me. As I was sweeping and cleaning dirty fabrication areas, I was always looking into what people were thinking. People talked about their bosses a lot. They talked about how they were behaving and why they liked some and didn't like others. They liked to have straightforward, tough people who were fair.

I should have brought headquarters in sooner. I should have invited them to one of the Garden Seminars. But I didn't. Often I get mad at myself because I didn't take the time to involve them. Maybe I was a little afraid. But they were a part of this—a part of the management, a part of the water channel. And they can restrict the water flow sometimes if they aren't a part of the process.

Vision for a Better World

I'm restless. I don't like to do standard things. I'm no longer at the plant. My vision now is to develop a totally new aluminum plant outside Norway, with the highest standards—the most profitable plant with the most motivated staff. It could be in Venezuela, Trinidad, Asia, or the United States. I'm convinced that these values work with all people.

I'm convinced that the only way you can develop a business or a society is to talk about what you want to attain in the future together. You cannot work with too-small steps. That's impossible because it doesn't motivate people. People need to see the whole picture—where you want to go, where you've been, and where you are currently.

I want to work with other international companies that share the same philosophy. This is a very unusual approach to running a business, and I think we can learn from each other and then tell our stories to the world.

Lessons We Learned

DreamMakers express vision and values. "I told them I wanted this place to be the best place to work in and the most competitive aluminum plant in Europe, maybe in the world. . . . I wanted people to work on improving holistically. We should focus not only on volume; we should work on everything—safety, health, environment, quality, cost, price, just everything."

DreamMakers engage others in their vision. "What was most fascinating was that the ordinary operators were talking exactly the way the well-educated engineers and economists were. And that was the most important result—the common language. The [garden] metaphor allowed everyone to be on the same level. So we had a shared vision. I believe if you start to speak a common language, as we did with the garden, to stand on something and describe what you say, it's much easier to change."

DreamMakers work with others to build a shared vision. "I told Marjie and Inger that I wanted to invite all the people in the whole organization to build our vision and figure out how to implement it."

DreamMakers support diversity and honor the integrity and contributions of all people. "I understood that if you want to do something, develop something, don't start with the top of the organization. Bring the operators with you. For example, we flew almost a hundred people to Japan on business class. They stayed at the best hotel in Tokyo. We treated them like managers or directors. That was one of my first significant learning experiences and perhaps the most important lesson for me: Treat people equally."

DreamMakers value and nurture interpersonal relationships. "Another very important result was that everyone started focusing on the customer and not just on the production systems. They were describing how they wanted to receive the customers: how they should meet them at the airport, how they should treat them, where they should stay, what they should serve them, and what they wanted to show them in the plant."

DreamMakers question and challenge the status quo. "I told them, 'Some of you will be very disappointed. The managers in the maintenance department were the big guys before, but in this metaphor you are just supporting the production people who are producing value added. We in management, the personnel department, the economists—we are all in support roles.'"

DreamMakers collaboratively transform and renew themselves and others. "I'm not a turnaround person like my predecessor. I think I am a transformation person. I hate to effect a turnaround and then stop and start on a new turnaround. It isn't healthy for the organization to do that. That's why I sought *continuous* improvement. When I became plant manager, my goal was to empower people to keep changing."

DreamMakers focus on education and continual learning. "I remember my first boss gave me some advice: 'This summer you will get a broom in your hands. That's not an important job, but sooner or later you will have a job as a manager. Look around and see how people are reacting to the different styles of managers. Learn from that.'"

DreamMakers trust feelings, emotions, and intuition. "When we first came up with the garden metaphor, I was nervous. I thought people would criticize me, especially people from the outside, like economists, lawyers, and people in our headquarters. I thought they might think it was a little frivolous to be talking about a garden. But we did it. The garden metaphor became how we defined everything."

DreamMakers demonstrate responsibility toward a larger community. "When it comes to the environment, we should always go beyond the regulations. We said that maybe the best way to assess our environmental impact was to have cattle and sheep grazing around the plant. Their health would immediately tell us if the environment was okay or not, whether we had a balance in nature."

DAVID COLE, *hi-tech nomad, conservationist, and budding philanthropist, has served as an executive of numerous companies, including America Online (group executive), Ziff Communications (president), and Ashton-Tate (chairman). He presently serves as a director of The Nature Conservancy, the Daily Wellness Company, Shiva Corporation, and the Virginia Eastern Shore Corporation. He also leads Sunnyside Farms, a producer of organic herbs and foods, and Aquaterra Corporation, the general partner for two investment firms.*

5

CONNECTION TO THE BROADER CONTEXT

David Cole, America Online

I met David Cole for the first time when I visited America Online, where he was at that time president of AOL's Internet Services Division. There was a palpable sense of excitement at AOL. Everyone seemed very engaged—participating, making decisions, and having fun. There was absolutely no sign of hierarchy. The CEO's office was a cubicle just like everyone else's, and David was shuttling from one cubicle to another. I found David to be a man passionate about values and principles, committed to leading with positive people values. Inside the company, he called himself the "ambassador of culture" and had chartered a group of employees to clarify the corporate values.

I went to his home for the interview. His wife, Maggie, met me at the door. David and Maggie's home speaks volumes about their values. The environment is open, bright, and innovative. Maggie guided me to a deck that circles the back of the house, nestled in the side of a large hill. We crossed a rope bridge to a beautifully designed, gazebo-like house—something like a Frank Lloyd Wright tree house. This family has a sense of play and imagination. It was clear that this man had made his dreams a reality.

The interview took place in David's home office, which opens into the house (unlike most home offices, it's not separate) and leads to an outside deck.

David seems to be one of those people who are always ahead of their time, sensing patterns and changes before the rest of us do. More important, he is able to grasp the larger picture, all of the interconnections, the broader context for what may seem to others like unrelated events. His commitment to sustainable development of the environment, people, communities, and organizations seems to be his quest. These qualities, combined with a strong sense of self-empowerment, have made it possible for David to realize many of his dreams for himself, his work, and the environment.

Defining Moments

Hawaii: Early Influences, Important Connections

David Cole: I grew up in a small town called Kailua, on the windward side of Oahu, the main island of Hawaii. Some of my earliest memories are of elementary school and my realization that people singled me out as a Caucasian. There are not too many places in America in the twentieth century where Caucasians are stigmatized simply because of their color. It helped me to become sensitive to how people see one another, based on some pretty trivial characteristics.

Those early years influenced my life values. My father was an inventor, a cool, calm, analytical guy. His most famous invention was the digital character generator, which is in all CRTs (cathode ray tubes). He was an engineer for RCA, and he got only $66 for his invention. I would ask him a question about something, and it would take him several hours to answer. He would always draw the whole picture—you know, all the forces that are at work. He always started with the big picture.

My mother is very expressive and driven—she had very high expectations of me and my three younger siblings. She grew up impoverished in Philadelphia and was really formed by that experience. She got her master's degree in social work and now directs a volunteer program for the state of Hawaii. I'm a lot like my mother in disposition.

I was greatly influenced by how I spent my childhood from eleven to thirteen, delivering morning newspapers for the *Honolulu Advertiser.* Today, increasingly, adults deliver papers in cars and on motor scooters. But what was really remarkable about life in Kailua for me as an emerging entrepreneur was that I was working this paper route in the wee hours of the morning, and it gave me lots of time to really get in touch with what was going on in the community.

And to get in touch with myself. You still had the stars out at 4:30 in the morning, and you had the creatures beginning to come out, so you saw all the beauty of Hawaii. If you come from Baltimore, for example, I think you have a really different view of your relationship to your environment than you do growing up in a place like Kailua, in the middle of the Pacific, in what is clearly one of the most beautiful places on earth. You have this deep sense of awe and beauty. There's this connectedness with the environment that we're in, and there was this kind of connectedness to the community.

I like being outdoors. It's a really important dimension to who I am and how I relate to myself. My notion of a vacation is to go far away, where there isn't all this kind of machinery, in a very broad sense—all these contraptions invented in the last century or two by our species. My sense of the natural environment is reflected in my work with the Nature Conservancy and with other environmental organizations.

The next big event in my life was meeting my future spouse. There are a couple of big decisions you make in life—finding your partner, your mate and lover, and finding someone you really trust to work with, to fill you out and extend you in your quest to make it in the world occupationally. I was fortunate that, by the time I was fourteen, I had met the woman that I felt comfortable with. She's a little older than I am—when I completed high school at age sixteen, she was a freshman at the University of Hawaii.

We plotted and schemed what we wanted our lives to be like. We were both from middle-class families. She had come to Hawaii because her father was an officer in the Marine Corps; she was accustomed to traveling. We connected and poured an awful lot of energy into our relationship, and it blossomed. The evidence of that was our first child, who was born when I was seventeen. Around this time, I started working as a carpenter in the daytime. At night, I attended the University of Hawaii.

Going to school was really a pleasure. I didn't think of it as drudgery. I was fortunate in getting to know a handful of professors very well, and it wasn't uncommon, while I was a student, for me to socialize with them. Two of those relationships have continued to this day; we're still very close. Relationships with my professors were important to me. I would see someone teaching, and I would try to look past the material. I connected with the person. When I talk with our children's teachers today, I don't talk about the syllabus, or how they calculate grades, or the schedule. Those are all extraneous, as far as I'm concerned. I'm really interested in what's happening with that person, what motivates him or her. How do they see their relationship with their students, and is it something that they're connected to? Is it something that feeds them? Because if it feeds them, it's going to be a much healthier relationship for our children.

My time at the University of Hawaii was very important to me. Hawaii was the staging ground for a lot of activities in Vietnam, and it was the only R&R center in the United States. There were protest activities in the local community, working with soldiers on R&R who were having second thoughts about the war. It became a place where the movement against the war became real, and we students were a real part of it.

We had a notion that we would change the world. We had this sense that justice was possible, and that you could achieve it simply by connecting with other citizens. We stopped a tuition hike. Sometimes we'd get arrested. But other people were dying for their beliefs. Kim Cha Ha, a poet in South Korea at the time, had been sentenced to death for writing a poem called "The Cry of the People." The notion of getting arrested in America is so much different than in other places—here it's not a life-threatening kind of event. We could actually make things happen. If we felt deeply that something was wrong, we could do something about it. We believed that the Cold War was not inevitable, that mutual assured destruction should not be a permanent policy, that poverty should not be a commonplace thing.

What amazed me at the time was that we could hear about something, and it could outrage us. Then we could call other people—seventy, eighty, a hundred people—and you could do something about it. You'd write a letter, and you'd copy it to the newspapers. You'd make it available: "These are our demands. This and that's not fair. We were not even consulted in this process. We're an important constituency."

I was involved in student government as the leader of the Committee for Students' Rights. It was the fighting party. The other parties consisted mostly of people dressing up their résumés to get into business schools: They wanted to emulate the state legislature in terms of their conduct, dress, and so on. Then there were those of us who were really saying, "Let's use these resources to promote change." We were driven by a vision and a larger sense of society undergoing radical change.

Law School, a Young Family, and a Search for Purpose

My next stop was Antioch Law School in Washington, D.C., with Maggie and a couple of kids. I can remember an ad in the student paper: "Come to the belly of the beast, Antioch Law School. Where change is really happening." All of us were student leaders, and everybody organized their own party. The Gay Student Lobby had two members, one male and one female. It was just amazing—a bunch of leaders in this place, and no followers. I loved it.

My days were spent going to law school and providing free legal services to the poor. It really was a work/study program. The Legal Services Corporation was in existence—part of the Great Society. At night I worked on the Metro system as a laborer—they called us miners. We worked underneath this big thing that drills tunnels called "the mole." It was this enormous machine that was not quite high enough for you to stand up in. You're laying railroad track, and it's moving through heat and darkness. It was like going to hell every night. I ran out of money and energy after about a year, and I could no longer imagine being a lawyer. It was a pretty bleak period for me. I was in a dark and morbid mood, just feeling run down and out of money with nowhere to go.

It was a tough time in our lives. I didn't know what I wanted to do, and we were broke. We had one car that was always breaking down. Even now when I pass people on the road whose cars are broken down, I remember that that was part of my daily life. You never knew if you could get from here to there. The buses would be late, and you would be late. We were slaves to all of these things. So I came from a situation where I thought I could really change things to one where our resources didn't match our ambitions. That was an interesting period for us and stressful, too, in our marriage.

Establishing a Career

I had this long list of things I'd never do for a living. I wouldn't promote products that had a planned obsolescence inherent in them, which covered most everything that I could see in America. I just couldn't work for a company engaged in peddling junk. I wouldn't work for a company that made pesticides or herbicides. And I wouldn't work for a company that promoted drugs or cigarettes or alcohol or that sort of thing.

So I ended up in the publishing industry because it was the only place that didn't pose any such ethical concerns. Prentice-Hall was an attractive company to me, the most successful independent educational publisher in the world at that time. I had been actively looking for a job for less than three weeks or thereabouts, and a recruiter contacted me. They were looking for people to sell textbooks on college campuses.

I had a great time, going from campus to campus and hanging out with professors, talking to them about ideas and showing them what kinds of products Prentice-Hall had. Soon after I started, I began working with acquisitions editors at Prentice-Hall, and I began to ask, "What kind of products are you looking for?" I was interested in creating more books, and in how new technologies would affect our society and the role of the citizen in our society. Would technologies result in an increased totalitarian kind of force in our society, or would they result in more empowered citizens?

This was a time when personal computers still hadn't been invented, but I'd been around talking to professors, and I knew that there was a major change coming in technology. I had the opportunity to become a specialist in engineering and computer science, which Prentice-Hall had correctly targeted as a major growth area for them. I became one of maybe a couple of specialists in the United States, and Prentice-Hall concentrated them where there were a lot of technical schools. I was assigned to the mid-Atlantic territory, which included Johns Hopkins, the U.S. Naval Academy, Virginia Tech, the University of Virginia, the University of North Carolina at Chapel Hill, Duke, and others.

I had my first "real" job, and I went on a mission to sign and encourage more authors, develop more manuscripts, and produce more books in this fast-growing area than anyone else. I developed good relationships with the editors and went through the Prentice-Hall training program, which was famous at the time as being very comprehensive.

At that point I said to my boss, "I really want to focus on doing software." My view was that there would be lots and lots of small computers, and fairly soon there would be millions of users of software products that would outstrip books in both revenues and profits. It had to happen.

That's where I got into my first business struggle. I had moved to Silicon Valley, in California, which violated a corporate rule—that was the first one. I said I had to move to where the talent was. And the company said, "No. Everybody comes to Englewood Cliffs [in New Jersey]. That's where we are."

Two weeks before I was going to leave, they said, "Okay. We'll pay for your relocation, and we'll stay with you on it." It was an important victory for me.

Then I said, "I could organize the best software developers in Silicon Valley to work with us." And I did, a whole team of them. It was an important accomplishment for me in that everybody had advised me, "Lay low, take your time. We'll get around to it. We'll do one or two software products at some point, and then, if it looks good, we'll grow from there." And I said, "That's not the right thing to do. We need a spectrum of products if we are to have a chance of success." Then they said, "Unwind all these agreements you put together to develop software, or you're out of here." And I said, "Well, I'm not going to unwind the agreements." So I continued to work with all these software authors to develop book/disk combinations, where we'd have products for the Commodore Pet, the TRS-80, and the Apple II, the three dominant personal computers at the time. That was the first time I was fired—which was without question my most important career development move.

I was then aware that I was in charge of my career. I wasn't going to react to what other people thought. I had only $300 in the bank, which did not allow a lot of maneuvering room. Maggie was just astonished. And all the people, all the relationships I'd built at Prentice-Hall, with the exception of one person at a subsidiary—they all said I was crazy. Only one person said I was doing the right thing.

I then consulted to CBS to develop a computer science list—it was a one-year contract, to pay the bills. On the side, I started my own business with a fellow who was a second-generation Mexican American, a really, really good quantitative analyst. The business that we started was focused on forecasting and teaching the economics of the software industry—an industry that hadn't even emerged yet. We had decided that the best way to learn about the industry was to teach it.

Byte magazine was the leading computer publication at the time, and we mailed seminar descriptions to all of their subscribers in New York, Boston, and San Francisco. We decided that if we got a certain response, we'd run a seminar. We sold out in all three cities, and we generated a lot of clients from those seminars. We ended up doing a lot of consulting work, primarily for Microsoft. And over the course of the year, we hired a number of people and went from two to about eighteen employees. We were doing nothing but selling our ideas, and the way in which we thought about the business, and working on specific product plans and documentation.

One of our clients was a company called SORCIM, which is "micros" spelled backwards, and I had an opportunity to go to work with them as a shareholder, and as somebody to direct all their marketing and sales efforts. They were all technical guys and had nobody who knew how to sell. They had a product called SuperCalc, which was going to be announced within the year in conjunction with the unveiling of the Osborne I "portable" computer.

It was my first management job in a high-tech company. I started selling software, learning a bit about the software industry, and I came up with this harebrained scheme of trading SuperCalc source code for other products. You don't want to be the only company with one product; you want to have a complete array of products. So you want to leverage your distribution channels across multiple products. This is what SORCIM wasn't doing at the time, leveraging its early position in the market. Exercise your first-mover advantage, if you can.

So I looked at the other software companies out there, and I went to them and said, "You need a spreadsheet product. We need a word processing product. I'll trade you." Micropro didn't want to do it. But Peach Tree did, and we swapped products in an airport. That's how PeachCalc and Super Writer were born. Then I went down to Software Plus, which had a database product called Vulcan. I offered to swap Vulcan for a spreadsheet product, and they were interested. But when I went back to SORCIM, they got cold feet.

So I moved from being a supporting player in the software industry to having a lead role as CEO of Software Plus, which eventually became Ashton-Tate, the marketer of DBASE II and DBASE III, the de facto database standard in the world. In my first few months there I met Miles Gilburne, who has become my partner in many of my business activities. Neither one of us does anything without the benefit of counsel from the other. In much the same way that I have a partner in Maggie, I also have a partner in Miles—who is a lawyer, a poet, and a Shakespearean scholar. He has a unique ability to rapidly formulate a dozen different ways to architect any deal.

Back to Hawaii and a First Love, the Environment

I returned to Hawaii after a stint as president of Ziff Corporation in New York in the mid-1980s. I decided that it was time for me to start investing more in something besides profit-making enterprises. I had been so consumed by my work that I ran the risk of losing my soul. It was time for me to seek some balance in my life, and I began searching for an environmental organization to meet my philanthropic needs. I interviewed Greenpeace, the Sierra Club, the Audubon Society, and the Nature Conservancy. I didn't want to be on lots of boards or spread a little bit of money in a lot of different places. I really wanted to hurry up and make a difference.

The Nature Conservancy was the far-and-away winner, in terms of their basic strategy, capabilities, and people. So now I have a partner in my activities in the nonprofit area—the Nature Conservancy. I'm presently involved with them in creating new initiatives. One, here in Virginia, is their first for-profit subsidiary, for sustainable development out on the Virginia eastern shore. Another initiative has been our active support for expanding the Conservancy's scope of operations throughout the Pacific region over the past seven or eight years.

A good part of my success is a result of not changing partners all that often. Miles and I continue to be friends and partners. I've worked with the same network of people, and that network expands slowly and very deliberately. It's not a transactional approach to building your community or your tribe. Our tribe has expanded very selectively, mostly because I think we're so intent on knowing whom we're dealing with. It's not "what"; it's all "who." And that brings us, of course, to values and basic beliefs and principles.

Vision and Values

Moral Compass

I have this moral compass for what the graceful relationship is between myself and others. The questions that I think about a lot when I'm looking at a new situation or a new potential relationship are "How does this help me understand truth?"—you know, the truth of a situation—and "How does it add meaning to my life?" I don't ask myself how it adds money or how it helps us get through this transaction.

When I went to Software Plus, I was a very rational, very analytical kind of person with a lot of juice, a lot of passion. It was an interesting mixture of characteristics shared by many at Software Plus. And it was chaos there. I'd been there about two weeks, and I thought, "There's something really different about this place. The people just work day and night, but they get along so very well that there doesn't seem to be a lot of conflict."

Then I found out that almost everybody who worked there was a Scientologist. One of the things that struck me was how they were unified by beliefs that transcended the business we were engaged in. They shared a belief about their relationship with the universe that really helped them in their relationships with one another. Quite remarkable. Although I did not share their religious beliefs, I could see the power of having a unified worldview. It was an early lesson for me, dropped out of the sky: People need a larger connection. They need to see how things connect in order to achieve their potential as a group. They need to share common values.

When Miles and I would get involved in companies, we would lead a three-day management retreat off-site. On the first day, we'd get all our beliefs out on the table. "What do we believe? What do we believe about the nature of our world?" By the end of the day, we'd ask what we believe about our market and about our competitors. The second day would be spent saying, "Okay. Given what we believe, where do we think our relative strengths and weaknesses are as a company?" In other words, how do we fit into the larger picture? We start with the bigger picture and move collaboratively down to our role within it. Not until the third day would we begin working on specific plans and strategies for the company.

Too many people only want the answer—really smart people out there, CEOs, they only want the answer. They don't understand that they can be faster than all of their employees, but if they don't include them in that process [of searching for the answers], in the end they're going to be slower than their competitors. You've got to start with the big picture—look at vision, values, and core competencies. Values must be inculcated throughout the company and relentlessly practiced at the top. Even if you have a company that's a $2 billion global company, if you don't answer the first question about who you are and what your relationship is to the rest of the world, you'll find yourselves in a precarious position.

Children as Teachers

I'm most passionate about my children at this stage in my life. I find myself thinking more and more about them. They drive me crazier than they've ever driven me before. They have more power over me than they've ever had, and I thought I'd end up with the upper hand. They are twenty-eight, twenty-two, twenty-one, and sixteen. My sixteen-year-old son and I spent five hours together last night. We went to a picnic with the Olympic athletes—which was great; they're all here in town—down at Wolf Trap. Afterwards we went to the Tracy Chapman concert. Then, at 10:30 at night, he's delivering his vision of his future to me: "This is what I will and will not do in my life." He's sixteen! All of them have a growing influence on me. They're at the point now where they're teaching me a lot.

One of my rules, Cole's Law: I tell people when I recruit them, "If you really want to learn twice as fast as your competitors, find a mentor half your age." So we hire a lot of really smart young people, and rather than telling them what to do, we tell them what problems we're grappling with, and we ask them, "How would you approach this?" We learn so much more that way. These young people in our company are some of the best people in the industry, and they weren't even in the industry last year. But they have this passion, and they have great intellects. And they're curious. Their eyes sparkle. They have lots of different ways of dealing with things.

Obstacles

Conventional Wisdom

Earlier in my life, I ran into obstacles—at Prentice-Hall, in law school—big obstacles. One was financial. But I always felt there was a way out. What was the worst thing that could happen? I could go bankrupt. I've never gone bankrupt, but the possibility didn't scare me. "Do I feed my children or do I pay this month's tuition?" was always an easy question to answer. I had a lot of creditors in the early part of my life, but I think they're all happy now.

The other obstacle was conventional wisdom, or practice, or customs that people wanted me to follow—somebody else's wisdom or customs. I decided to disregard the conventional wisdom or custom, or I would opt out. I would say, "Those are your obstacles. They're not mine." It was the perspective we had in college: I wasn't sentenced to die like Kim Cha Ha. The worst they can do in America is fire me.

I told Steve Case when I went to work with him at AOL that I do have one policy: "If I have three bad days in a row, I'll leave." By that I meant I won't be engaged in irrational power politics. I cannot be engaged in some process where I feel that decision making is corrupted by forces that have no relevance to the issues at hand.

I've had lots of failures, made lots of mistakes, and learned lots of lessons from them. In order to produce one Shiva or Macromedia, two or three failed companies are left behind. They fall into a couple of categories. There are companies like the living dead: They don't lose money and they don't make money; they just keep going. And then there are those that just didn't connect, and you have to let them go—mercifully. You try to do it in a humane fashion, but you want to do it quickly. We missed with our product, or we were outgunned, or we bet on the wrong management team, or there's no time to get back in the market, or whatever. That sort of stuff happens when you push the envelope.

In conservation matters, you don't win a high percentage. So you have to be careful that you don't end up focusing on small things that make no difference, a green measle that's going to disappear no matter what you do. You make sure you get to a sufficient scale where you really can make a lasting kind of impression. At the same time, don't risk so much that it's unlikely you'll ever get anything done. You can do lots of feel-good, easy things, or you can really gun for big projects. To be a conservationist, you have to be fairly optimistic.

Instead of saying, "The world is going to hell in a handbasket," you have to go beyond that as a conservationist and say, "We can do something about this. We can change our relationship to the Earth. We can change our relationship to God."

When there's disconnection inside of people, there's a disconnection in their relationship with the outside world. I think that a lot of the violence we do to the landscape—when people litter, for example—is a manifestation of noise inside us. When people scar the Earth or don't think through the implications of cutting a forest, they manifest a deeper imbalance inside.

We inflict on children what we do to the outside. If you put children in the middle of broken glass and detritus from all parts of our industrial society, they, too, will feel like detritus. They will feel alienated from what could be a warmer kind of experience in the human community. And they carry that around. You can take those children and move them to a pristine paradise, and immediately they will create the shards of glass and the rusted cans because that's who they are. There's not a hard line between where we are sitting at this moment and that forest out there.

The Business of Hope

I would say to young people, to those losing hope, "You need to recognize that you're not alone, that you have soulmates out there." Sometimes, if you're very lucky, you can turn to religion. I'm not religious. My conception of God is not something that materializes in a certain way. My spirituality revolves around a whole mystical sense of wonder, rather than a reified framework for religious belief. That's what works for me right now.

But some people are very lucky. They have a religious relationship they can carry with them, and I think that's wonderful, a special relationship with a larger force. But if you don't have that, one way to build strength is to find others and invest in others. It's not the number of people. In a way, you end up with lower self-esteem by having more and more people that you surrender to, or trust, or just give yourself to. It's really more important to find people who share some of your pain. One of the things that's successful about, say, Alcoholics Anonymous, is that it shows people who have temporarily lost hope how other people have conquered that dilemma, people who have made it to the next step.

One of the great things about information technology is that it really helps you to find people with similar interests. The Internet can help you find people who have similar interests, and who have suffered similar pain. Pain is just a part of life; find others who have gone a step past where you are now. Similarly, if you can find people who need your guidance, you can shepherd them through something you've already been through. That would be good for both of you.

I think that's how you build hope: by seeing living evidence of people who have done it. Some programs are good. Maggie's involved in the Boys and Girls Club. They're in the hope business in a big way. The way we've organized our lives with our children and our own hope business is by creating a foundation that targets funds to individuals who are themselves in the hope business. We're creating environmental entrepreneurs, people who try to build sustainable businesses in relationship with the environment, so that organizations don't degrade the environment in the normal course of their business.

I've been inspired by Jeffrey Jacobs, president of HARPO Entertainment, who's created a group called Civitas to deal with the problem of child abuse and the cycle of parents abusing children, who then grow up and, in turn, abuse their children. Jeff went to his alma mater, Loyola Law School, and said, "I think it's important for us to understand the rights of abused children. I want to devote funds to people who want to specialize in the rights of abused children." Then he went to Baylor University and said the same thing to a psychiatrist there, who developed a program dealing with post-traumatic stress disorder in abused children. Then he went to the School of Social Work at the University of Michigan and established a work/study program in the summer, stipends and all, to develop social workers who really think about this problem and how to break the cycle of abuse. So he's creating Civitas scholars.

He's really quite an inspiration. As I listened to him at the Investors' Circle (a group I belong to, made up of people who invest their own money for dual dividends in new enterprises), I thought, "We could do the same thing for environmental entrepreneurs." And that's what we're working on now.

Vision for a Better World

One of the things I wrestled with after I left law school was the question of what's good for us as a species. I had the notion that if you get people more information, and they can participate in determining what to look for, what to learn, and when to learn it, they will become better citizens, people who can set agendas and have a higher sense of responsibility for their community in a broad sense.

Will technology result in an increased number of totalitarian elements in our society? Or will technology be a mechanism for empowering citizens to do more and take more responsibility for their decisions? I'm currently laboring under the assumption that by building broad-scale information networks, you actually empower people. People end up with an ability to perceive a lot of events remotely, to discover virtual communities of people who don't have to be close to one another yet can share experiences as groups and touch other communities and other worldviews.

I'm really trying to understand the nature of humankind. Are we capable of restraining our urges, deferring gratification so that other parts of our world can survive? I believe that we can move away from a near-term view of what's good for us to a longer-term view. We know that certain Native American cultures had a rule for guiding them in making major decisions affecting their tribe: They tried to think about the seven generations that had preceded theirs, as well as the seven generations yet to come. If adopting a certain course of action would benefit and/or be approved by all of those preceding and following generations, then and only then would they do it. How different this approach is from the typical American focus on short-term business results. In America, the comparable guiding question might be "What did you do for me yesterday?" Yet if such an enlightened attitude—focusing on the welfare and values of past as well as future generations—can be present in certain human cultures, why not in others?

Is this the winning strategy? I don't know. I'm hopeful, though, that we can influence how the mature world-historical trends unfold: the rise of corporatism, and the alienation of our souls. They're very big forces, and we have yet to figure out where the rudder is. Can we change some of our behavior? To the extent that we can help organizations rethink the ways in which they relate to the people that compose them, we can help them see that they are part of something larger than themselves, communities outside corporations.

Look at corporatism. Suppose I strike a deal with you and say, "I want tax concessions to put a plant here." And you go to all this trouble as a local government in a local community to attract an employer. You build a lot of trust in that relationship. Suppose I then decide that when my tax concessions run out I will leave. The company has a different set of values, which is "This is a transaction. As long as it's cheaper here, this is where we'll stay. When it's not cheaper, we'll leave." But once a company builds a plant, it has a new group of stakeholders, all of the people in that community.

The way in which we think about articulating the responsibilities companies have toward stakeholders—indeed, who the stakeholders are—can affect the way in which people relate to one another and even the way in which we relate to our environment. You can't just treat everything as a transaction. There has to be the principle of a lasting relationship, and not the overriding kind of logic that says run to the cheapest spot at any given time. Eventually that approach runs us all down. It dehumanizes us all.

On the environmental front, there's a need for us to rethink our definition of capital, so that it doesn't include only conventional notions of where capital goes—the money you put in and what we buy with it. The Earth is not viewed as capital, yet it is. You would never dip into principal as a responsible financial steward, yet we dip into our environmental principal all the time when we use fossil fuels, deposit toxic waste into the Earth, clear-cut forests, desecrate coral reefs, and so on—as if the Earth were an unlimited resource. My view is that we need to redefine principal to include our own planet, which means that we can think about spending nonrenewable resources, but let's account for them and know what we're doing. Capitalism isn't completely broken. It simply fails to account for the real costs of many enterprises.

Another thing—and this is where we're investing some of our resources—is that we need to build a new kind of entrepreneur, one who really knows how to build teams and create new businesses explicitly oriented toward yielding dual dividends: dividends in the traditional sense of a return on capital, and also in the sense of what's sustainable and good for the community. We can introduce sustainability into the method by which we calculate what good enterprises are. I would like to see business schools teach that in much the same way as they now teach ethics.

I think that sustainability and compatible development are new areas that will emerge in the next twenty years that will be very, very important to improving the quality of our lives. So as a change agent, you ask yourself, "How can I find the point of maximum leverage?"

Finally, we need to reconceptualize our relationship to the great mystery or creator and our delicate living tapestry on Earth. The old hierarchical view of God, humankind, and then all the lesser creatures at the bottom of the pyramid is fatally flawed. We must move toward a circular or spiral relationship with other living things, where we recognize that both our spiritual and our physical well-being are not safe in a scorched and sullied world. Our souls cannot flourish without the extraordinary diversity and beauty of our natural world.

Lessons We Learned

DreamMakers express vision and values. "You've got to start with the big picture—look at vision, values, and core competencies. Values must be inculcated throughout the company and relentlessly practiced at the top. Even if you have a company that's a $2 billion global company, if you don't answer the first question about who you are and what your relationship is to the rest of the universe, you'll find yourselves in a precarious position."

DreamMakers understand that we are all connected and interdependent. "The old hierarchical view of God, humankind, and then all the lesser creatures at the bottom of the pyramid is fatally flawed. We must move toward a circular or spiral relationship with other living things, where we recognize that both our spiritual and our physical well-being are not safe in a scorched and sullied world."

DreamMakers value and nurture interpersonal relationships. "A good part of my success is a result of not changing partners all that often. . . . I've worked with the same network of people, and that network expands slowly and very deliberately."

DreamMakers tap in to the extraordinary potential in all of us. "We hire a lot of really smart young people, and rather than telling them what to do, we tell them what problems we're grappling with, and we ask them, 'How would you approach this?' We learn so much more that way."

DreamMakers make their dreams a reality. "I was then aware that I was in charge of my career. I wasn't going to react to what other people thought."

DreamMakers focus on education and continual learning. "I tell people when I recruit them, 'If you really want to learn twice as fast as your competitors, find a mentor half your age.'"

DreamMakers follow a moral compass. "I had this long list of things I'd never do for a living. I wouldn't promote products that had a planned obsolescence inherent in them, which covered most everything that I could see in America. . . . I wouldn't work for a company that made pesticides or herbicides. And I wouldn't work for a company that promoted drugs or cigarettes or alcohol or that sort of thing."

DreamMakers believe in a higher power and purpose. "Then I found out that almost everybody who worked there was a Scientologist. One of the things that struck me was how they were unified by beliefs that transcended the business we were engaged in. They shared a belief about their relationship with the universe that really helped them in their relationships with one another. Quite remarkable."

DreamMakers demonstrate responsibility toward a larger community. "I decided that it was time for me to start investing more in something besides profit-making enterprises. I had been so consumed by my work that I ran the risk of losing my soul. It was time for me to seek some balance in my life, and I began searching for an environmental organization to meet my philanthropic needs."

DreamMakers are committed to making the world a better place. "My view is that we need to redefine principal to include our own planet, which means that we can think about spending nonrenewable resources, but let's account for them and know what we're doing. Capitalism isn't completely broken. It simply fails to account for the real costs of many enterprises."

Just as we have seen business leaders choose a different path from the norm for their lives and their organizations, so we will find here stories of individuals who have decided to pursue community good as personal fulfillment. Guided by their vision of "what is possible" rather than "what is" or "what is expected," these DreamMakers dream big and have achieved those dreams for themselves and the communities they serve.

Sharlonda Gillis' youth was troubled and her future threatened by circumstances largely out of her control in her earliest years. When she is confronted with the consequences of her worst nightmare—stabbing another girl in self-defense when only fourteen herself—she can choose darkness or light. With a willingness to accept help from others—something many of us find difficult to do as we tend our own pride—Sharlonda is able to achieve the same degree of self-empowerment that we have seen in highly accomplished business leaders. She develops a new vision for her own life that encompasses the work of the Warren Conner Development Coalition and the possibilities

Part 2

DREAMMAKERS BUILDING COMMUNITIES

SHARLONDA GILLIS
Youth on the Edge of Greatness

MARILYN KING
Beyond Sports

SURRY COUNTY, VIRGINIA

JULIET CHIEUW AND JOYCE BARTELS-DAAL
The Aruba Quality Foundation

for all youth. She reaches deep inside and pul to the surface the values toward which she had always gravitated: learning, respect for people and life, and love.

From "wannabe" athlete to Olympic champion to leader of the Peace Team—it's an unlikely story, but it truly and completely belongs to Marilyn King. Marilyn makes radical strides in learning about the power of personal vision, confronting her fears of failure time and time again, making herself vulnerable to the help and guidance of others, and transferring each lesson learned to the next and larger challenge. Her inner strength resonates with that of Sharlonda. But more than anything, Marilyn has grasped a complex and deep understanding of vision combined with a passion for action and good information: "If people everywhere who want to live in peace will dare to imagine the world they want to live in, envision it in great detail and do something every day to work toward that goal, we will achieve it."

A handful of wise and compassionate leaders in Surry County, Virginia, refused to accept the agenda they had been handed and organized themselves against incredible odds to re-create a community that honored the human potential in everyone. Four of these leaders tell a story of overcoming prejudice, economic hardship, and deprivation in almost every human service area one can think of. Through belief in a higher power, themselves, and the basic capacities of all people, and through the ability to co-create and share positive visions and deeply held values, they were able to reinvent their county's educational, health, housing, job assistance, recreational, and economic systems. They were even able to close the county jail, which they believe was so substandard that it did not honor even the most basic standards of humane treatment. They believe, as much as anyone represented in this book, that "our greastest asset is our human resources, our people."

From two different pathways, Joyce Bartels-Daal and Juliet Chieuw step into a journey with the people of Aruba to co-create a vision for the future of their island that they can all be proud of. Their faith in one another, in their network of colleagues and friends, in the basic goodness of human beings, and in a higher power "holding us very gently" gave them the courage to pursue a mission of such enormous magnitude—involving all 90,000 people on the island, including the children, the government, the business and education communities, and the spiritual leaders. Now many people in Aruba are working on shared priorities of national pride, health, safety and security, quality service in all sectors, environmental stewardship, education, and personal development "so that we can contribute to the global health of the planet." Others in this book would find a comfortable and reassuring port in Aruba.

Each of these stories speaks to the great power of community, to the hope that can emerge when people understand their relationships with one another and with their environment, and to the creativity and fortitude that are possible when a great diversity of people with enormous respect for one another is allowed to flourish. Each of the individuals you are about to meet provides the rest of the world with a model of hope and achievement against all odds.

SHARLONDA GILLIS *is Warren Conner Development Coalition's youth development director. She has been actively involved for over a decade in this community-based organization focusing on improving the quality of life on Detroit's east side. As a leader at Warren Conner, Sharlonda serves on the management and transition monitoring teams, and she heads the Youth on the Edge of Greatness program, which changed her own life when she was a troubled teen. She is also involved in several other Detroit youth programs, and she runs her own small events-planning business called Shar-P.*

RESILIENCE AND EMPOWERMENT

*Sharlonda Gillis, Youth
on the Edge of Greatness*

I was talking with my oldest brother, Teddy, about some of the fascinating DreamMakers I had come across while writing this book, and he said, "You have to talk to this young lady I just read about in the *Detroit Chronicle,* Sharlonda Gillis."

When I arrived at Sharlonda's apartment on the East Side of Detroit, I was not at all prepared for the remarkable person I was about to meet, nor for the incredible story I was about to hear. Sharlonda is courageous, open, determined, and wise. She is committed to helping young people in her community see their possibilities and reach for their potential. She works with many young people who fear they won't live past the age of eighteen. I sat in awe of her insights, her strength, and her insatiable desire to learn and turn her mistakes into positive, life-giving actions. Growing up, she beat all the odds and overcame obstacles no child should have to face. Today, at the age of twenty-four, she is director of Youth on the Edge of Greatness.

Sharlonda is an example of what we called at Herman Miller a "frantic learner"—one committed to lifelong learning, open to ever new possibilities, acquiring new perspectives and competencies at a startling rate. It is ironic, therefore, that she was permanently expelled from all of Detroit's public schools when she was in her teens. Think about that word *permanently:* It sounds like a life sentence. Fortunately, Sharlonda found the support and internal strength to get beyond that setback.

Angela Wilson, former deputy director at Warren Conner Development Coalition and a key mentor in Sharlonda's life, also participated in our conversation. She helps us see the challenges Sharlonda faced and the unique strengths that sustained her.

Sharlonda shares with us an inspiring story of the power of her own personal vision. She takes us back in time from her present situation—one of great hope and enormous contribution—to her period of deepest despair and desperation, and shows us how she got out. Her story gave me hope for our youth and their tomorrows. I listened, I learned, and I was moved.

Defining Moments

The Present

Sharlonda Gillis: I'm the youth development director for Warren Conner Development Coalition, working with young people between the ages of twelve and fourteen. We take them through a comprehensive program, where they talk about issues related to their lives, and we teach them life skills, giving them information that helps them make good everyday decisions. We take them through job readiness to get them prepared to go through a job search, fill out an application, and keep a job once they get one. We also offer entrepreneur training for those young people aspiring to start their own businesses. We provide academic support, attracting tutors from different universities and other volunteers. We take them through social and cultural enrichment that focuses on pride in their African American heritage, and we expose them to other cultures, so they have a sensitivity and respect for people of other backgrounds. We take them on field trips, offer recreation. We also have a family development component, where we promote positive interaction between the young people and their families.

In 1995, after a five-year demonstration, the program won national recognition, resulting in our receiving a grant from the Center for Substance Abuse Prevention. However, this grant was cut in the recent federal budget cuts, and we would not still be running the full program if it weren't for a grant from the Skillman Foundation. That's great news that I just found out about.

The name of the program is Youth on the Edge of Greatness. Young people come to us from teachers, parents, churches, the juvenile system, and community organizations. If they've had some experience with the juvenile justice system, their probation officer might refer them. We always end up with too many young people, and, unfortunately, we have to turn some away. However, we do try to refer them to other programs. We work with eighty young people a year.

Career Decisions

Sharlonda: I have been youth development director for the past year. I went through the program myself when I was fourteen, and I stayed around after I graduated and volunteered for a while. At seventeen, I worked as a youth supervisor, but it was a part-time position. I had to leave because I needed to make money. I wanted to go to college and needed to move out of a bad home situation. So I left and worked at a bank for five years. Then a position came up at Warren Conner that fit me to a tee. But I said to myself, "Maybe it's not time to leave the bank. Warren Conner doesn't have a 401(k), so maybe I should stay."

Then I went to a conference, the Development Leadership Network, in New York. I convinced Maggie DeSantis, executive director of Warren Conner and my mentor, to send me there, mainly because I wanted to go to New York. I got there and listened to people speak about their transitions from working in the community to working in corporate America and vice versa. I was really intrigued by what people said. Working at the bank was fine, but for me there was no direct service to people. The bank serves a purpose, but Warren Conner serves a higher one. So I followed my heart and went back to Warren Conner.

Angela Wilson: Sharlonda never really left Warren Conner. She always volunteered here, and when the job of coordinator came up, she knew she could do it. She told us, "I can do that job. I want it." Now, the salary was less than what she was making at the bank, and there was no guarantee that it would go up or that a better position would become available—we're a nonprofit and constantly raising money. But Sharlonda took the plunge.

Sharlonda: I started out planning events, and I just loved it. I'm an implementer: I love to make things happen. I was promoted within six months to manager, so now I planned events and also did membership development and volunteer recruitment. Then I was asked to think about what other things I could do for the program. The issue of school reform came up. I thought long and hard about it. I thought it would be amazing if I worked to reform the same school system that had rejected me ten years earlier—and I decided to do it. So I became the school reform manager. During this time, I also entered my master's program at New Hampshire College. I majored in community economic development, which was all related to my work— school is work and work is school.

Then Warren Conner needed a youth development director, and Maggie asked me to do it. I was really scared. I wondered, "Can I really do this justice?" I hadn't finished my degree. Now I am comfortable and confident that I know what I'm doing—I have the vision. I knew Maggie thought I could do it. My supervisor, Donna Johnson, thought so. I remembered when I was afraid before, and they said, "You can do this," and they were right, so I decided to trust them and myself. Now I'm shaping and forming these new programs. Sometimes it's overwhelming—at twenty-four I'm doing this.

A Troubled Teen

Sharlonda: When I was fourteen, living on the East Side of Detroit, I was probably your average teenager making the transition from middle school to high school. That was a big transition for me. In middle school, everything is much more structured. In high school, you could leave when you wanted and you were responsible for getting to all your classes. If you're not there, the teachers aren't going to look for you, which wasn't good for me. I chose to skip sometimes.

I had this friend—we always walked to school together. One day we were walking to school, and she was eating a pear. She had a pear knife. She asked me to carry it for her, because she was always getting in trouble. I put it in my jacket and forgot about it—probably had it in my pocket for three days. Even when I tell this story, it sounds unbelievable, but this is how it happened.

One day there were these two girls in the lunchroom, and we were looking over at these little girls and laughing at them. It was silly—it was a teenage thing. Then I went to my world history class, and a senior came charging at me. She said, "I heard you've been messing with my cousin." Now, she was a fairly big girl, and I knew I should have run. She started swinging, and peer pressure prevented me from running. So we started fighting. The next thing I know, I'm on the floor, and this big guy picks me up and takes me into the hall. I'm in tears by this time, and I was going to call my mother. I go up two flights of steps to the phone, but I'm so nervous and so upset, I dial the wrong number. I never fought in school—that just wasn't my background. Then this girl is coming up the hallway and starts running at me. I remember saying to myself, "How do they keep letting this girl loose?" She's on me, and the next thing I know I had stabbed her. I just couldn't believe what I had done. Within five minutes it felt like my life was over.

Angela: In the early 1990s, kids started writing on their intake forms that their greatest fear was not living to be eighteen years old. A lot of kids were into drug trafficking and dropping out of school. They saw it as a way to make money. When I got to the center in 1985, kids were writing on their intake forms that they were afraid of not graduating or of failing the tenth grade. Around 1989, kids started saying they were afraid of being shot on the way to school, afraid someone in their family was going to be killed. Kids started carrying guns. The behaviors that brought kids to the program were different. Parents were afraid their kids were becoming involved with gangs, whereas in previous years they were having trouble in school or not interacting with their peers. It was obvious there was a more violent atmosphere.

Sharlonda: I ended up in juvenile for a week. All I could do was cry and think, "What have I done?" This is very hard for me to talk about. I had to watch my mother in pain when she visited me every day. She was alone, my father was strung out on drugs somewhere, and my mother was raising four children alone. This was really hard on her. They didn't know if the girl I stabbed would live at that point, but finally she was okay. She survived, thank God. I am really grateful for that. I remember not caring what they were going to do to me, because I felt I deserved to be punished. The whole thing was overwhelming.

Next I had to go through the school system's disciplinary process. I went to a hearing, and they wanted to set an example, because the schools were becoming violent. So I was one of the young people permanently expelled from all Detroit public schools. We didn't know what to do. For a while, I sat at home, but my mother kept telling me, "You have to go out and do something." That created a lot of pressure for me. Sometimes when we get older, we forget about all the pressures a young person feels. I was overwhelmed. I actually got to the point of considering selling drugs. I remember crying that night and thinking I had very few choices. At least if I sold drugs, I could send money to my mother, but I knew then I wouldn't be able to see my family that much, because the drug dealers used the girls and women in the drug houses to watch the drugs. I cried all night.

An Opportunity Opens

Sharlonda: The next day—it was a blessing—my sister came home with this little card that said "Youth on the Edge, please apply." My old science teacher had sent it. The only reason I applied is because it said that they provided part-time jobs for young people. I saw dollar signs, and my mother had told me to get a job. School wasn't even an option, so I went. I found a community of people who helped me, and I really got excited about having someplace to go and something to do.

Angela: When we started the program in 1985, we started with ten kids through fifteen sessions. We found out quickly that if kids saw some value in the program, they wouldn't go away. You couldn't beg them to go away. We tried to bring in a new group, and the old group told us, "That's not fair. You can't kick us out. This is our program." We had to adjust and find a way to keep those kids and still expand the program.

The program is comprehensive, and kids see value in it. Some of these kids have never been out of their neighborhood, they don't see very much. One summer we took the kids to grocery stores outside their community, and they were stunned that the stores were clean and brightly lit. That's sad. They didn't even know there was another world that other people experience every day. We used to take them to the theater, horseback riding. Exposing kids to what's available is important. I have seen a lot of kids turn around—go on to decent jobs and living decent lives. Some don't.

I was there when Sharlonda came into the program. She was a loner, very vocal, and would tell us what was on her mind. I remember taking the kids to a formal dinner. All the boys had to wear jackets and the girls had to wear dresses, but Sharlonda refused. She said she didn't even have a dress. Finally, she went home and had her mother buy her a dress. She was always real determined, always set her own agenda. She clearly wanted to go to school and get an education. Getting her in school was the challenge. We struggled with that. We were never successful with the public school system, but we got her a tutor, and we had her tutoring an eight-year-old. We wanted her to give back by teaching someone else and to stay connected to education.

Sharlonda: I was still discouraged because I was not in school. Finally, I told Angela and Maggie, and they tried to get me reinstated. They were unsuccessful at getting me back into school, but they were successful at getting me a tutor, a teacher named Mrs. Strickland. I was so excited. I thought, "Wow! She doesn't have to do this." I felt people cared about me. The big problem, however, was that you couldn't take the high school equivalency exam until you were eighteen. Here I was only sixteen, so I started taking college prep courses at Wayne County Community College.

Angela: Sharlonda knew when she came into the program at fourteen that she wanted her education and not just a high school diploma. She wanted to go to college. I remember her talking about that. It was important to her, and so it was important to us. When you have a kid telling you, "Hey, I want to go to school!" but you can't get them enrolled, it's really frustrating.

Sharlonda: So things were happening. I ended up getting my associate degree. Then another blessing happened. I went to Chicago to help plan a conference for that same organization that had influenced me to go back to Warren Conner, the Development Leadership Network, and I met Woullard Lett, an administrator at New Hampshire College. He told me that I had enough credits from college and from my experience in community development to enter a graduate program at New Hampshire College. So I went. I flew to New Hampshire once a month and received my master's degree in March 1997.

Help Along the Way

Sharlonda: The science teacher who originally sent the "Youth on the Edge" card to me, her name was Mrs. Herbert, now Mrs. Abbott. I saw her sister at

Hudson's department store one day and realized I had never told Mrs. Abbott that sending that card to me saved my life. I told her sister my story. She was so excited, she said, "This is why we stay in the education field." Then she pulled out her cellular phone in the middle of Hudson's and called her sister, and I told her my story and thanked her. Her sister is still active with me in school reform.

Angela Wilson has always been supportive, has helped me find a place to live, and helped me think through day-to-day decisions. And Maggie DeSantis helped me to create a vision for myself. She also helped me when I messed up. I got all these credit cards and messed up my credit rating. She had me give her all my cards, cut them up, and then helped me to repair my credit. Jurutha Kennedy, a board member of Warren Conner—as part of the program, they would hook the young people up with a board member—she became my mentor and still is today. I just saw her a couple days ago. We go to lunch and talk. She helps me understand why some things occur. She challenges me to think deeper about what it is I'm doing. When I get upset about something, she says, "Think about it, why is this happening?" As a result of having people like those three around, I can be successful. I've now made it a permanent part of the program to match all the young people up with mentors, because I know how important they've been to me in my own life and development.

My mother was always there, and even if she didn't have the answers, she never gave up on me. My Aunt Peggy has always helped me pay for school. My grandmother just gives me inspiration because she always has really nice things to say. You'd be surprised how many people don't have nice things to say. My sisters, Melinda, Vernetta, and Sharmaine, are my closest friends.

And I guess I should say my father, to the extent that he has lived a life where he has made a whole lot of bad decisions that I've learned from. I used to have a lot of anger for my father, and I still have some, but I also see the pattern he fell into. He was pretty much raised in the same kind of environment and neighborhood that I was. I can understand why he fell into selling and using drugs. It actually helps me when I'm working with young people. I see these young guys and understand that my father was one of them at one time, that he was confronted with the same difficulties and unfortunately didn't get the kind of support I did.

Sharlonda: My primary personal goal is to live a decent life, to make decisions that are socially responsible. Another is to be a role model for other young people, so they have something to look forward to. Look at where I've come from, and look at where I am now. Sometimes it's so hard to see outside the box that you're in if you don't get exposed to other things. I'm most passionate about, and committed to, always working in some capacity to further opportunities for young people, to stimulate young people to see their possibilities. The young people we work with live in neighborhoods just plagued with violence, drugs, and all kinds of bad influences. They don't see anything else. We offer these young people alternatives. My goal is to help them to see themselves in their best light and to provide them with environments where they feel comfortable learning and growing.

When I was in the program, one of the ways we got paid was by delivering newspapers. I remember one day our supervisor asked, "Can somebody come up with a better plan to deliver these papers?" He said we were going to try everyone's idea, and that was the most empowering thing. They tried my plan, and it made me feel like my opinion was valued and I was validated. That was one of the best builders of my self-esteem. They ended up throwing my plan out, but that didn't matter. What mattered was that they valued my ideas enough to try them out.

My vision and values are connected—respect for people. My number one value is respect for life. So much that happened in my life has helped shape the way I think about things now. It's been ten years since I stabbed that girl in high school. I feel like life is short, and just the fact that I could have taken someone's life is really scary. It bothered me for so long. I always felt like something was missing. I would go to church because I do believe in God, and it would make me mad. I had done all these things, had all these accomplishments, and still I felt as if something was missing. I had always prayed to God to forgive me for bad things I had done in the past, but I had never asked Him to forgive me for stabbing her. This was a year and a half ago. So I prayed for forgiveness. I don't consider myself a religious fanatic, but I prayed for forgiveness. I cried for two hours, and from that day forward, I have never felt that I was missing anything in my life. It allowed me to forgive myself. Sometimes your worst enemy is yourself. I learned a lot from my mistake, and I am able to forgive myself, and I know I can help other young people to avoid making some of the same mistakes that I made.

I also value friends and family. You've heard me talk about all these people that have influenced my life.

I value learning. I don't happen to believe that formal education is the only type of education. I believe in learning from all situations—from others, from elders, from young people—but always challenging yourself to learn about something. I still have to struggle with that today because sometimes we get comfortable, and it's like, "I've done this," but don't get comfortable. Continue to try to learn.

I believe in God, in a higher power. That's important to me.

I value being able to love people and care for other people. That's really important to me. Also being able to be happy for other people, being happy when something good happens to them or they accomplish something. This is new for me, too. Just two years ago one of my good friends did something, and I was happy for her, but at the same time I felt irritated. I said to myself, "What's wrong with you?" I had to really challenge myself to deal with that. I think when you get to the point where you can really be happy for others, there's a lot of value in that.

Obstacles

Sharlonda: I believe I beat the system. A lot of people bet against me, wrote me off. If you're a young person with no skills, out of school, what are your chances of success? It's not just about winning all the time, but when you have to fight so much and so often with the perceptions of other people, their negativity, as well as your own fears and doubts, it makes you feel good to move on and have a better vision for yourself. Their vision of you can't dominate yours. It's about really beginning to know who you are and understand where you want to go. I actually think I was able to learn so much because I didn't go to high school.

I spent a lot of time around wise older folks. I was at the office every day and I learned to listen a lot. Now I talk a lot, too—talking is like a hobby to me—but I learned to listen to these wise and caring older people. I owe them a lot. That's why it became my goal to succeed, because the people at Warren Conner supported me and believed in me. It became my job to make them and my mother proud of me.

My message to young people is this (it actually comes from something Angela once said to me): "There's a whole world out there; don't limit yourself. Challenge yourself to continue to learn and grow. Find someone who is doing what you want to do and attach yourself to that person. Then create a vision for yourself."

Vision for a Better World

Sharlonda: I'm always asking, "How can I create more opportunities for young people? What can I do to contribute to those young people's lives?" If I can work to improve a system that will affect a whole generation of young people, then I need to be doing that.

Lessons We Learned

DreamMakers express vision and values. "My vision and values are connected—respect for people. My number one value is respect for life."

DreamMakers support diversity and honor the integrity and contributions of all people. "When I was in the program, one of the ways we got paid was by delivering newspapers. I remember one day our supervisor asked, 'Can somebody come up with a better plan to deliver these papers?' He said we were going to try everyone's idea, and that was the most empowering thing. They tried my plan, and it made me feel like my opinion was valued and I was validated."

DreamMakers value and nurture interpersonal relationships. "I've now made it a permanent part of the program to match all the young people up with mentors, because I know how important they've been to me in my own life and development."

DreamMakers collaboratively transform and renew themselves and others. "One summer we took the kids to grocery stores outside their community, and they were stunned that the stores were clean and brightly lit. That's sad. They didn't even know there was another world that other people experience every day. We used to take them to the theater, horseback riding. Exposing kids to what's available is important. I have seen a lot of kids turn around—go on to decent jobs and living decent lives."

DreamMakers make their dreams a reality. "A lot of people bet against me, wrote me off. If you're a young person with no skills, out of school, what are your chances of success? It's not just about winning all the time, but when you have to fight so much and so often with the perceptions of other people, their negativity, as well as your own fears and doubts, it makes you feel good to move on and have a better vision for yourself. Their vision of you can't dominate yours."

DreamMakers focus on education and continual learning. "I believe in learning from all situations—from others, from elders, from young people—but always challenging yourself to learn about something."

DreamMakers foster creativity and hope. "I'm always asking, 'How can I create more opportunities for young people? What can I do to contribute to those young people's lives?' If I can work to improve a system that will affect a whole generation of young people, then I need to be doing that."

DreamMakers believe in a higher power and purpose. "I don't consider myself a religious fanatic, but I prayed for forgiveness. I cried for two hours, and from that day forward, I have never felt that I was missing anything in my life. It allowed me to forgive myself."

DreamMakers demonstrate responsibility toward a larger community. "I'm most passionate about, and committed to, always working in some capacity to further opportunities for young people, to stimulate young people to see their possibilities. The young people we work with live in neighborhoods just plagued with violence, drugs, and all kinds of bad influences. They don't see anything else. We offer these young people alternatives. My goal is to help them to see themselves in their best light and to provide them with environments where they feel comfortable learning and growing."

MARILYN KING *is a two-time Olympic athlete and a former head coach at the University of California, Berkeley. Through her work with Beyond Sports, the consulting business she founded in 1981, she provides business leaders and educators with thinking skills that will serve them for a lifetime. Her clients have included American Express, Apple Computers, AT&T, Hewlett-Packard, IBM, Sun Microsystems, and Xerox Business Services. She has also presented at over 200 national and international education conferences with academicians and researchers who are designing schools of the future. She is the creator of an inner-city youth empowerment program called "Dare to Imagine." Her most pioneering work, a joint Russian-American venture called the Peace Team, prompted two invitations to speak at the United Nations.*

OLYMPIAN
THINKING

Marilyn King, Beyond Sports

Marilyn King and I had been intending to meet each other for about two years—we had not even talked by telephone. Our acquaintance was through mutual friends and colleagues, who knew we had much to learn from each other. Even though our lives had taken us down very different paths, we shared a passion and belief in the power of vision and values.

One day I was down in Aruba, meeting with the folks at the Aruba Quality Foundation, helping them create a shared vision for their country. It was my first visit to the island. The foundation was filled with excitement, activity, and chaos. Juliet Chieuw and Joyce Bartels-Daal had been overwhelmed by the tremendous response from the people of Aruba after their invitation to contribute to a vision for that country. So much was going on that when the phone rang, no one answered it. I hesitated, not wanting to overstep my bounds, but then felt that I should do something. So I picked up the phone and said, "Aruba Quality Foundation." A voice said, "This is Marilyn King. May I speak to Juliet Chieuw?" I said, "Marilyn King, the Olympian Marilyn King?" She said, "Yes, who is this?" I was speechless. I had traveled thousands of miles to an island off the coast of Venezuela to finally connect with Marilyn King.

Within three months, I was in Aruba again and so was Marilyn. She was doing a business leadership seminar for the foundation, and I was meeting with Aruba's Vision Steering Committee. We shared our ideas, our vision for the world, our business strategies, and our friendship. Our connecting in Aruba is an example of what Carl Jung—and, more recently, Joseph Jaworski—called "synchronicity" at its best, and what I call God's work: The needs of this small island had been a catalyst for bringing us together to do something special. And our union gave me the chance to learn about and shine a light on Marilyn's story.

Defining Moments

Marilyn King: When I think about being considered for inclusion in a book called *DreamMakers,* I get a big smile on my face. While being an Olympian was a dream come true, mine would be a very different story if I had been someone destined to be a great athlete. I wasn't.

My father was in the military. We moved a lot, and I was basically shy and had trouble meeting people and making friends. I was always the new kid in town, so I got involved in sports and athletics as an easy way to make friends and create community. And it was always very wholesome. I wasn't a great athlete—I wasn't the fastest or the strongest, I wasn't the one who learned the quickest, I wasn't the team leader, but I was slightly above average. But while I wasn't a great, I was a great competitor. There was something about how I used my mind that allowed me to compete with those who were better athletes than I. Sports were really a good socializing activity, and it worked for me. I ran on a lot of relay teams and had a lot of fun.

Then my life took an unexpected turn.

The Eastern States Pentathlon

At a competition one day, they announced the Eastern States Pentathlon Championship (five track-and-field events: 100-meter hurdles, shot put, high jump, long jump, and 200-meter race). Only two girls had entered, and they needed three for a legal competition. I asked my coach for permission, and he let me volunteer. At the end of the day, lo and behold, I was the third best on the whole East Coast. Until this happened, I had never even heard of a pentathlon.

I had always thought of myself as a clunker—you know, an aspiring athlete, but an "also ran." Then, all of a sudden, I'm the third best on the whole East Coast in something. And it changes your thinking to be recognized as good at something. So I thought, "Gosh, if I train for this, who knows, maybe I could beat them." And I did. The same two girls showed up the next year, and I became the Eastern States Pentathlon Champion, which was a very big deal on Staten Island in New York, where I was from.

So they send me to the National Pentathlon Championships alone, and I am just blown away to be there. There are around sixteen contestants from the whole country, and I place in the top ten, and my mind is tripping. I'm in the top ten in the whole United States in something I'd only heard of a year ago! Then the Olympic Committee shows up and invites a number of athletes—including two women I had beaten—to the Olympic Training Camp. And they skipped me. Well, I'm from the East Coast, my coach is not there politicking for me. Nobody had ever heard of me.

An Olympic Dream

You talk about a defining moment in a dream. The Olympic dream came into being in a nanosecond. I thought, "Wait a minute, not only did I beat them, but I'm a better athlete than one of them. If the Olympic Committee thinks this person can go to the Olympics, and I'm a better athlete than she is, then I could go to the Olympics, too." And that was it! That was it! That moment—that one new thought—shaped the rest of my life. I could go to the Olympics! That one moment, one new, outrageous thought, one flickering of neurons, created a paradigm shift that changed my whole life. When you hold on to an image of something that matters to you more than anything else, your world changes.

I went to college in southern California because I knew that all the great athletes were on the West Coast. But I made a mistake, selected the wrong coach. He just wanted to tell me what to do. After taking his orders all day, I wanted to understand why I had done certain things, and he said, "Because I said so." I knew this was not the coach for me, although technically he was the best in the country. So I left him and went to train with Ed Parker in northern California. This was really the coach for me. He was, I can't say egoless, but it sure seemed like it. He was there for us; he was a lifelong learner. Every conference we went to, any time a speaker came, he always picked that person's brain. He was always picking the brains of other coaches, trying new things. He wanted to know, and everything was an opportunity to learn.

So I went to train with Ed Parker in the Bay Area, and went to Cal State University at Hayward, which had a great kinesiology department and physical education program. I made the Olympic team in 1972 by the skin of my teeth, experiencing my first conscious awareness of imagery impacting performance. I had placed at the Olympic trials high enough to qualify for the 1972 Olympic team, but you also have to score a minimum number of points. Two of us in the top three hadn't scored enough points. So they set up another competition for us, against the Canadians, before the Olympic team left for Europe, so that we could score the points. It poured buckets in Champaign, Illinois, and the humidity made it an ugly, ugly day to try to make the Olympic team.

Going into the last event, I needed a time that equaled my lifetime best in the 200 meters. We were drenched, we were exhausted, we were beat. My very fast, tall friend, Gail Fitzgerald, was also trying to make the Olympic team. They put her in the lane next to me, and I knew that if I could be side by side with her when we came out of the turn, I could use her to pull me through. The gun went off, and when we came off the turn, Gail was gone. She was so far ahead that it seemed she was nowhere in sight. I was in deep trouble. Then my mind created this amazing, spontaneous image. I saw my friend Gail on the back of the Staten Island Ferry, pulling away from Staten Island with New York City in the background. She was waving good-bye to me. And my mind said, "You're not going without me." And I ran like I was going to jump onto that ferry. I crossed the finish line and went straight to the three timers for my lane. Two of the three watches had clocked me in exactly the time I needed. Gail and I both became Olympians. The combination of daring to imagine I could be in the Olympics and envisioning Gail pulling away on the ferry had landed me on my first Olympic team.

Munich

The Olympics in Munich were pivotal for many people. They are forever etched in my mind and in my heart for so many reasons. It was memorable and joyous for me because every kind of person was there. You could walk around that village, and there were 300-pound shot-putters, seven-foot-tall basketball players, 72-pound gymnasts—people from just about every country, every race, every religion, and every political persuasion. It was truly the global village, and it remains a key experience and motivator in my work now. For a moment in time, I knew and experienced that it was possible to live in peace. Then came the terrorist attack on the Israeli team, and it was as if the outside world was saying, "You cannot have this." But inside the Olympic Village, as Olympians we all had respect for ourselves and for one another at a very deep level. I came to believe that, with respect as a core guiding principle, we *can and will* live in peace.

The Olympic Committee said that the games must go on. Olympic athletes are highly skilled at directing and focusing their attention, and so we focused solely on the competition. Going home, and not having a chance to debrief from that experience, resulted in post-traumatic stress-like symptoms for many Olympians, including me. Not being able to talk about that experience interrupted the needed cycle of grieving and healing. I had been very rudely awakened and profoundly impacted by the depth of the Munich experience—and I became deeply passionate about my experience and totally confused about the world. It took me nearly a year to recover emotionally, and the next three years were really about training for 1976. A dozen Olympic veterans, including Bruce Jenner, gathered in San Jose to train for Montreal. It was a great training situation, which resulted in my placing thirteenth in the pentathlon, and for me that was quite an accomplishment.

Training for the 1980 Moscow Games

At the Montreal games, I was inspired by the European women—by their speed, their strength, their commitment to excel. I decided to train for one more Olympics, to complete my career by setting aside the year before Moscow to do nothing but train. I did not believe I could actually win a medal, but I wanted to end my career saying, "I did it." I wanted to push the limits of my abilities and find out just how good I could be.

In preparing for 1976, I had watched Bruce Jenner take his solo morning runs during which he imagined himself crossing the finish line in Montreal, winning the gold medal, setting the world record, and retiring. He played the same movie in his head each morning. Bruce won the gold, set the record, and retired after the 1976 games. I decided to do the same thing. I'd take an apartment by the track, and just spend the whole year training for the 1980 games and envisioning success and retirement.

My plans for 1980 were abruptly altered in November of 1979, when my car was hit from behind by a truck. While it wasn't a catastrophic accident, it was enough to give me a bulging disc in my lower back. And that literally incapacitated me. I could not move. I couldn't turn over, couldn't sit up. I certainly couldn't spend six to eight hours a day training for the Olympic pentathlon. I now understand what it means to be a great competitor—my mind was my strong suit. I now understand the power of what happened in my mind. I didn't think that this would be a life-threatening or career-ending injury. I assumed we'd find out what the problem was and that it would go away. So I just kept telling myself, "I'm getting better every day, and I'll be in the top three in the Olympic trials." I said that over and over like a mantra. But my back problems did not go away. I spent four months unable to train physically.

So I watched films of the world record holders in all five of my events. I watched those films for many, many hours, in slow motion, frame by frame, even backwards. I was not able to train physically, so I trained mentally. As I propped myself up in the chair and watched the films, I could feel every movement in my body. I could smell the grass and feel the wind on my face, hear the sound of my feet on the runway. I could feel the rhythm, the pace, what muscles were moving. When I got bored, I would lie down on the couch and envision my events.

Before the Olympic trials, the United States' policymakers decided the team was going to boycott the Moscow games because of Russia's invasion of Afghanistan. As athletes, we continued to train, hoping that we were going to be allowed to go to Moscow. With almost no physical training and a boycott looming, I placed second in the pentathlon at the Olympic trials for the Moscow games. Somehow, I got exactly what I had envisioned: to finish in the top three at the Olympic trials. Unfortunately, I did not get what I had intended. I had not paid any attention to points, and I didn't score enough to meet the minimum qualifying standard. So when they named the Olympic team for Moscow, I wasn't on it.

I did learn something very important about the power of imagery: When used consciously, it's both a science and an art form. One of the things I've come to understand is that imagery is very, very specific. It's almost like the imagery mind can't take a joke: You get what you envision, not what you intend. The universe has repeatedly taught me this same lesson about specificity. I've had a number of experiences of aligning the three elements I teach as "Olympian Thinking," and I've accomplished what I had envisioned but not what I had intended. I aligned a very deeply held passion with a very clear vision and followed through with all kinds of action that brought what I had envisioned to fruition. I am very, very respectful of the process of aligning passion, vision, and action. I believe that I will get what I envision, if it is passionately held and I follow through with action. It makes me very cautious about what I envision. I had said to myself that I would finish in the top three at the Olympic trials, and that is exactly what happened, but it was not what I had intended.

Grandmother

I think the biggest influence in my life was my grandmother, my mother's mother, Marceline. She was French Canadian, and grew up in a large family in the late 1800s. Her sisters became teachers, but she was pulled out of school in the fourth grade to iron the handkerchiefs and bake the biscuits for the men who would go through my great-grandmother's boarding house. She never really learned to read and write. But she did sit up at night playing checkers with these men who were worldly-wise, and that's where she got her education. She soaked it up. My grandmother became quite worldly-wise, but she loved to play. She was a good athlete and loved to dance.

The one story that was pivotal in my experience of learning the power of what I now call "Olympian Thinking" was the story of my grandmother's coming to this country from Nova Scotia. She told my mother to go out and slaughter the chickens and packed up these suitcases, and made chicken sandwiches. Everyone was saying, "They'll never let you in the United States during a depression with no visible means of support, six kids, and pregnant." My grandmother just looked them straight in the eye and said, "No man is going to stop me." No one at Customs was going to keep her from finding my grandfather, who had left for Boston to find work but had never sent for her and never sent her money. She decided she was going to find Grandpa Fred. She arrived in Boston and bumped into this very well-dressed man who looked at her and looked at all of those kids and said, "Are all these kids yours?" And she said, "Would they be with me if they weren't?" And he said, "Well, what are you doing?" She said, "I'm looking for my husband, Fred Gillis." He said, "I'm looking for Fred Gillis. I'm his boss. We go out and sober him up every two or three days, get him to work, and pay him, and he disappears again." This man took my grandmother and all the kids, found my grandfather, sobered him up, and brought him home. My grandmother told me many, many stories like this that show you what happens when you align passion, vision, and action.

The Power of Imagery and Vision

After placing second at the Olympic trials for the 1980 Moscow games without physical training, I knew something extraordinary had happened. I knew immediately that I was not interested in using what I had learned to help people run faster and jump higher. I researched the areas of imagery, visualization, and mental rehearsal—skills often referred to as "the master skill of high achievers." I discovered that people were teaching these skills to cancer patients, because what we envision affects every cell of our bodies. The field of psychoneuroimmunology is based on the body-mind connection. Hypochondriacs do not just think they are sick: They often manifest diseases because of negative thoughts they have. What we envision affects our health and well-being. We can affect our healing and health by what we think. I hope someday we teach kids in school about how our natural body-mind connection works for promoting optimal health.

I also learned in my exploration of what happened to me that not only do the images that we create in our minds affect our physiology, but they also affect our performance. That's why they were teaching astronauts, salespeople, public speakers, actors, and all kinds of people to use imagery to improve their performance.

Then I discovered that imagery also affects our future, both individually and collectively. One of the people who most affected my life regarding this issue was Willis Harman, a futurist with SRI International and president of the Institute of Noetic Science, which was founded by the astronaut Edgar Mitchell. Willis Harman showed me that what I had done in my Olympic career was just one use of the master skill of high achievers. I was profoundly moved by how the same tool that I had used was being used in such dramatic ways by people in other professions—and had been for centuries. Writings by the ancient Egyptians about how images held in the mind have the ability to affect the physical universe tell us that the awareness of the impact of imagery is not new. Roger Sperry, who won the Nobel Prize, said, "Consciousness is a causal reality." This is not voodoo California hot-tub stuff. Our mental images affect our physiology and our performance, and I came to understand that they also affect our future. That's why I work with what some people call "at risk" kids. They're at risk because social conditions have put them at risk and they have not had the privilege of people assisting them in making images of healthy, productive, satisfying possibilities. Their images of a positive future are limited or in some cases nonexistent. There is very little positive modeling for many of them.

Images of our own futures affect what we do on a daily basis; our daily thoughts direct our actions, and our actions determine our results. If you're in an abusive situation—whether in society or in a relationship—and you can't imagine changing it or leaving, then you probably won't. But those who dare to imagine that they can make a change become creative problem solvers in the service of their dreams. In my work, I very strongly underline and talk about the critical issue of courage. "Olympian Thinking," which is what I teach, is the alignment of passion, vision, and action. Passion doesn't happen by default. It takes great courage to dare to imagine your dream coming true. To look inside and ask yourself the questions—"What is it that really matters to me? If I could do anything, what would I do?"—it takes courage to accept the challenge of what you find when you ask those questions.

World Peace

One new thought changed my life forever, when I asked myself the question "What am I passionate about?" For one of those rare moments in my life, I got quiet and waited for the answer. Instantly three thoughts occurred in my mind. They just flew into my mind, forever indelible. They were, in this order: my grandmother, human potential, and peace.

I easily recognized the appropriateness of the first two, but when peace occurred to me, I was shocked. I had never been involved in any peace efforts. Then I saw the three icons that I use in my work—a heart for passion, the drawing of an eye for vision, and a little stick figure of a running person for action. All three are required for exceptional human performance. When people push the envelope, individually or collectively, all three of those things must be present. Passion and vision without action is just a dream. Passion and action with an inappropriate or inaccurate vision is an exercise in futility. And if there's no passion in the system, you don't even step up to the plate.

Regarding peace, I immediately saw that there are almost six billion people on the planet, and that the vast majority of them want to live in peace. So I thought, "We've got one out of three of the requirements for living in peace. We don't have to go manufacture passion for peace, we just have to unearth it." People are out there trying to do things, but a lot of people don't do things because they just don't think it will really make a difference—that's their negative vision. Among those who do have a clear vision of the goal, many cannot imagine realizing it. But if people know what to do and can see how their actions accelerate our progress toward peace, will they take action? Of course they will. The willingness to help create a world at peace exists, and people are beginning to see that their contribution is part of a larger, viable plan for peace.

We're two-thirds of the way there on achieving this vision. What's missing is information. The media treats things—huge, global things like the end of the Cold War, the eradication of diseases, the dawn of global communication capabilities, strides toward ending hunger and reducing infant mortality, waves of change sweeping through large corporations—like isolated incidents. For example, people don't understand that superpower-supported wars all over the world stopped because the superpowers were no longer propping up regimes and supporting guerrilla armies. While many of those conflicts have evolved into ugly, more local power struggles, in many ways that is a de-escalation, easier to resolve than the Cold War. When you treat such a change as an isolated incident, you can't really understand what it means. When you treat the end of apartheid and the election of Nelson Mandela to the presidency of South Africa as an isolated incident, you commit a grave injustice. You fail to see these as pieces of a larger story in the evolution of humankind.

Look at what people are doing in your city, in your own community. There are answers. I get emotional about this, because most people don't have the privilege to see what I see, to know what I know. What I know leads me to realize that we could very well see peace in my lifetime. Willis Harman said, "The negative belief that peace is not possible is the greatest impediment to peace." Regardless of how passionate they may be, people who do not believe peace is possible will rarely become the creative problem solvers in bringing about peace. As people everywhere who want to live in peace dare to imagine the world they want to live in, envision it in great detail and do something every day to work toward that goal, we will achieve it. The reason that this particular moment in time has never existed before is that we now have global information technology. For all the things that are problematic about technology, it allows us to share accurate information about our tremendous progress, and to share answers. The majority of problems that exist on the planet have creative solutions that already exist and that can now be shared with others working on the same problem.

The cynics will say, "Yes, but what about this, what about that?" I don't have all the answers, but I have to share one story about one of the "what abouts." A friend told me a story about a man in South Africa. After Nelson Mandela became president, this man's brother was shot in the back—a hate crime, a Black man gunned down in the driveway of his new home by a White man. You would think that this man [the surviving brother], who had fought his whole life to end apartheid, would be bitter. Yet he has such deep love, and such a passionate commitment to living in peace, that he wants to share those feelings, share that depth of knowledge about forgiveness and healing with people in other parts of the world, like Rwanda and Bosnia. He wants to become a powerful force for peace and assist others to transcend their own anger and pain.

When I had my "aha" about the possibility of peace in my lifetime, I felt like a crazy person. I had never heard anyone talking about things in that way until I heard Willis Harman. Though internationally respected in the futures field, he was very gracious when I approached him. Shy as I was, I had to talk to him because I didn't know who else I could talk to who would understand the implications of our collective negative beliefs about the possibility of peace. He invited me to his home. In the two hours or so that we spent together, he treated me with such great respect and dignity and had questions and new thoughts. He was really in a dialogue and an exploration with me. When I went out and sat in my car, I was dumbfounded. I had made Willis Harman think! Whether or not that was true, I felt that way when I got back in the car. It made me believe that perhaps I had something to contribute to our thinking about peace. Willis's life, his words, his belief in the power of ordinary people to collectively, consciously shape our world continue to give me the courage I need to pursue this work.

Vision and Values

Olympians Sound the Call for Peace

We will see peace in our lifetime when people take time each day to align their desire to live in peace with how they think and what they do. Peace is, first and foremost, a state of mind. We can change our minds in a nanosecond. Olympians as messengers can sound the call for that one minute—I know that when people understand the power of envisioning, they will be willing to take one minute a day to envision the world they want to live in. That image, that one minute, will guide their actions differently from their previous images of nonpossibility. As we each do our part each day, a little bit more each day, people will reconnect with and strengthen their desire to live in peace, their images will become more clear, and their actions will become more effective. There are people around the world who already each day take time to stop, take a breath, and envision the world they want to live in. Their images of peace guide their daily actions.

The strategy to ask Olympians to create visibility for World Peace Day and the power of that act of envisioning is to engage more and more people in the realization that we are all on the same team. I may disagree with your politics or your strategy or your lifestyle, but we can find a way to live in peace and move toward peace a little bit more each day, pushing the limits like an Olympian in training to become the tiniest bit more peaceful each day.

This is the work the Brahma Kumaris World Spiritual University has done. They have gone into 126 countries, asking people for their visions of a better world. It doesn't matter what race or religion or political persuasion or socioeconomic level they come from. People all say the same things about the world they want to live in. This is what is so exciting to me. There is already a common vision—it just isn't being spoken. So, in fact, passion, vision, and a willingness to act already exist, waiting to be aligned and mobilized.

The Peace Team

I have been working on this now for seven years, talking to people, designing materials, planning how the outreach will happen, keeping logs of companies that I think should be partners in this effort, creating relationships with people in those organizations. Who are the people already 100 percent on this virtual peace team? I want to know who my colleagues are, who my peers are, who the people are out there trying to figure out their best contribution to peace and then doing it. What are they doing and how can I support them? How can we use the International Day of Peace as a truly global holiday to report on our progress toward peace, shine the light on what is working, and log the commitments people make to peace for the next year?

I am priviledged to know many people who have made major contributions in the world and are now coming together to focus on what I call "the only game in town." The name of the game is Peace, and Peace is the only Gold.

The Role of Business

One of the things I learned from my esteemed colleagues is that the biggest player on the planet in determining the quality of life for all people in the twenty-first century is not government but business. Business is now the prime mover in the world, and it shapes our destiny. For some people that elicits a cynical response. They say, "No wonder we're in trouble, look at the values and impact of business." There's certainly some truth to that view, but my work teaching Olympian Thinking has profound implications for organizations and has brought me into contact with companies that are setting new standards for the twenty-first century, companies like Xerox Business Services, by far the most profitable and innovative division of Xerox. They have determined that to become the "premier learning organization" is their competitive advantage in the next century.

Their process for learning faster than their competitors and the marketplace is called the Change Strategy, which is all about creating a place where learning and creativity flourish, where people want to live and work and play, where people take responsibility for their own continuous learning based on a shared vision and shared values that inspire and guide their actions. I've come to tell my clients that if you are in a company where people come in and punch the time clock and push buttons, you won't survive in the twenty-first century. Companies need to be quick and agile, engaging the best in all their people. There's no way that you can survive in the twenty-first century if creativity and innovation are only coming from a chosen few up in the glass office. They must also come from people engaged in the day-to-day business of the company. It is engaging the heads and hearts, as well as the hands, at the shop-floor level that will bring prolonged high performance to an organization.

I have found five explanations for why people are passionate about work. One, they make a lot of money, but research tells us that money alone doesn't bring out the best in people and isn't sufficient for sustained high performance. Two, they care about the company, just as people at IBM in the first thirty years were proud to be part of that company and its values. Three, sometimes the product itself generates passion—when Apple Computer came into being, people believed that they would change the world by creating these funny little boxes and putting them on people's desks, and they were right. Four, it is sometimes because of the challenge—because people just love to be around high achievers and be inspired to be their best. And five, it's about the community, the people you work with, the relationships and feelings created at work.

So Olympian Thinking teaches us that if you want an agile, high-performance, creative organization in the twenty-first century, you should be drawing on all five of those areas to enlist people's passion. Different people in the organization are there for different reasons. But if you build an organization in which you pay people fairly, if you're a high-integrity company that people are proud to work for, if you create a quality product that's of value, if you challenge people to grow and change, and if you do all of that while also fostering a strong sense of community—then you're going to have people who are passionate, creative, committed, and proud to be part of your business.

There was a fabulous write-up about Xerox Business Services in *Fast Company,* a relatively new business magazine. Chris Turner, chief architect of the Change Strategy at XBS, was asked, "What's your vision?" She said that she wanted Xerox Business Systems to set the standard for what it means to be a twenty-first-century company. When I talked to Chris on the phone a few weeks later, she said, "Marilyn, I don't want to change the company, I want to change the world." So when I express hope and optimism about peace in my lifetime, it is in part because business is the biggest player in defining the quality of life in the next century. Everywhere I go in the corporate world, I find companies that understand the need to engage the whole person—body, mind, and spirit. Many of them are multinational trendsetters experimenting and challenging themselves to lead the way to a desired future for all.

Obstacles

On Being a Female Athlete

Olga Connely, the five-time Olympian in track and field, was a powerful role model for me in 1972 and helped me understand some of the obstacles I faced. One of the things I did find very difficult was the multiple messages that rained down on me as a young female athlete back in the 1960s. People would say when they saw a tall, lean, athletic person working out, "Is that a boy or a girl?" And the boys weren't interested in having you be their girl-friend. In high school I had a lot of guys who were good friends of mine, but being a strong female athlete was a very, very mixed experience in those days.

I met Olga Connely at the 1972 Olympic games. She was a discus throw-er, five-foot-ten or -eleven, maybe 170 or 185 pounds, a very powerful, beau-tiful woman, very articulate, very intelligent. She was highly revered and respected. That meant a lot to me, that Olga—a Czechoslovakian—was born in a country where to be a big, strong, powerful, beautiful, intelligent, artic-ulate woman was very sexy and attractive. Confident men were attracted to her. She didn't have to compromise: Olga stands proudly and firmly on all of who she is. So she was a great role model for me. She stood for the real pur-pose of the Olympic Games, and the U.S. team recognized this by selecting her to carry our flag in the opening ceremonies.

Dealing with Fear

Unfortunately, while I had a powerful message and fine delivery, I didn't yet understand how to make a living in the business of speaking and consulting. I was very disempowered and felt guilty about not being able to make good on so many things that I believed so passionately about. My greatest obsta-cle has always been fear, with all of its many faces. It heartens me to under-stand the importance of courage in peak performance. But fear of not being loved, fear of not being accepted, fear of being ridiculed, fear of becoming so successful—fear is disempowering. I have friends and colleagues who went from being total unknowns to having global notoriety, and that shift was not the most positive thing that happened in their personal and emotional lives. I have seen people be absolutely devastated by fame, popularity, and success. It terrified me on some level. I saw friends whom I respected get torn apart in the press by things that weren't true. So to be successful did not look too good to me. Especially since I am by nature a shy person.

How do you overcome fear? This is a great question—and an ongoing challenge for me. I have two ways. One is to confront it head on, because it's more the feeling of fear itself that you need to come to grips with and not the thing feared. I ask myself the question, "What's the worst thing that could happen, if you decide to go for it?"—like going to the Olympic games. I envision the answer very clearly. After identifying the worst outcome, evaluating it, and consciously deciding to take the risk every time the fear surfaces, you remind yourself that you have dealt with the worst-case scenario and refocus on the goal.

The other way is to just go into it, and stop resisting. I had to overcome a tremendous history of never quite being solvent in my business. After years of struggle I gave in to the fear—that I was a failure. I was devastated by a particular incident when a client decided not to do this project we had planned. The decision had nothing to do with me, but it really threw me. I just started beating myself up. I just gave in to feelings of abject, utter despair. I went out on the lawn and lay down after that telephone call and embraced images and feelings of failure for the first and only time in my life. After about three hours, I looked up and saw my house, and I thought, "Well, you're not a complete failure, you have this wonderful house in the hills."

Then I thought about my relationship of eighteen years, and I thought, "Oh, okay, you've got a nice house and a great relationship, your health, great friends. Okay, you're a business failure." Then I thought, "No, that's not true. You have a highly respected technology, you're a great speaker. So, okay, I'm not a business failure, I'm a financial failure." Then I thought, "Well, not exactly." And I finally got it down to exactly what kind of failure I was. And it really wasn't so bad. I knew that I was either going to get back on the horse or give up my business and go to work for somebody. I created a strategy to determine if I should be in business for myself, learned what was missing, and put it in place. I am now financially successful and able to produce results at a much higher level.

Vision for a Better World

If everybody on the planet had the chance to achieve their potential, we would live in a very different, very exciting world. For that I would be willing to jump into the volcano. What drives me is the opportunity for everyone to achieve their potential. The world I want to live in is peaceful, prosperous, and proud.

My vision for humankind is guided by the Global Peace Team image. I want to live in a world at peace. Because this goal is not impossible, that means it is possible. I want to make my best contribution, accelerating our progress toward peace. I want to be a person who walks the face of the Earth, and when I'm done the world is a better place—I don't want to consume more than I give back.

My vision is also about respect. If there is one word I could put in everyone's mind with a wave of my magic wand, it would be *respect,* the kind of respect that I experienced in the Olympic Village. First and foremost, respect for myself—my physical body, my mind, and my spirit. And then respect for others in body, mind, and spirit. Third, respect for the world I live in, for the birds and the bees and the trees and the water and the air and other resources. Respect for the history of the land I live on right this moment, where less than 200 years ago, indigenous people knew how to live in harmony and balance with the spirit that enlivens the trees and the birds. I have respect for my ancestors, and I also have respect for those who will come after me.

To the young, the cynics, the hopeless, I would say, "Be aware that our actions are shaped by our thinking, our attitudes, our beliefs, and our opinions." And be very, very careful about what information you base your beliefs and attitudes and opinions on, because my personal experience is that we are all getting incomplete information. The good works that you hear of someone doing in your city or community are not isolated events and are part of the larger story that's emerging from people all over the world who are doing their part.

The history of the world is not just the history of wars. It's the history of peace and courageous people taking a stand for what is right. Of the almost six billion people living on the planet right now, most of them are trying to live in peace. So take the whole picture into account—see the good things— and let them affect you and influence you, because your attitudes, your opinions, and your thoughts dictate your actions. To the hopeless and to the young, I say, "Dare to imagine. Find something in your heart that matters to you, and find others who are daring to imagine things that matter to them. Surround yourself with kindred spirits, and go for it."

As people everywhere begin to communicate the courageous stories and creative solutions, more and more people will be inspired to do their part. There are more of us than there are of them. Soon we will all recognize that each day each of us must step forward and create the world we all want to live in. As we take responsibility for being made in the image and likeness of God, and for the fact that we too are creators, we will live in peace.

Lessons We Learned

DreamMakers express vision and values. "If you build an organization in which you pay people fairly, if you're a high-integrity company that people are proud to work for, if you create a quality product that's of value, if you challenge people to grow and change, and if you do all of that while also fostering a strong sense of community—then you're going to have people who are passionate, creative, committed, and proud to be part of your business."

DreamMakers engage others in their vision. "The strategy to ask Olympians to create visibility for World Peace Day and the power of that act of envisioning, is to engage more and more people in the realization that we are all on the same team. I may disagree with your politics or your strategy or your lifestyle, but we can find a way to live in peace and move toward peace a little bit more each day, pushing the limits like an Olympian in training to become the tiniest bit more peaceful each day."

DreamMakers understand that we are all connected and interdependent. "If there is one word I could put in everyone's mind with a wave of my magic wand, it would be *respect*, the kind of respect that I experienced in the Olympic Village. First and foremost, respect for myself—my physical body, my mind, and my spirit. And then respect for others in body, mind, and spirit. Third, respect for the world I live in, for the birds and the bees and the trees and the water and the air and other resources."

DreamMakers tap in to the extraordinary potential in all of us. "I researched the areas of imagery, visualization, and mental rehearsal—skills often referred to as 'the master skill of high achievers.' I discovered that people were teaching these skills to cancer patients, because what we envision affects every cell of our bodies."

DreamMakers find unprecedented opportunities for transformation and renewal in the current climate of rapid change. "Their process for learning faster than their competitors and the marketplace is called the Change Strategy, which is all about creating a place where learning and creativity flourish, where people want to live and work and play, where people take responsibility for their own continuous learning based on a shared vision and shared values that inspire and guide their actions."

DreamMakers make their dreams a reality. "The Olympic dream came into being in a nanosecond. I thought, 'Wait a minute, not only did I beat them, but I'm a better athlete than one of them. If the Olympic Committee thinks this person can go to the Olympics, and I'm a better athlete than she is, then I could go to the Olympics, too.' And that was it! That was it! That moment shaped the rest of my life."

DreamMakers are both passionate and compassionate. "'Olympian Thinking,' which is what I teach, is the alignment of passion, vision, and action. Passion doesn't happen by default. It takes great courage to dare to imagine your dream coming true. To look inside and ask yourself the questions—'What is it that really matters to me? If I could do anything, what would I do?'—it takes courage to accept the challenge of what you find by asking those questions."

DreamMakers demonstrate responsibility toward a larger community. "That's why I work with what some people call 'at risk' kids. They're at risk because social conditions have put them at risk and they have not had the privilege of people assisting them in making images of healthy, productive, satisfying possibilities. Their images of a positive future are limited or in some cases nonexistent. There is very little positive modeling for many of them."

DreamMakers are committed to making the world a better place. "As people everywhere who want to live in peace dare to imagine the world they want to live in, envision it in great detail and do something every day to work toward that goal, we will achieve it."

WALTER N. HARDY

is a retired supervisor of Gwaltney of Smithfield. He is a member of the Surry County Board of Supervisors, and has served as both chairman and vice-chairman. He is a member of the Surry Assembly, and a member of the board of trustees of the Chippokes Farm and Forestry Museum.

C.P. PENN

has been superintendent of the Surry County Public School Division since 1977. He is active in church and in many fraternal, civic, and civil rights organizations.

TERRY D. LEWIS

has been a county administrator of Surry County since 1988. He was formerly a county planning director of Isle of Wight County, Virginia, and Surry County Planning and Development Director.

THOMAS S. HARDY

is retired from the Norfolk naval shipyard and is a current member and former chairman of the Surry County Planning Commission. He is currently president of the Surry Assembly and chairman of the board of directors of the Surry Family Health Group.

COMMUNITY
BUILDING

Surry County, Virginia

I was 90 percent sure that I was going to write this book when I decided to call one more precious ally, Frances Hesselbein, former CEO of the Girl Scouts of America, current president of the Drucker Foundation, and a good friend and advisor for some seven years.

When I discussed this book with Frances, she told me, "Of course you should write this book, and I have a DreamMaker for you—the County of Surry, in Virginia." In their research into the plight of Black men and boys in America, Frances and an advisory group to the Kellogg Foundation had uncovered this incredible community in rural Virginia, where a remarkable collection of people had created miracles. They transformed an area with severe educational, housing, and public health care challenges—a county whose population was 65 percent African American but with no Black representation among its political or community leadership—into a community working in harmony, a community with representative leadership, a community to marvel at.

The day of the interview, I drove from Washington, D.C., to Surry, Virginia—three hours of excitement and anticipation. I walked into a room of distinguished, proud Black men, who seemed to be as excited to talk with me as I was to hear and share their story:

Terry Lewis, the county administrator

Dr. C. P. Penn, the superintendent of schools

Walter Hardy, vice chairman of the Board of Supervisors of Surry County

Thomas Hardy, president of the Surry Assembly and a member of the County Planning Commission

These leaders have made their dreams come true through courage, resilience, and a deep commitment to their vision of a community that cherishes and nurtures all of its people, especially children. Their vision, values, and belief in God combine to form their North Star.

Postscript: Thomas Hardy told me that he was supposed to write a history of Surry County, but never did. For those who would like more information on Surry County, one of his daughters wrote a dissertation at Howard University Law School entitled "The History of Surry's Struggles and Injustice to Blacks, Plus the Many Accomplishments the County Has Made Since Gaining Black Control." At this writing, she is serving as general counsel for Hampton University in Hampton, Virginia. NBC News did a program on the county that was carried on the evening broadcast. Surry has also been written about in the *San Francisco Chronicle*, the *Chicago Tribune*, the *Washington Post*, and the *Toronto Star*.

Defining Moments

Creating the Assembly and Getting People Registered to Vote

Thomas Hardy: Back in the 1960s, during the time of Martin Luther King, we in Surry County worked in the civil rights movement. Back then we had an organization called the Surry Improvement Association. We had struggled to get more voter strength in the county among the Black majority population, which was approximately 65 percent at that particular time. But we didn't seem to be getting very far in registering voters. At that time, we in Virginia had to pay a $3 poll tax to vote. A lot of our people really did not have the $3, and this held back our voter registration drive. But with the help of the NAACP and the Surry Improvement Association, we did make some inroads. The first Black elected official in the county was my wife, Gladys Hardy—a write-in for justice of the peace—but that was as far as we got. We kept meeting to determine what the problem was, but we couldn't get all of our people together.

Terry Lewis: I guess the Surry story sort of parallels the modern civil rights era. What took place here was similar to what was taking place in many other areas. We were trying to utilize political power that communities gained at that time through the federal legislation that gave African Americans a greater opportunity—gave all people the vote. Of course, Virginia, up until that time, had a number of ways of keeping citizens from voting—including the poll tax and the literacy test. There was also a liberty tax. But with the advent of the legislation that came about in the 1960s that abolished these obstacles to voting, many people looked for ways to mobilize the political power they saw in minorities and poor people. Surry County was one of the communities in which such an opportunity existed.

Thomas: Then Don Anderson came to Surry, and with Don's help we organized the first Surry Assembly in 1969. Don had been working with U.S. Representative Adam Clayton Powell in New York. He founded an organization called the National Association for the Southern Poor. We were highly suspicious of Don. In fact, at first we accused him of being a Communist. We wondered why he wanted to come to Surry County. We questioned him extensively, and finally he was able to convince us to organize the assembly. Charles C. Pettaway, a civil rights leader and pioneer of the success Surry enjoys, was the first president of the assembly.

The Surry Assembly is the strength of our community today, really the secret to the whole thing. The assembly is built on the structure Thomas Jefferson used: Each community divides itself into wards and sets out to solve its own problems. The meetings are designed and modeled after the British House of Commons, where you have a president and a speaker of the house. The organization consists of one representative out of each ward.

It's a structure built to truly engage the people—a problem-solving design that gives everyone in Surry County a voice. The ward representatives have seven committee members, and those seven pick seven people in their immediate community. In the end, every voice in the county is represented.

One of the things that helped us a lot was that the representatives had to make sure that each member of their community became a registered voter. That's when we started the voter registration drive. Abraham Lincoln said, "Among free [people], there can be no successful appeal from the ballot to the bullet, and those who take such appeal are sure to lose their case and pay the cost." This quotation influenced me a lot.

Once we had our meetings and got our reports back from each of the five precincts in the county, we found that we had enough registered Black voters in at least three precincts to elect a Black supervisor. So in 1971, three of the five members of the Board of Supervisors were Black—we were finally represented.

Walter Hardy: When we first elected three Black men to the county Board of Supervisors, there were a lot of challenges. And to be honest with you, we didn't know anything about government. After we were elected, we started looking at each other and saying, "What do we know about local government?" We had gone to the board meetings and had seen what they had done. But I will say that the Ford Foundation set up seminars in Richmond and gave us the opportunity to go and learn something about government and about what we needed to do. And on the advice of Don Anderson, we employed Gerald Poindexter as our county attorney, one of the first in Virginia.

Focus on Education

C. P. Penn: One of the first things the newly elected Board of Supervisors focused on was education. They knew that Surry lacked even adequate education in the public schools, and they had a vision of a better system. They also had the courage to be critical of the educational system, and with that, a lot of folks were insulted, even when they received constructive criticism. When the new board took over and discovered that the county was going to build a high school without an auditorium, they stood up and objected. We built the auditorium. And on just this past Saturday, we used that auditorium for one of our employees who passed away, since the funeral was too big for the church.

I came here in 1977. At that time people called Surry's school system the "sorry" school system. I think we had not won a football game. We had no band uniforms, no bleachers. We had built a new school and put $100,000 worth of lights out on the field, but not one bleacher. Why? Because it was a protest—the school was intentionally designed to not work. When the gymnasium filled up with people, fans were turned on that pumped heat inside. It made the gym feel like it was 200 degrees—filled up with people and 200 degrees. But that was out of anger. After the assembly, they had to listen to other voices, Black voices—99 percent of the students in the Surry School System were Black. The White students went to the Surry Academy, a private school. So the power shifted, and we wanted changes so that all our children could be educated—and we were able to change things. Today, 92 percent of those White kids are back in the public schools. And we haven't had one bit of trouble.

We made a lot of changes. Number one, we enhanced the educational program by ridding ourselves of undesirable teachers. We had the longest school day, the longest school year of any place in the state, and yet we required less of teachers than any other place, and we were paying our teachers a good salary. We had no requirements for teachers, but the grass was cut, the shades were drawn, and the lights were cut off. Those were the things that were important, and they happened.

We had a number of teachers that weren't certified for anything. They were just on the county's payroll. The first thing I did was ask to have everybody's records put in front of me. They were given contracts for another year, even if they didn't have valid teaching certificates. But we told them they had a certain amount of time to get them or their contracts would be null and void. That gave us room to go out and hire teachers from other places and do some things that needed to be done. We went to all of the colleges and universities that we could find—North Carolina, Virginia, Yale, Princeton. We have people teaching here now from Cornell and other universities who have come and want to stay. Our teacher turnover rate is 2 percent, and that is only because somebody gets married or retires. When they come, they come to stay. That helped.

We started including the parents in the educational programs. We tested every child; we developed an individual educational program for every child.

That's usually done for special education students, but we did it for every child. We were able to tell the parents where the children had needs and where the children had strengths.

With the new philosophy came a "can do" attitude. Now our kids are very proud of everything they participate in. Kids give you what you expect. If you expect nothing, you get nothing.

I have an informal test for hiring teachers: I don't like to hire teachers who don't want a kid to touch them. Black children are people-oriented. White children tend to be task-oriented. That's just something I've come to observe over the years. But that Black child who is born to a mother becomes the family's child—Grandma holds him, Granddaddy holds him (or her), aunts, uncles—everybody wants to hold that baby. Now, when this child goes to school, it's the first time that child is away from the family. When a teacher hugs that child and tells him or her, "You can do it, I know you can," that child will work.

But a teacher who sits that child on one side of the room and directs, gives directions, doesn't touch, is cold, factual—pretty soon you have a dropout. The child feels nobody cares. It's traumatic. We want teachers to teach children but also to show them feelings, to care for our kids. We insist upon that, and our children have consistently done better as a result of this approach. When I first got here, in 1977, Surry's students were testing nationally in the lower 10th to 27th percentile on the secondary level, and in the lower 17th to 27th percentile on the elementary level. Today we are testing in the 45th to 75th percentile on the elementary level, and in the 38th to 55th on the secondary level. Before the changes, our dropout rate was about 14 percent. Today it is slightly over 2 percent, and 90 percent of our students are college-bound.

We really do believe that "it takes a village to raise a child." We know about each other's children, and the students take a great deal of pride in everything they do. Today we have a hundred-piece marching band and a football team that's ranked fourth in the state of Virginia. We have little country boys here, but they're tough, they're really tough. We went down in August to scrimmage a team in Henderson, North Carolina, and the University of North Carolina had some scouts that were looking at two boys from Henderson, a triple-A team. We're a single-A team. We have fewer than 400 students in the high school; Henderson has 1,200 students. We went down there, and we beat them. And now the University of North Carolina is calling for three of our boys.

Improving Health Services

Terry: After education, the assembly has had to concentrate on improving the health of the citizens of Surry County. I can't sit here and give you percentages, but Surry County, like many other poor communities, had a high infant mortality rate, and a large number of babies were born underweight. And there were many health problems within the community with such diseases as diabetes, hypertension, and cancer. We had only one part-time doctor in the county back in those early days. And when we say part-time, the office was actually only open when that doctor wanted to open the office, which was infrequently. We had very, very poor medical service at that time.

Through the efforts of citizens and the Board of Supervisors, the county created a health organization, an organization that Mr. Thomas Hardy headed as president for a number of years: the Surry Family Health Group, which had as its mission to build a health center and staff it with doctors. We went from having only one part-time doctor available to the county to as many as four doctors affiliated with the program, a dentist, and a nurse. The center was filled with health care providers and even equipped with a trauma room. If an accident victim had to be brought in, that person could receive emergency room–type care before being moved to a hospital. We really have a grand facility created from the energies and efforts of the citizens of the county, in particular the assembly along with the Board of Supervisors.

Recreational Services

Walter: Recreation was another of the main concerns of the assembly back in its infant days. The assembly embarked upon constructing a community center, and in 1976 a facility opened. For the first time, the county had an outlet for recreational activities. Through the community center we're now able to have a senior citizen program, recognized as one of the best in the nation. We have an extremely active summer recreation program, which helps to provide structure for our children, a place where they can go so they don't have to hang out on the street or be in situations where they can get in trouble. The center also houses a number of other programs for citizens of the county—arts and crafts, games, organized sports for adults, drama presentations, musical presentations, a place where you can hold your family reunions. And remember, Surry County, being as old as it is, happens to be home, we like to say, to the first Black folks who came to America.

We have any number of youth programs located at the community center, including organized sports such as football—we actually field fully equipped youth football teams to play in various leagues—baseball, softball, soccer, and basketball.

Housing

Walter: Another one of the early concerns was housing. Back in those early days, a lot of people were still living in conditions worse than those of sharecroppers: They were just farm tenants, which meant that they were really at the mercy of the farm owner. We have people who can tell you about some atrocious conditions they lived in during those early days. I know about one case where the individual lived in a house with a dirt floor. And again, the assembly assisted the county in this particular effort tremendously. Back in those early days, the 1970s, the state constitution actually contained provisions that prohibited local governments from spending money on housing, from contributing money to people to improve their housing. The only way that you could do it legitimately was through a housing authority. And to create a housing authority you had to conduct a referendum so that voters could decide whether the county would establish one. The assembly was able to serve as a nonprofit corporation to get around that law. So the Board of Supervisors in essence could seek money from federal and state sources, for that matter—donations, whatever—which it could then pass to the assembly to improve housing in the community.

One of the earliest successes was winterizing and rehabilitating houses, and helping people to understand how to make good choices as far as selecting replacement housing. So we found houses that could be rehabilitated, upgraded to reasonable standards, and at the same time we helped some people to improve their condition by moving them on the road toward purchasing a new home. As a result of the winterization program sponsored by the assembly, we received an award from the state of Virginia for winterizing more homes than any other county in the state.

Job Training Through Welfare Reform

Terry: Today you hear a lot about welfare reform on the national and the state levels. I'd like to report that Surry County has really been working on welfare reform for a number of years, although we have implemented it in a slightly different way. We have tried to help people move off the welfare rolls. People are not on welfare because that's where they want to be. What they want is a chance in life to earn a reasonable income for their families. In Surry we emphasized job training, so that people could develop job skills that would enable them to hold jobs within the community—not just skills for any and every kind of job, but skills that would enable them to obtain the jobs readily available in the community. The training programs that we've had here have been highly successful, with a large number of people participating in them. People from other communities actually seek to be involved in the training programs that Surry has been providing.

One of the most successful of these was a computer training program. The county entered into a partnership with one of the area's private job-skill schools to provide the program. The young people who participated in it were some of the highest-scoring students graduating from the school, both here on the Surry campus as well as on the main campus back in Newport News. These young people wanted a chance and, after receiving the opportunity, demonstrated that they had the capabilities necessary to compete for jobs. The county's welfare system also provided child care and transportation. If you get trained and there's a job out there, what do you do about your children? Well, again, Surry County has been on the cutting edge, matching child care with the needs of the family so that the family not only has the skills required for a job, but also assistance in taking care of their children so they can actually move into a full-time job.

Closing the Jail

Terry: Surry is blessed in being a rural community, a community of families where people all know one another. We tend to have a relatively low crime rate. If you put a lot of effort into trying to improve the abilities of people, the quality of life for them, then you tend to have fewer people doing things not acceptable to society. If you're able to channel your children into an early childhood program, then when they come out of it they're more likely to succeed in high school. They are also less likely to commit crime and are more likely to mature into socially responsible adults, with less drug abuse and fewer problems as teenagers.

All of those social ills tend to be decreased very much by early investments—in education, recreation, better health care, a social services system that is extremely responsive to the needs of families, the support from churches, and the support from family members. By having these kinds of support services, Surry County has a lower crime rate than other, similar communities.

The Surry Board of Supervisors made the decision years ago to close the jail, to tear it down. This was done because of the inhumane conditions that people had to endure when they were in that facility. So rather than continue to put people into conditions that were not acceptable, the board made the decision to place our prisoners, if we had them, in other facilities that were more modern. Now, other communities came to that decision after a lot of Supreme Court cases that challenged the conditions and demanded that certain jails be closed. But Surry made this decision at a much earlier time, believing that all humans deserve to be treated as well as we can treat them, even if they've committed a crime.

The Present Challenge: Economic Sustainability

Terry: We're looking at the economic arena now as where we need to make some progress. Of course, as anyone will tell you, when people begin to make some economic progress, they are able to sustain themselves, and they have greater belief in the system that helped bring about the change. Then they begin to take action to sustain the system.

We are trying to attract new industries to the county and are working on developing an industrial park to help in that effort. The Board of Supervisors a few years ago acquired roughly 200 acres of land for that purpose. We are constructing a shell building in the park, so that we can actually have something to market to prospects who come to the county.

The board has done a number of things to try to stimulate the economy in this county. It has worked with Hampton University in Hampton, Virginia, for instance, to establish a rural business assistance center, through which we're working with citizens of Surry County and surrounding communities on ways to develop businesses for themselves. Surry citizens, like citizens in a number of places, have some good ideas about starting businesses that they can own and operate. This center is helping them put their ideas on paper in the form of a business plan that can be presented to a bank to obtain funds to start a business and get it off the ground.

The Board of Supervisors recently joined other regional organizations through which the board hopes to induce new businesses to come to Surry County. We're working on upgrading the road system so that the community can be more accessible to the airports and seaports some fifty miles away, in Richmond to the north and Norfolk to the south. We are also looking to stimulate the development of more housing in the county and to provide better-quality housing to attract newcomers.

Vision and Values

Terry: You've got to see where you're going to know where you're going. And you've got to know *why* you're going there. If you're not going anywhere, any road will take you there. You can't teach what you don't know, and you can't lead where you don't go.

For the future, we want to do those things that will enable Surry County to continue to blossom. And I have a saying: "We want to grow from within." We want to do the things here that will allow our people—all the citizens of Surry County—to profit from them, to make the county attractive and desirable for our citizens, especially for our young people to continue to live here. We want to create the opportunity for people who desire to remain here in Surry County to do so. And we will benefit from those talents, and by benefiting from those talents, Surry County will begin to blossom into an even more successful community than it is today. After all, our greatest asset is our human resources, our people.

My core values really go back to an old spiritual that says, "If I can help somebody along the way, then my living has not been in vain." And I really would like to feel that I have been there in this life to help people.

Walter: I feel very strongly that through the Supreme Being, Surry County has been selected as a place to let the world know that Black people can run a government. That's my strongest conviction.

Certainly all of us working together, with the same beliefs and everything—that's really been our success. And I'm proud of it, and I hope that it will continue for many years to come. Of course, if the Lord's willing.

My term will expire in the year 2000. My prayers are that the person who replaces me on the board will have the same values.

I want to see a good fiscal government operating here, something that will satisfy all the people. I don't think there should ever be a person in Surry County homeless or without food on the table. Local government has to get into that—see that a child is fed or see that that child has a place to live.

Terry: People in Surry County have come a long way in understanding that we're all human, that we all have in essence the same blood running through our veins, the same intellectual capacity, and the same feelings. Since we are that way, we might as well treat each other with respect and work together to create a place we can all be proud of.

Ethics and Fairness

C. P.: I'd like to say that I think that the overriding factor in our success has been the honesty, fairness, and integrity of the people in office. People respect integrity. People have found that this majority Black leadership is more effective than the previous leadership. They've gotten their roads paved, they've gotten a number of things that they wouldn't have gotten had their requests fallen on deaf ears.

Terry: One of the key issues that Dr. Penn has touched upon is the fact that county officials, the Board of Supervisors in particular, have bent over backwards to try to treat everyone fairly. The fact that Black elected officials are inclined to treat people fairly and respectfully led to the election of the current Black treasurer over a White incumbent.

Shared Vision
and Participation

Terry: If you go right back to the very earliest days of the assembly, it was all about uniting people—pulling them together, giving them a mission, an idea, a vision. By following that vision, we are seeing many kinds of success. We want to continue those successes right on into the future.

We have active board meetings. The things that the board is called upon to make decisions on are relatively routine. If you went to other communities, you probably would see very few people involved in routine matters. But in Surry County, the routine becomes the extraordinary for a lot of people—they want to be involved.

One of the great things about Surry County is that we have an extraordinary number of people participating in local elections. We perhaps have the highest voter registration rate in the state, and we have a very, very high percentage of voters that actually vote in the elections—approximately 76 percent—which is much, much higher than the national average.

We interest people in participating in elections at an early age—at least by high school. We have student government for a day, which gives our students an opportunity to work with all of the elected and appointed officials. And then the officials all come to the high school for lunch. When it's over, these kids want to be part of something—of Surry, their home, of which they are very proud.

And at graduation time—we're probably the only school system in the state that does this—all the county officials get invitations to come and be with us. All of our elected and appointed officials and others are invited to come and sit on the stage with us and be there when these children receive their diplomas. All of that inspires total commitment from the community.

We really have an extremely participatory government in Surry County. The structure of the assembly generates an awful lot of participation—for example, we were able to create the kind of school system that we wanted because of the involvement of the citizens who demanded that the system be improved. Now, in order for that school system to continue to be what it needs to be and to be what the citizens of the county want it to be, the school system has to participate in the process. And it does so by encouraging students to become full citizens, voting citizens of the community. They are able to continue this progress by regenerating the whole system. That's the key to what goes on in Surry County. The next major effort is creating opportunities so that we can keep these good students, these good citizens, right here in the community. If we're going to be successful as a community, we've got to continue to regenerate. And we are only going to regenerate by keeping our students here. That is a major part of "growing from within."

Thomas: The fact is we are very much concerned about national elections, and we are participants in those elections, but the elections that affect us most are local. So we put special emphasis on our local elections by closing schools, by encouraging our students to be poll workers or what have you, and by getting the students to help people get out to vote. We feel like we're trying to educate the whole child so that he or she is involved in all the things that affect his or her life. That's what it's about. And quite often, if they can participate in something memorable and pleasant, they'll want to do it over and over again.

Obstacles

Thomas: I had no intention of ever becoming any part of the political arena. But my political activity really started when I went into the service. I was going to fight for our country. I was just a young fellow, raised up on the farm. When I came back to the United States from the Korean War, I was assigned to a processing station at Fort Meade, Maryland. I processed out and was reassigned to Camp Pickett, Virginia. Luckily I had made sergeant first class on the front line, and I was in charge of a convoy of troops traveling from Fort Meade to Camp Pickett. The captain gave me a meal ticket for 175 troops and told me when I got into Richmond to stop at a restaurant and feed them. So I walked into the restaurant. The manager asked me how many Black soldiers were in the convoy. I said approximately twenty. He said, "I'm sorry, they can't eat here." I think because I had a light complexion, he thought that I was Caucasian. So I told him that I was a Black, and that the check would not be any good unless I signed it. I said, "I'll get the troops back on the bus unless everyone is allowed to eat, including the Blacks." I was determined not to let them eat, but he called me back and told me to bring them in. That rested heavily on my mind because I had been in Korea fighting for my country. I have never forgotten that humiliating incident.

When my daughter was going to high school, she came home one day and said she wanted to be a doctor. Then she said, "But, Daddy, the laboratory at L. P. Jackson High School has only one Bunsen burner and little laboratory equipment." I went up there and observed the laboratory, and my brother can tell you, they didn't have anything for biology students. And so through the assembly, Don Anderson got her a scholarship at Chatham Hall, an all-girls school in Danville, Virginia. She went on to the University of Virginia and from there to Howard University Medical School. Today she is a very successful OB/GYN practicing in Annapolis, Maryland. She has established her own business, Women's Health Care Associates, and has a staff of three doctors. I am truly proud of her success. But she had to go outside the public school system to do it.

My daughter's experience made me decide to do something about the public school system. I said, "If this is my country, and I was willing to go away and die for it, then I should be willing to make some type of contribution when I'm back home." I hadn't wanted any part of politics, but this experience ignited a spark in me.

C. P.: If it were not for the assembly and its continued vested interest in the community, its vision of what is and what ought to be, then we would have faltered. Many communities did what we did back then, but over time, their efforts dissipated. Today there are only seven Black superintendents of schools in the state of Virginia, out of around 135 school districts. Ten years ago, there were twelve of us out of 135. But as the communities forgot, they've gone backward. Surry has continued to hold its own. Governmentally, we've been sound in every way, including fiscally. We've been able to do what we've needed to do and continue to do things right.

Terry: Today we have four Black supervisors out of five. We have increased the Black strength on the Board of Supervisors, at a time when the percentage of Blacks in the population has actually declined. We have a county government here that is operating as well as or better than any that you will find across the nation—for all its constituents. We've also increased the number of Blacks in constitutional offices—for example, we now have a sheriff who is Black. Three of five constitutional office positions are filled by people of color.

C. P.: Five years ago a White board member who felt threatened by our advancements started an investigation of my expenditures [as school superintendent] over a three-year period. The investigators questioned $6 million worth of expenditures. I believe they thought that a Black man could not be expected to handle anybody else's money. So they said, "He's been here long enough, we've surely got him now." And they ran an investigation for six months, and they found that out of $6 million, there was only $283 questionably spent. The community then pretty much said to leave me alone. But during that time, these men—Walter and Thomas—were asked to join in the witch-hunt, and they refused. They continued to support and encourage me.

We did have a small problem a few years ago when one of our Black elected officials embezzled some money. Then the seed was sown to never elect another Black treasurer of the county. They appointed a White lady in the interim, and most folks thought the citizens were going to hand the job to her. But when the election rolled around, a Black man was elected—who, by the way, has done an outstanding job. This community did not blame all Black people. When President Nixon had to step down, the country didn't blame all White folks. We're all going to have some folks that make mistakes, but that doesn't mean we ought to give up hope for all others. What are we telling our Black children if we do so?

Vision for a Better World

Thomas: I guess the thing that I could pass on to other communities—something I strongly feel and know—is that counties in North Carolina, Georgia, and Mississippi are in the same predicament today that Surry faced back in the 1970s. It's hard to realize, but it's true. I think that Blacks and poor Whites in those communities should band themselves together to solve their own particular problems as we did here in Surry. That way you gain more respect, and you build good race relationships. And it comes from helping poor people learn to help themselves.

There's a proverb that says if you give a man a fish, you've fed him for a day, but if you teach him how to fish, you've fed him for a lifetime. The simple fact is that people should get involved in their community activities, get their people organized. I still say the power resides in the ballot box. One of my favorite Biblical quotations is how can you love God, whom you've never seen, and hate your fellow man that you see every day? Love and leadership can help our communities be more successful.

Terry: People are your treasure. They are a storehouse, first of all, of ideas, of how things should be, can be, and how to go about making those ideas realities. You have to listen to people, listen to what they are saying, and try to develop a plan of action that focuses on those things. In the end, they're going to be the ones to actually carry the mission out. If a vision is going to be successful, you've got to have supporters. Progress doesn't come about through the efforts of one individual; it doesn't come about through the efforts of a few individuals. It takes everybody's shoulder pressed to the stone—or, I should say, the more shoulders we have pressed to the stone, the easier it's going to be to get that stone to roll.

Lessons We Learned

DreamMakers express vision and values. "My core values really go back to an old spiritual that says, 'If I can help somebody along the way, then my living has not been in vain.' And I really would like to feel that I have been there in this life to help people."

DreamMakers work with others to build a shared vision. "The Surry Assembly is the strength of our community today, really the secret to the whole thing. The assembly is built on the structure Thomas Jefferson used: Each community divides itself into wards and sets out to solve its own problems. . . . The ward representatives have seven committee members, and those seven pick seven people in their immediate community. In the end, every voice in the county is represented."

DreamMakers support diversity and honor the integrity and contributions of all people. "People in Surry County have come a long way in understanding that we're all human, that we all have in essence the same blood running through our veins, the same intellectual capacity, and the same feelings. Since we are that way, we might as well treat each other with respect and work together to create a place we can all be proud of."

DreamMakers tap in to the extraordinary potential in all of us. "People are your treasure. They are a storehouse, first of all, of ideas, of how things should be, can be, and how to go about making those ideas realities. You have to listen to people, listen to what they are saying, and try to develop a plan of action that focuses on those things. In the end, they're going to be the ones to actually carry the mission out."

DreamMakers make their dreams a reality. "Today we have four Black supervisors out of five. We have increased the Black strength on the Board of Supervisors, at a time when the percentage of Blacks in the population has actually declined. We have a county government here that is operating as well as or better than any that you will find across the nation—for all its constituents. We've also increased the number of Blacks in constitutional offices."

DreamMakers trust feelings, emotions, and intuition. "I have an informal test for hiring teachers: I don't like to hire teachers who don't want a kid to touch them. Black children are people-oriented. White children tend to be task-oriented. That's just something I've come to observe over the years. . . . When a teacher hugs that [Black] child and tells him or her, 'You can do it, I know you can,' that child will work."

DreamMakers follow a moral compass. "The Surry Board of Supervisors made the decision years ago to close the jail, to tear it down. This was done because of the inhumane conditions that people had to endure in that facility. So rather than continue to put people into conditions that were not acceptable, the board made the decision to place our prisoners, if we had them, in other facilities that were more modern."

DreamMakers demonstrate responsibility toward a larger community. "We want to create the opportunity for people who desire to remain here in Surry County to do so. And we will benefit from those talents, and by benefiting from those talents, Surry County will begin to blossom into an even more successful community than it is today." [p. 172]

DreamMakers are committed to making the world a better place. "My daughter's experience made me decide to do something about the public school system. I said, 'If this is my country, and I was willing to go away and die for it, then I should be willing to make some type of contribution when I'm back home.' I hadn't wanted any part of politics, but this experience ignited a spark in me."

JULIET CHIEUW *is co–managing director of the Aruba Quality Foundation. She has a Ph.D. in educational foundations and policy studies from Florida State University, and her areas of professional focus are macro strategic planning using large group processes that tap into the group's innate creativity and potentials, program design, workshop facilitation based on accelerative learning, presentations, and consultation. Her professional mission and personal desire in life is to codesign and facilitate collaborative processes that support human systems toward whole systems perspectives and integrative ways of work, not stovepipe thinking and fragmentation. In this way, she aspires to contribute actively in a local way to the global changes afoot in creating a different future built on a more life-enhancing and life-supporting vision.*

JOYCE BARTELS-DAAL *is co–managing director of the Aruba Quality Foundation. As a mother of three, she believes that family values help children become better citizens of the world. Together with her husband, Mathias, she is cofounder of a local restaurant and of a consultancy company that focuses on continuous quality improvement. She has been actively involved in various projects promoting the growth and well-being of children, and she believes her role in life is to be the best she can be to help others grow, especially the children of the world.*

PARTICIPATION

Juliet Chieuw and
Joyce Bartels-Daal,
The Aruba Quality Foundation

In August of 1995 I received a call from Juliet Chieuw of the Aruba Quality Foundation. She was referred by Rita Cleary, president of the Visions of a Better World Foundation. Juliet called because she had read the book Rita's foundation had published, sharing the visions of people from 127 countries around the world. Rita told her to call me because of my work on vision and values. That call spawned a fascinating learning, sharing, and growing experience for me—and a love and admiration for a country of people that I believe have volumes to teach our world.

Aruba is a country of 90,000 citizens from fifty-two nationalities who have discovered a way to create a shared vision that reflects and at the same time transcends their ethnic, political, and religious differences. Led by an integrated team representing every sector and major institution on the island, they are creating their future. The Aruba Quality Foundation is the guiding light and facilitates that creation process. Through exceptional leadership, commitment, and excitement, Joyce Bartels-Daal and Juliet Chieuw ignited a fire in the spirit of the people of Aruba.

Juliet initially invited me to simply come to Aruba for a conversation about vision and values. I literally became caught up in the journey itself and now feel a part of a wonderful community and an exciting new experience that could have wonderful implications for the rest of our world. Joyce and Juliet tell the story.

137

Defining Moments

Personal Journeys: Preparing the Way

Joyce Bartels-Daal: Looking back now, I can see that there were things in my life that allowed me to be able to join this vision for Aruba. Earlier this year, I saved the life of a two-year-old little boy in a pool, and I just knew and sensed that he was there. It's sort of a confirmation of a gift I see that I've had since I was little—both seeing and knowing that certain things are going to happen. I've started to learn not to fight that gift, but to be proud of it. It's a gift of feeling deep inside myself that's guiding me. I don't have it totally defined yet, but it's much more about what I am here for, and I think I'm here for children. And I know that is why I'm here right now.

Juliet Chieuw: I think there's one key turning point in my life. I've always been a pretty reflective person, thinking and being by myself and wondering, "What's my purpose in life? What am I to do? Why am I here?" I've been a searcher from a very early age.

When I was in my early teens, I discovered how libraries can open all parts of the world to you, and I read everything I could get my hands on (since I was an introvert and didn't talk to anybody). I loved biographies, and by the time I was seventeen I had read everything on the library shelves about Black American activists, such as Angela Davis, James Baldwin, and Eldridge Cleaver, and about the Zionism movement. I remember admiring such figures as David Ben-Gurion, Golda Meir, and Moshe Dayan. I was a very impressionable young person and loved reading about all these very courageous people. I also had a very active fantasy life. There was this tremendous contrast between my very mundane life and my wonderful imaginative life. And I thought, "Life must be more than this. I must have a purpose." I remember as a student driving around Tallahassee in my car, waiting at the traffic lights and thinking, "What's my purpose? Why am I here?"

I went about searching for my religion. I came across a book called *The Tao* that made intuitive sense to me, because it talked about the spirit that resides in basically all of life, the trees and the rocks and the mountains and the seas. It was such a natural religion and philosophy that I said, "Okay, that's it! I'm a Taoist, that's what I am."

Then my youngest brother got ill with cancer, and he came over to the States on a vacation and ended up with me in my one-bedroom apartment in Tallahassee. He was always considered the weakest in the family, not very bright, rather slow, very introverted. He really lived a life full of fear, and he did poorly in school. I grew up the oldest child in the family and rather arrogant, a smart kid. I always felt like, "Gosh, why is he around?" But during that last year of his life we bonded.

And so I—with my "project" mind—took him on as my project. But I learned the biggest lesson in my life, that the one I thought was the weakest and with the least gifts in the family actually had the greatest gifts. When he was in the hospital, he had a stroke and couldn't speak. But he attracted everybody in the hospital. I learned so much love from my youngest brother. And I learned about courage and learned to care really from him—he was twenty-eight. I learned also that I loved him very deeply. And I understood how much damage we can do in our families by holding back so much. When I look back, I really feel very strongly that we must have made a pact that he was going to facilitate my awakening, he was going to wake me up from my sleep. And I was going to facilitate him out of this life.

That really was a turning point in my life. Somehow the universe was kicking me and saying, "Wake up, you dodo bird. Wake up from your fantasies and your dream life and your imaginary life." And then things started to accelerate.

I read a book called *A World Waiting to Be Born*, by Scott Peck—actually, I read only the introduction and the conclusion because the book was too fat—and at the end of the book was this section on community building. I promptly booked a flight to Denver and sat in a community building workshop that lasted four days. Within the first two hours, I thought I had made a big mistake. "There must be a whole bunch of crazy people in this room," I remember thinking. Well, I stayed for the four days and realized that I had not begun to deal with so many things in my life. I hadn't even grieved over my brother's death.

I learned that when people sit together in a circle and spend time together talking, something happens where you begin to tap deeply in to something that you don't have access to on a conscious level. I truly believe that when you sit there together long enough and begin to share your hearts and souls, you open up to what the great psychologist Carl Jung calls the collective unconscious. You begin to tap in to a greater soul that you are part of. My brother's death plus the community building experience really started me off on my own personal journey.

In the last few years, I've come to deal with fears. For me, the greatest fear is the fear of my own gift and what I must do. With this gift comes a responsibility, more like a calling. Part of my vision, I think, is fulfilling my calling. Part of my search has been to discover my calling.

I have learned that I am body and spirit, and that I do have a calling in life, just as everybody else has a calling in life, and that at a critical point in time you are called. And if you pay attention, you will hear the calling and then you must respond.

I've also come to understand that this is the time of the rise of the feminine. Not the feminine in women, but the feminine in all of us—that part of us that is nurturing, caring, and has great love. If there's one thing that I fear besides my own power, it's love. Because with love comes great responsibility.

All of these things were very important in my journey. If I had not had that development, I would not be able to do the work I'm doing right now. I do this work with total faith that what we are about is needed not just for Aruba, but for our times.

The Aruba Journey Begins

Joyce: The Aruba journey started in August 1994. I was just back from Holland. Two days after I came back, a good friend of mine called and asked me to come meet with the newly elected minister of tourism, who wanted to put quality on the national agenda. The first function was going to be an event in September of 1994. Would I be interested in helping Myrna Yansen from the Aruba Tourism Authority set it up? I said, "Sure."

After meeting several times, we started to see that this thing was going to be big, that what we were doing was much more than just organizing events. So we said, "Okay, fine. Let's do this event in December, but then as soon as that's over, let's sit down and plan how to proceed."

So we organized another event in December and invited this representative from the Disney World University to be there. At that time our plan was to have seminars every two months on the subject of quality. We had a session, and 400 people came. Everybody was saying, "This is good, but what are you going to do next?" So one day, Tico Croes, the minister of economic affairs and tourism, called and asked me to come to his office. He said, "You know, I'm getting so much positive feedback from commerce, from the community, who are calling my office and saying that this whole emphasis on quality is very important, that it should continue. I think we should set it up, and that you should give it structure, so let's create a foundation to guide this whole thing. Would you be interested in leading it?"

So I had to go and think. I went to my restaurant, which is where I go to think. I wanted advice from my business partner, Gladys, at the restaurant. I started talking to her a little bit about this whole offer and what to do with it.

Juliet: I hadn't planned to come home for Christmas—this was in December—but my father got ill, and I booked a ticket to come home [to Aruba]. The night before I was due to fly out to come back to Aruba, my father died. My mother lives alone now on the island. So I thought, "Okay, my mom is alone, I will have to come back to Aruba more often. I can't come back ten times a year on vacation, so I might as well get a consulting sort of assignment." I went to the different departments in government and spent quite a bit of time just talking their ears off and trying to sell myself with absolutely no luck. Then that last night before I was to leave, I met my friend Sonya and we went [to Joyce's restaurant] to have dinner and chat.

That night I saw Joyce [for the first time]. I had just finished dinner. The food was good, service was great. I came up to her to compliment her on the experience, and then she said to me, "What do you do? Where are you now?"

That was the beginning for me.

Joyce: Juliet gave me a card that said the Center for Quality and Learning. I thought, "Quality, learning—this is nice." I took her card, and she went back to the table. You know, the design of the card caught my attention. It was different from regular business cards. The coloring was nice. So I said, "Can we talk? What is the Center for Quality and Learning?" So it started, and we had a conversation for one hour outside. We couldn't stop. When I was listening to Juliet, for that one hour—we didn't know each other before this—I knew we needed her. We needed her scientific background also. There was chemistry there. Immediate chemistry.

Juliet: I was excited and thought, "Here's an opportunity—I could be coming home, this may be it." We were talking big right away—learning communities, systems thinking, quality. Joyce was reading *The Fifth Discipline*, which I had read. So we had a shared point of reference, and she got all excited about that. I talked to her too about community building. It was two sparks, then an explosion.

On the flight back to the United States, I had a book with me called *Future Search Conferencing,* by Marvin Weisbord. I sat there and thought, "I don't know enough for what we need to do. I need a big process, a big one." And I knew several—open space, community building—but I thought, "There needs to be a little bit more structure because of the conservative nature of Aruba." I looked through the table of contents and thought, "I need something here that is not theoretical. I need it practical." For some odd reason, I flipped to this chapter called "Planning the Energy Sector in Colombia." Ordinarily that would not have appealed to me, but I started reading this chapter and thought, "This is it. This man is operating from a conceptual framework that I recognize: He's using chaos theory."

Joyce: After Juliet left, I went back to Tico [Croes] and decided to take on this project. I brought Juliet's card, and I told him that she needed to be involved in this work, and he said, "Great, yeah, no problem." In January I called Juliet, and we sat down and started planning this thing.

A Leadership Retreat

Juliet: We wrote a proposal specifically for improving quality in the tourist industry—that's how we understood our charge. One of the first activities we planned was a leadership retreat. The whole idea was to bring the top leadership of the country—the parliament, the ministers, and so on—and begin to give them an introduction to quality, to learning some of the new brain research, really take this as a whole system. We were thinking twenty-four people. But as we got closer to the date, the number kept growing to include all sectors—business, government, health care, and community leadership. By the time of the retreat, we had something like eighty-nine people.

Joyce: As I look back, I think we must've been crazy. Here we were planning an event for the island, and I'd never seen Juliet in action. We were planning a two-day event to which we were inviting the prime minister and the whole world—as high-profile as could be.

Juliet: A couple of days before the retreat, I was thinking that I would like to see a conch shell. When we do the closing, we pass something. I wanted something of the past, the present, and the future. When I was a kid and used to go to the beach, there were tons of those shells. But today, you walk and you cannot find one whole conch shell anymore. And so I thought, "Where am I going to find one?" Well, on the morning of the second day of the retreat, Nancy Dalton from AT&T went walking on the beach. She came to me and said, "Juliet, look what I found!" A conch shell—she had found a whole conch shell!

Joyce: When we started—you have to understand, these are traditional people—I'm sitting there saying, "I really trust this girl, and this thing is going to work." And I'm saying, "Just do it." Juliet brings in all these objects, chimes—people here are not used to this stuff, you know? So she does chimes, she does a little game, she does music, she has people running around to do all sorts of stuff. So I'm looking at their faces, and I see Tico Croes for the first hour not looking too happy. And then suddenly I see people getting to like all this stuff. Juliet had them playing games, and then she did an exercise called concentric circles where you put people in two circles facing each other, and she had five questions that built up to a larger vision. The first question would be very personal, like, "What were the greatest achievements in your life?" You get three minutes to talk to each other. And then you rotate, you just move to the left. And the next person asks the second question. It really helps people go from the very personal to something much further removed. They liked that. They wanted to continue and keep on going around the circle. At the end, it was quite emotional. This whole process to me was so full of magic.

Juliet: Out of those two days, task forces emerged: on vision, education, training, coordination, and one dealing with the products of Aruba. We tried to categorize and prioritize all the issues that emerged. We said vision was the most important, but people didn't realize it. People then self-selected into groups.

Joyce: That was the beginning of community involvement and excitement in the process. We planned to meet again in three months and have a follow-up and have the task forces report the issues that they discussed, any recommendations, and any ideas on how they wanted to move forward. The whole idea behind this process was to make it very participatory. That was a struggle. When you throw people who have not had any experience into participation, they protest. They'll sit there for a while, look at you, and ask, "What do you want us to do?" But it began to work, I have no idea how.

A lot of the sessions became gripe sessions, but people wanted this to happen, and they would come back time and time again. So it went ahead, struggling, painful, with an underlying hope that something positive was happening. We were constantly checking with Juliet—by fax, phoning—Juliet was still living in Tallahassee. In June when Juliet came back for the second leadership retreat, there was progress, movement.

Creating a Vision for Aruba

Juliet: In June 1995 all the task forces met and shared ideas—it was happening! Then Bill Smith, whom I had contacted from the beginning, said to me, "Juliet, I'm going to give you the number of a person who I believe can help you. I think you ought to talk to her." And he gave me the name of Rita Cleary.

I called Rita. I felt she was a very special person. She talked about her work on the Visions of a Better World Foundation and then sent me the book entitled *Visions of a Better World.* I faxed the appendix and the vision statement to the Vision Task Force. It immediately spoke to them. There was an immediate click and a good feeling about the book, about the way and the process.

Joyce: So Rita's ideas guided the Vision Task Force, gave them an idea of what this whole thing was going to look like, what the process should be. They started to design the campaign, to get the involvement of everybody on the island. Juliet came in September and kicked it off—the campaign to get the Vision for Aruba.

Juliet: In June I was already beginning to feel that I needed to come home [to Aruba]. This opportunity was so exciting. I would be in Tallahassee thinking I needed to go home, but at the same time I was afraid—I was leaving things behind. Yet I had a strong feeling that this was the opportunity of a lifetime.

Next I was asked to develop a ten-year strategic plan for the island. It was hard work—comparable to writing my dissertation. Just as the Vision Task Force was closing one meeting, we presented the strategic plan to the leadership of Aruba and closed with a poem from Nelson Mandela's inaugural address. When they left that room, people had tears in their eyes. They walked out and said, "We can do this, we can do this. We can be the beacon of light to the world." The poem was translated into Papiamento, our native language. In Aruba, the official language is Dutch, since we're still a Dutch colony. But our love language and our language of intimate communicating is Papiamento. It has a lot of Spanish, some English, some Portuguese, and a little bit of Dutch. It's our own language.

A Massive Campaign

Juliet: The campaign to create the Vision for Aruba was massive. We mailed an invitation to every household on the island to give us their vision for Aruba in the year 2005. We had articles in the newspapers, we went on the radio, we went on television, we had leaflets put in containers in all the major places like banks and supermarkets and hospitals and whatnot.

We asked our people what their vision for a better Aruba was. Write it and send it to us, and please make it positive. Don't use negative words. We also wrote a letter to the school boards, all the teachers in every single school, with a poster, asking them to please use this with your kids—you can even do a project with your children. And the teachers did. We hoped to get 2,000 responses from an island of 90,000 people. We got 1,175.

We went all out and did a major campaign. And the responses started trickling in. Finally we had a box full of this stuff. The whole team sat down and took a couple of weekends to read through it all so that we would have a sense of what was being said. Then the analysis began. We had two approaches. We had two people who are very analytical—Helen Guda, Joyce's sister, very much research-oriented, and another person called Antjie, a member of the board of the Aruba Quality Foundation. They went through all this stuff and started counting how many times certain themes came up. Very quantitative, very scientific, very proper. I can't work that way. My mind is too chaotic for that.

While they did that, I took the stuff and read it and got a holistic sense of the major, underlying deep currents. I had a theoretical framework in my mind, the dynamic value systems developed by Don Beck and Chris Cowan in Texas. I knew that you go from the very individual, to family, to organization, to community, to the world. And I was thinking, "Will I see that scope of perspective in the data?" And I did. I knew that you have to have the global perspective. You can't have your vision focused only on family. It's too limited. Or only on your community here. It's too limited. Or your cultural identity. It's too limited. You've got to go beyond your boundaries and into the world. But only 1 percent of what we got had a global perspective. Most people's visions would be centered around what was very immediate to their cultural identity, their language, their family, and their community.

When I formulated the seven vision statements, I went back to Helen and Antjie and asked them to compare them to their quantitative results. It was remarkable, but they said everything matched. Then it was a matter of pulling out the pieces to exemplify the vision statements. When you read it, you really have a sense of, "Wow! This is the vision that we want."

I had this picture in my mind of a book, a beautiful, elegant book—not ostentatious, not academic—a book that you would hold and be proud of. If I were an Aruban in Holland, I would have this book, and I would be proud to say, "Look, this is what my people in Aruba did." A book that a diplomat from Aruba could carry as a gift to other nations and say, "This is our country—not the economic plan, but a shared vision." And the world could say, "Look, this is what a nation is doing for themselves."

Joyce: Then we had this great idea for a party, a huge party to give the vision back to the people. So we had this beautiful party on April 4th on the Plaza. We asked people who were working on the different segments already, working on making this vision come true, to talk to people. It was just beautiful. The vision book was officially given back to the Aruban community, and we had a beautiful video made called *The Aruba Vision 2005.* We had songs and we had the various stands representing people in our community already making this vision come true. And that was beautiful.

Making Visions Come True

Joyce: People started to share what they were doing to achieve the vision. For example, the Foundation Against Child Abuse was already working on statement number 7. Another group was working on spiritual, mental, and physical well-being. We had another group that dealt with our environment, from the Department of Agriculture—vision statement number 5, which deals with flora and fauna.

Those people who came and saw the whole connection were just beautiful. They said to themselves, "I am already working on making Aruba a better place. I feel for this place, and I'm part of it."

This is a movement from us to us. It is not a movement that should stay in a little group in a little office. I think it is important to hold a vision out there, which you can start by doing yourself. The challenge is to take this movement—a positive movement—to take it out to other people. Just bringing the messages, showing the linkages, showing the good things that are happening already, and just continuing to accentuate the positive and letting people feel that their actions are part of the vision of making Aruba a better place.

Just One Example: Education Reform

Juliet: Part of the vision is the new education reform—it's not really new. It had been stuck in the old planning model: Five education experts sit in a room and lock themselves up for a year. They come up with this wonderful thick plan, present it to the teachers, and say, "*Voilà*—now we're going to do this." But the whole teaching field just sits there and then rebels. That had been the history and the experience of our educational reform.

But the Aruba Quality Foundation, through the Vision for Aruba, has got an enormous opportunity to begin to help shape our community for the better—through our kids. I really believe that the key leverage for change in the long term is through education and the youth. The more you work with and the more time you spend with kids, the more you realize that they affect everybody. We are now involved with educational reform at the primary level, the secondary level, and the vocational/technical level. So now we've gained respect in the education field. Before they were suspicious that we were just another fad. But no, we're serious. The quality movement is similar to education: The education sector is moving from what Paulo Freire used to call a banking education to a more dynamic, living model.

In 2005 we want to have an educational system that allows the young and the old to be creative and prepared for constant change. The education field is definitely moving big-time as a sector, toward achieving our vision for 2005.

Vision and Values

Vision for Aruba

Juliet: The goals [of the Vision for Aruba] are universal. They are deep. The heart of our vision touches a lot of people.

Joyce: Number one, we are proud of our multicultural background and of our language, Papiamento. Number two, we have respect for each other, and we live in a healthy community. Number three, we have leaders who respect and manage laws that produce a safe and secure society. Number four, we deliver quality service in all sectors of our community, and we are proud of a job well done. Number five, we protect and safeguard our environment and our flora and fauna. Number six, we have an educational system that allows our children to be creative and innovative and that prepares them for a changing world. And number seven, we work on our personal, physical, mental, and spiritual development so that we can contribute to the global health of the planet. The banner is that we want Aruba to be a safe, beautiful, and peaceful island with good-hearted people.

Personal Vision and Values

Joyce: I have always seen that people can be so much more if they can just let go and become themselves, if they don't get stuck in structures and ways of thinking. People can become so much lighter, so much happier, so much more productive, so much more in love with what's inside them and what's outside of them. But in our society today, I see many people like zombies—they are shackled. I see that in children in school, and I have always seen it in organizations that I've been working for. So I sometimes imagine people liberated from this you-have-to-do-it-this-way attitude. That's why I used to get rebellious. I would say, "Stop all this shackling, just stop. Why in the world are we doing this to ourselves?" I experienced this when I was in school, a teacher keeping us down. So I said, "Why do you keep us down? You don't have to do that. Be nice to us. You're keeping us down by your structures, by your roll call, by the rigid roles that you stick people in."

What I care about most—it sounds naive—but I want to be a good person who does things that are basically good for the people around me. I put a lot of importance on integrity and on being a good person. Many times when I explain that, people say, "Yeah, yeah, yeah." But I think if I try every day to wake up and be a good person and to take into consideration how the other person feels and what that other person needs, then I think I am connected—and that can only be for the good of the world.

Juliet: I care most about respect for life. One of the things that has been a stumbling block [in my own life] is the issue of self-worth. I had to prove that I was worthy, I had to prove that I had value. What helped me move beyond this was the understanding and the belief that all of life deserves respect: Just because I am here, I have value.

We devalue people by putting different tags on them. "You must have this or have that." We just lose sight and miss the other stuff, because we're looking in the wrong places. You know, the word *respect* means to look again and to pay attention again. To notice. Respect is about taking the time to notice, and taking the time to reconsider, because so very often we dismiss things offhand, quickly, and move on.

Joyce: For me, a lesson learned is that for you to be able to think about vision and values, you have to constantly work on yourself. You have to look for changes in yourself every single moment, no matter how difficult it can get, or how challenging, or how frustrating. I will always have to go back inside myself if something doesn't go as planned. You have to look for strength and resilience inside yourself. Go deeper and deeper, and then you know that the challenges and difficulties are not about you. Then you realize that what you are doing is absolutely not about you or who you are. You look for that courage, that passion, that wisdom, that craziness. But you look for all of that inside.

Juliet: Connected with that for me is the constant question "Who am I serving and why am I doing this?" We are serving the whole, we are serving the island, but not just the island today. We are serving the future. And in doing that, we serve the world.

I think another lesson is that you have to believe in what you're doing. You've got to have a kind of naive idealism. You have got to believe that what you're doing is great and is going to flower and is going to be something wonderful. If we didn't have that belief, we would have packed up a long time ago, because financially we're a mess. Physically and emotionally sometimes we're exhausted. Now the two of us, we could jump on each other at times. If you look at all those things, any businessperson would say, "You're crazy. Close it down, it's bankrupt." But we don't. We don't because we just feel that we have a total, complete obligation and responsibility to continue.

Joyce: You know, the old people on this island say that Aruba has always had God's hand over it. I personally feel that we do have somebody higher up somewhere, I really do. I see two hands holding us very gently—big, big hands holding us and allowing a vision to happen. And I do think that there are unseen forces at work—for this island and for this world—so that we get a chance to try something with which we can help the rest of the world. I do feel that makes Aruba special. People come and go, the mortals come and go, but something larger remains. It has to do with this hand. That's why the vision for Aruba is happening. It's not because of us.

These hands hold a wonderful diversity here. We have fifty-two nationalities living on this island—diversity is sky-high. Aruba truly is a microcosm of the world. My mom says that you never know what to expect when you're pregnant. Because you can have a rainbow child. In one family, a person might be half black, half white, half whatever. The traditional Caribbean family is based on the fact that diversity really means that there's intermarriage. Here nobody thinks or talks about race—not in your passport, not on your driver's license, not on your application for a credit card. The first time I was supposed to write down my race was when I got to the United States. Here you're just Juliet or Joyce.

Juliet: It's really as Martin Luther King said: Here you're judged on your character, not on the color of your skin. That's why I say we are special. That's why I see those hands. Because we tend to take that for granted. That is the beauty. That is the way the world should be. Historians have always called the Caribbean the New World. We are the new world here. Our island, I think, is one of the only islands in the Caribbean without a history of bloodshed. We have not had major slave plantations here. This is a peaceful island.

Joyce: Violence is something to be avoided and has been and will be avoided at all costs. People will back off from a confrontation, because there is a deeper sense of respect for people and for the island. If you really feel that way, and you feel you are in a special place, you will really take care of it, right? People here, no matter what all our problems are, really take care of this little rock. Maybe that's the real reason we are making a vision for Aruba come true.

Juliet: My message to the young is that you're never alone. You are *never* alone, even though you think you are. You are part of life, and life wants you here. You have a gift, you have a calling, and you need to pay attention to that very quiet voice in your head to find out what it is. And when you least expect it, that voice will speak to you.

Joyce: To the children, the hopeless, the cynical, I say, "Dream, dream, dream. Dream and work on yourself." I think those two things are so important. I basically think life is fun. It has to do also with dreaming. I dream up so many things. I just live dreaming about how Aruba is going to look in 2005. I like to close my eyes and dream about how I see my children, how I'm going to be a grandma, all of that.

Obstacles

Joyce: There have been lots of mistakes—many having to do with me—my arrogance. Mathias, my husband and best friend, whom I have been married to for many years and have known since I was fifteen, and Gladys, my business partner, have helped me with that. I'm still working on myself, and I have a long way to go. But if there's something that stops you, it's going to be inside of you, it's not going to be outside of you.

Juliet: If there has been an obstacle, it's been my own self-perceptions. So very often we carry tapes inside of us that tell us we're not good, we're selfish, we're arrogant, we're this, we're that, you don't match up. I had those tapes running for years. And they're so weakening and paralyzing—it is pretty horrendous. Now if I do something stupid or silly, I won't say, "That was a stupid mistake." I just say, "Oops, that wasn't very wise."

Vision for a Better World

Joyce: I want a world that respects children, a world where children play a much more important role. So many times, we say we listen to children, but we don't. I see children being part of making major decisions for the world. I see them sitting on councils for schools. Children want this world to be good because they see it much more clearly than we do. My children help me see more clearly. So I see a world where we really, really listen to them and where they help design the future. And that's why I see much less violence. I also see a world where there are no boundaries like race and religion. You know children don't have a problem with that, but we adults do.

Juliet: My vision of this world will have cities, and countries, and nationalities and all of that, but there will be an essential difference. People, through their education and through their lives at home and at work, will be nurtured and fostered to look at a side of themselves that is not just money-making or career-achieving. They'll be fostered and nurtured to look into their reflective life. They'll be able to tap into a reservoir of insights and talents and potential. There will be a time when groups will actually have a dialogue and become skilled in tapping in to their gifts.

The world we create is not just from our brains. It'll be a much more caring world, much more respectful, much more joyful, actually, because there will be humor in what we see. I have a friend who says the universe is laughing at us. So there will be greater propensity to laugh and not be so morbid about things. And because of that, there would be really no reason to fight, if you can laugh together and smile together.

And in doing so, we will create heaven on earth, because what we've done with the paradigm that we've inherited for the last couple of hundred years is really to create hell on earth. We have become experts at that. We even have academies of war like West Point. In the future we will have academies of peace, and academies on the art and science of love, and where we come from, and where we go. Heaven is not a place far away that you go to when you die. It's a place where you can experience human love and live and act and play and learn together, really from the depths of your soul.

Lessons We Learned

DreamMakers express vision and values. "Number one, we are proud of our multicultural background and our language, Papiamento. Number two, we have respect for each other, and we live in a healthy community. Number three, we have leaders who respect and manage laws that produce a safe and secure society. Number four, we deliver quality service in all sectors of our community, and we are proud of a job well done. Number five, we protect and safeguard our environment and our flora and fauna. Number six, we have an educational system that allows our children to be creative and innovative and that prepares them for a changing world. And number seven, we work on our personal, physical, mental, and spiritual development so that we can contribute to the global health of the planet."

DreamMakers work with others to build a shared vision. "The campaign to create the Vision for Aruba was massive. We mailed an invitation to every household on the island to give us their vision for Aruba in the year 2005. We had articles in the newspapers, we went on the radio, we went on television, we had leaflets put in containers in all the major places like banks and supermarkets and hospitals and whatnot."

DreamMakers understand that we are all connected and interdependent. "I learned that when people sit together in a circle and spend time together talking, something happens where you begin to tap deeply in to something that you don't have access to on a conscious level. I truly believe that when you sit there together long enough and begin to share your hearts and souls, you open up to what the great psychologist Carl Jung calls the collective unconscious. You begin to tap in to a greater soul that you are part of."

DreamMakers support diversity and honor the integrity and contributions of all people. "I have always seen that people can be so much more if they can just let go and become themselves, if they don't get stuck in structures and ways of thinking. People can become so much lighter, so much happier, so much more productive, so much more in love with what's inside them and what's outside of them."

DreamMakers collaboratively transform and renew themselves and others. "This is a movement from us to us. It is not a movement that should stay in a little group in a little office. I think it is important to hold a vision out there, which you can start by doing yourself. The challenge is to take this movement—a positive movement—to take it out to other people."

DreamMakers focus on education and continual learning. "I really believe that the key leverage for change in the long term is through education and the youth. The more you work with and the more time you spend with kids, the more you realize that they affect everybody."

DreamMakers trust feelings, emotions, and intuition. "You have a gift, you have a calling, and you need to pay attention to that very quiet voice in your head to find out what it is. And when you least expect it, that voice will speak to you."

DreamMakers believe in a higher power and purpose. "I think another lesson is that you have to believe in what you're doing. You've got to have a kind of naive idealism. You have got to believe that what you're doing is great and is going to flower and is going to be something wonderful."

DreamMakers are committed to making the world a better place. "Connected with that for me is the constant question 'Who am I serving and why am I doing this?' We are serving the whole, we are serving the island, but not just the island today. We are serving the future. And in doing that, we serve the world."

There are issues in this world of such enormous magnitude that only the most optimistic and visionary people could even dream of tackling them. These issues include the kind of prejudice, hate, and fragmentation of our collective consciousness that can and does result in killing, war, and even genocide. They include how we view ourselves in service to each other and the world. They certainly include how our children are cared for, their opportunities, their learning environment, and their future. And these issues include how nations can work together to create a better world for all. Those with the courage to take on these issues demonstrate the very same strengths and capacities we have seen in the previous sections of this book: the power of vision, the strength of self-knowledge, and the ability to make connections and see the whole.

Part 3

DREAMMAKERS FOR A BETTER WORLD

JOE BRODECKI
The United States Holocaust Memorial Museum

MICHAEL LANE
The U.S. Customs Service

JOHN ABBOTT
Education 2000

RITA CLEARY
Vision for a Better World Foundation

MICHELE HUNT
Vision & Values

Joe Brodecki was a child of Holocaust survivors, but it took many years and many experiences of revisiting that devastating time before he knew what he needed to commit his life to. He had to create a mechanism—the United States Holocaust Memorial Museum—to ensure that we never forget. "If we can teach the world about the dangers of anti-Semitism, bigotry, racism, and prejudice, maybe we can prevent this from ever happening again to my children or somebody else's children. If we can truly educate this country and the world to the dangers, maybe we can prevent the Holocaust from happening to others." Because he was able to articulate his bold vision over and over, because of his personal sense of commitment, and because of his great compassion for the human condition, he was able to overcome obstacles of every size and shape to achieve his mission.

While the U.S. Customs Service might seem a strange choice for this section, its ability to see itself in a much larger context—truly a global context —of service led me to include its story here. And, of course, the Customs Service story is the story of a leader with huge convictions about our connectedness and our potential to solve big issues together. Michael Lane has looked for the higher ground, the larger purpose, all his life, and then directed his efforts always in that direction. Using his own ability to learn from others and engage others in the process, Michael was able not only to reinvent the Customs Service but also to bring relief to difficult situations in Bosnia and at the Olympic games. He does things because they are right, because, as he says, "It's what we're supposed to do."

After decades of seeing our children go through an educational system that thought it was perfectly okay to break the world down into unrelated, disconnected subjects—to break the web of life into fragments—John Abbott decided to engage whomever he could *in the world* to change this approach. John understands how children learn: He understands that they need to see things in context, to get the "why" questions answered holistically, to see patterns in complexity rather than be shielded from that complexity, and—not least of all—to be loved and cared for in a community context. To do nothing to change education entails too great a cost, in John's mind— the cost is the creation of a world not fit for children to grow up in, the kind of world that might have swallowed up Sharlonda Gillis, a world that would close its eyes to more genocide, and a world that would continue to devastate the environment. Thus John is pursuing Education 2000, undaunted by cynics, compassionate toward the hopeless, and committed to the children of the world.

Rita Cleary, after experiencing, at an early age, the death of her mother, spent years searching for her heart and for how she personally could relate to the whole of what went on in life. Rita introduced me to Aruba's Juliet Chieuw and Joyce Bartels-Daal; she suggested John Abbott for this book as well. Indeed, Rita has found that her mission in life is no less than to help create visions for a better world by bringing people together to tell their stories, to engage in dialogues, and to support the learning process of the largest organization in the world—the world itself. One of the values Rita articulates resonates with all the stories we have heard so far and is "of utmost importance to people of the world . . .—learning and staying open so that we can together, collectively, learn how to do that which we have dreamt of for the well-being of all people."

The well-being of *all* people—children; people of different ethnic, cultural, religious, and political backgrounds; people who have lost hope; people who cannot see yet where they fit in or how they can help; businesspeople; athletes; the wealthy who are poor in spirit and the poor who are wealthy in human dignity—this is the scope of Part Three, "DreamMakers for a Better World." The power of vision of the individuals you are about to meet, their well-grounded values, their moral compass, their sense of being part of the web of life, and their great love and hope for the peoples of the world and the world itself will empower them to bring about sustainable, life-giving change.

JOE BRODECKI *is a financial advisor with Sanford C. Bernstein and Co., Inc., an investment management firm in Washington, D.C.*

TENACITY

Joe Brodecki, The United States Holocaust Memorial Museum

I had lunch with Janet Smith one afternoon and told her about my decision to write *DreamMakers.* I had hardly gotten the title out of my mouth when she said, "I know a wonderful DreamMaker: Joe Brodecki." Janet told me all about him and strongly encouraged me to contact him. It seemed as if everyone knew a wonderful DreamMaker who should be in the book—which left me with a pleasant dilemma to have: too many DreamMakers. But Janet was persistent, so I decided to call Joe. After a brief telephone conversation with him, I understood why his story had to be told—and why he needed to tell it.

I arrived at the Brodecki home to find Joe going through articles, memos, and memories of his United States Holocaust Memorial Museum journey. Joe's story touched me deeply. I'm a person who likes to look forward; I rarely ponder the past. And I prefer to focus on the positive impact of values, not the negative consequences of the lack of value, or, as Joe would say, "no moral compass." From Joe and my visit to the Holocaust Museum, however, I learned the critical importance of looking the past squarely in the face and understanding its profound and painful messages. Joe's life and work are committed to creating a better world. His large vision, and the pain and suffering in the world, have fueled his passion to make a difference.

Defining Moments

Joe Brodecki: The Holocaust Museum was not yet there when I started. There were three of us in charge—the government person, the museum person, and me, the executive director of the Campaign to Remember. We all had our expertise, and we came together on a regular basis and worked under a kind of shared leadership. I don't think I could have succeeded if I had had to report to anyone. When I began, there was not adequate staff or resources to mount a national, grand-scale campaign.

I began the campaign in July 1988 and knew that between $100 and $200 million had to be raised in time for an April 1993 opening. Our headquarters were at 20th and L in downtown Washington, D.C., and I started getting on the phone and calling people and trying to garner support. Though the effort to build the museum had begun years before, it had not gone very far. There had been several false starts, and the museum-to-be desperately needed money. And we needed it fast. We made the decision to initially go after only contributions of $50,000 and above. We could not afford to solicit smaller gifts. The day-to-day talking to people about the museum was a challenge. They would say, "What are you talking about? There are so many more important needs. The homeless need money." And then as money began coming in, I started building a national staff.

Prior to building the museum, I led the highest per capita fund-raising campaign among Jewish organizations nationally. And I was the first recipient of the Vivian Rabineau Award, for best campaign director in the country, voted by peer professionals. I tell you this not to impress you but to impress upon you that though I had been involved in successful campaigns, nothing had prepared me for the Holocaust Museum job.

A Personal Journey Toward Destiny

Eighteen months before she gave birth to me, my mother was a slave in a Nazi concentration camp. So was my father. I was born in the displaced persons camp where they met. I grew up knowing about the Holocaust, but it wasn't an obsession. My father was born in Warsaw in 1921. His mother died when he was eight, and he was raised largely by his aunt. His father was an accountant and didn't want to leave Poland. My father played soccer, rode bicycles. It took him years to understand why American people were interested in baseball. He and his older sister actually tried to escape to Russia. Everybody else in his family was killed; only he survived. He was in Auschwitz. He was liberated from Theresienstadt. He was a member of the Jewish police in the refugee camp. The Jews had to have their own police force, because after what they went through, many wouldn't accept authority from anyone after the Holocaust. They were very tough to deal with, and understandably so.

My mother is from a town in southern Poland called Sosnowiec, from a very wealthy family, probably a little more religiously observant than my father's. She was much younger when all this happened. She was also in a ghetto and in different camps, but not the same camps that my father was in. My father has numbers the Nazis tattooed into his arm. She doesn't. My mother was a dancer, almost like a child star. She danced for the people in the camps. After the war, she tried to go back to her hometown, but they were killing the returning Jews, and she barely escaped with her life. In 1949, we immigrated to Richmond, Virginia.

My father goes disco dancing every night—seventy-five years old and a Holocaust survivor and he still goes disco dancing every night. He's in excellent shape. Does not concern himself with a lot of things, does a certain amount of speaking on the Holocaust, but primarily just has fun. He naps from about six or seven p.m. until about nine. He goes out about ten every night. It's a real problem for me when I go to Richmond, because it wrecks my schedule. One of the places where he dances, he met Jack Lemmon. Since then, he's been in a dozen movies. There's a myth that Holocaust survivors are difficult, negative, very tough people. Some of them are. On the other hand, most, like my parents, are warm, relaxed, very positive people. The Holocaust experience affected each survivor differently.

The messages my parents taught us growing up were not to hate, to be positive, and that you can make a difference. They're not philosophical people, however. I remember being taught in fourth grade that prior to the Civil War, the slaves loved their masters. The school was teaching about what they called "the War of Northern Aggression." Remember, Richmond, now a great city, was the capital of the Confederacy. When I told my father about what I had learned in school, boy, was he angry. He hit the ceiling.

About the same time, all the parents in the neighborhood got a letter asking them to sign a petition to keep our school segregated. Other parents signed the petition, threatening not to send their kids to school, but my parents refused to sign. It was because of the Holocaust and what they'd gone through. They said, "We didn't go through all that and survive to discriminate against somebody else." But other than that, and not having grandparents, the Holocaust didn't come up much. There was no effort to avoid the subject, but it wasn't our focus.

I worked on social issues in my career but not issues relating to the Jewish community. I had a master's degree in industrial psychology and had been a consultant to businesses, a lot of my work having to do with discrimination problems. I remember a factory that had 2,000 employees, and all but a handful were women, but no women were in supervisory positions. And I remember a furniture company where when I walked in, they said, "Oh, you're the guy that's here to force us to hire niggers," or something like that.

For a long time, all I wanted to do was be a professional baseball player. But my father wouldn't let me sign a contract out of high school.

The impact of the Holocaust really hit me when I went to the Middle East as a volunteer civilian replacement during the Yom Kippur War in 1973. While I was over there, I learned to love Israel, and I saw what was happening, so many countries trying to destroy little Israel. You had to be there to believe it. There were large lots with hundreds of captured enemy tanks. An international military effort had been mounted against the Israeli people, people just trying to raise a family—just like you and me. And many of these were Holocaust survivors and their children and grandchildren.

I remember saying to my girlfriend, when we were raising the money to go over to Israel, "Six months from now we'll be back to our normal lives." But that never happened. Everything changed. Israel opened up a new world for me. From then on, I wanted to get involved, maybe because I was born in the refugee camp in Landsberg, the same town where Hitler wrote *Mein Kampf.* My mother has always been convinced that since I was born in the town where Hitler gave birth to the Holocaust, I was destined for great things.

And so when I returned to the United States, I got involved in the Jewish community. I earned a second master's degree, and I was trained in what was the foremost Jewish community organization, the Jewish Community Federation of Cleveland. I met my wife in Cleveland. After seven years there, I moved to Minneapolis as the associate executive director of the Minneapolis Federation for Jewish Service.

In 1985 I went to a Holocaust survivors' conference in Philadelphia. There was one film from the Holocaust with a scene that got to me and affected me more than all the horror. There was a little four- or five-year-old boy—actual footage—the Nazis were filming all this. There was a mother and her little boy, and a Nazi was separating them. The little boy kept trying to get to his mother, and the Nazi kept pushing him away. I know that ultimately she was probably killed and he was probably killed, but the indignity of the way, in front of this little boy, the Nazi just kept kicking this mother in her behind like she was nothing really disturbed me. Little children think their parents are omnipotent, but that boy's mother was powerless—she couldn't do anything. For weeks, I couldn't get that scene out of my mind. The soldier probably had his own kids and probably went home at night and was a loving father—yet he was doing this to someone else's child.

I remembered a story that my mother had told me about when she last saw her mother, how it was raining, and how *her* mother, who couldn't do anything to save her, put a shawl on her shoulders to protect her from the rain and said good-bye. I kept thinking, "This story's got to be told." Three years later I was raising money for the museum that would tell the story.

When the firm hired to find candidates for the Holocaust Museum job asked me why I thought I could do the job, I said, "It's destiny. I've worked in top fund-raising campaigns, I was born in a displaced persons camp. For me, the campaign is the right place, at the right time, right now." I know that's a bold, overused statement, but I was sincere. They didn't ask me anything else after that.

The Work Begins: Mr. Meyerhoff

And then I met Mr. Harvey M. Meyerhoff. He's one of the museum's unsung heroes. Mr. Meyerhoff of Baltimore was the chairman of the Holocaust Museum. It was around Passover when I got a call from Korn/Ferry, the firm conducting the search for the campaign director. I had been on vacation, visiting my parents in Richmond. I had to buy a white shirt, and I went to New York for the interview. I picked up a tie at Paul Stuart—someone told me they had nice ties. At the interview, I met Ann Kern and Esther Rosenberg, the search firm representatives. I can never repay their confidence in me. When I called my wife later that evening, she said, "A man named Mr. Meyerhoff just called and would like to meet you. Go to Baltimore tomorrow. Mr. Meyerhoff has all the details, but you must call from the airport before you leave, because his wife is ill, and if you're going to be late, he wants to spend more time with her."

Now my big problem was getting the white shirt cleaned and pressed in time to make a mid-morning flight. I found a place to do the shirt, got to the airport, and picked up the phone. Mr. Meyerhoff's assistant said, "Mr. Meyerhoff's wife is dying. But he insists that you come in." And I said, "How can I?" She said, "He insists, and he is coming directly from the hospital specifically to see you." Now, when you're talking to someone about a job, you want to show fire and enthusiasm. But how do you show enthusiasm to someone whose wife is dying? You can't. But I flew up anyway and walked into his office. I could see that he hadn't slept and that he was holding back his feelings. I looked at him and said, "Mr. Meyerhoff, we don't have to do this today. We can talk another time." He looked me in the eye and said, "My wife told me that building the Holocaust Museum is the most important thing I will ever do in my life and that I must go to the meeting. I promised her I would. We'll talk now!" And so we did. It was the most memorable encounter I've ever had.

That moved me. And it also played into my feeling about destiny and fate. A few minutes later, I said to him, "Mr. Meyerhoff, you're the chairman of this campaign. What have you done for the project?" You know, leadership. In the Israeli military, they have a philosophy, *icharei*—"Follow me, after me." Since the officers go into battle first, they make damn sure what they're doing is important. They don't just send people into battle. Leadership takes the first step. If you're not going anywhere, nobody can follow you, and if people don't follow you, by definition you're not a leader.

I said, "Well, Mr. Meyerhoff, what is your contribution?" He used very colorful language. "I have contributed six million dollars," he said. "What do you think about that?" I almost fell off my chair. I'd been told by the people who had already worked with this project and by virtually all my professional colleagues that taking this job would be professional suicide—the false starts, the controversy, the negative press every day, the mistrust many had of the government, the lack of money. All of a sudden, I'm looking at this man I've just met, and I'm thinking about my mother languishing in a displaced persons camp, never dreaming that her son would be in this position. I'm thinking about this man who's seeing me as his wife is hospitalized, gravely ill. I'm thinking about his generous contribution. And I'm saying to myself, "This is it. I really want to do this. And I'm going to do it, and it doesn't matter what it takes. No obstacle will stop me." I have always believed that if you truly know *why* you are doing something, you will figure out *how* to do it.

That's the stuff that keeps me going. I know it sounds trite. I told the head of the organization in Minneapolis that I was leaving. He didn't even want to announce it at the next board meeting because he thought I was ruining my career.

Evolution of the Holocaust Museum

The Holocaust Museum is not a Jewish museum. It's a museum created by a unanimous act of Congress. It started in the Carter administration. President Carter appointed a commission. I believe they started the project because our country was selling jets to one of the countries vowing to destroy Israel. So I believe President Carter wanted to find a way to keep good relations with the Jewish community. He established a commission, chaired by Elie Wiesel, which said our country needed a living memorial to the Holocaust. But it must be more than a memorial—it must educate. They established the United States Holocaust Memorial Council, with its most important goal to build the museum.

Then Ronald Reagan came into office, and by another unanimous act of Congress the land was set aside with the proviso that all the money to build the museum had to be raised privately. Ronald Reagan became the honorary Campaign to Remember chairman, and the honorary campaign committee included Father Theodore Hesburgh, the Rev. Billy Graham, Jean Kirkpatrick, baseball commissioner Bart Giamatti, Supreme Court Justice Warren Burger, Walter Annenberg, Lane Kirkland, and other prominent people. Holocaust Council membership required appointment by the president of the United States. So the first people were Carter people, then there were Reagan people, Bush people, and Clinton people. And the interesting thing about a process like this is that you get a mix of people, some knowledgeable and committed to the subject, and some who got appointed for political reasons. Most were financial contributors to the museum. A few weren't. I went to one person and said, "Look, you're a leader, you're a member of the Holocaust Council. I'm asking you as a leader to contribute a quarter of a million dollars to the museum." He said, "Wait a minute. That's what I gave politically to get here!"

Some sophisticated persons whom you tap for lots of money rightfully want to have a hand in deciding how the money will be used. One of the challenges for me was that even if someone gave a million dollars, I couldn't guarantee that that person would be appointed to the council, because one had to be appointed by the president. One fellow submitted letters supporting his appointment from sixty-five senators but was not successful. Five senators and five representatives were on the council. One time I had an urgent issue and I pulled one of the senators on the council out of a U.S. Senate Appropriations meeting, and said, "Look, you've got a responsibility. You've got this title on your résumé and you're not doing anything. You have an obligation to help." He agreed.

This was a team effort—it had to be. Nobody could have done this alone. And working as a team, everyone achieved more. Even though sometimes we had what Chairman Miles Lerman called "naked conversations" when we went at each other, we all shared the vision in our own ways. There is a man named Adam Starkopf from Chicago, whose mother told him when he was a boy that a Jewish life was worth less than a penny. He was collecting six million pennies for the museum. There was a story about a nun who inherited $3,000 and left it all to the museum. There are so many stories. Others helped in other ways. Ted Koppel of *Nightline* narrated, as a volunteer, a fund-raising video for us.

The way you build a museum and the way you raise funds are two different things. We needed top scholars, top people in the world, because we wanted to tell a story that was unchallengeable. But in terms of fund-raising, you find people, tell them the story, and hope they give. I found early on that convincing some of the major million-dollar prospects could go on and on and on. Some of the pledges took three years to close. But it's like anything else—90 percent of your efforts don't produce anything, 10 percent do. The problem is you don't know which 10 percent in advance, so you have to do it all.

The campaign raised nearly $200 million—including eighty gifts of $1 million or more, and a thousand of $50,000 or more—and nearly 300,000 contributors from all walks of life. The campaign to build the museum had corporate, labor, military, Holocaust survivors, church, direct mail, fraternity, entertainment industry, and many other subcampaigns. I worked with more groups and constituencies in this single fund-raising campaign than most fund-raisers work with in their entire careers. People of all ages, from every conceivable race, religion, industry, and occupation, supported the United States Holocaust Memorial Museum Campaign to Remember.

Vision and Values

My initial feeling when I started was that we needed two components, vision and immediate action. It's easier to take day-to-day rejection when you have a vision. If you can see your vision, and can get other people to see it and internalize it, not only in terms of today but in terms of what it will mean for this country and the world and, more important, for them, their families, and their future families, they will persist through the roughest times. I think about the technology that's out there today. Think what good and what harm could be done. Can you imagine if the Nazis had the technology we have today? Values are so important.

That's why the museum had to be on the National Mall—to remind us, to educate us. Putting something like this on the Mall in the center of all those wonderful institutions that celebrate culture and technological achievement serves as a stark contrast and a reminder of what can happen when all these wonderful achievements are turned the wrong way. And it keeps in front of us the importance of moral values.

First, Remember

You see, the Holocaust didn't start with the killing. We wanted to tell a story of how it happened. We wanted a story told in a way that the average person could understand. We wanted that story to be unchallengeable—irrefutable, with authentic evidence—and that's why our people went all over the world and gathered the artifacts. This was at a time when eastern European governments were changing, when Communism was failing. Miles Lerman and Dr. Michael Berenbaum and Jacek Nowakowski and other people scoured eastern Europe to get the artifacts to support the story.

With technology and the media today, something like the Holocaust could happen again overnight. So we wanted to show that it didn't just start with the killing. It starts with a little brushfire. You've got to put it out right away. You've got to be alert. The cancer has to be cut out right away. If it goes too far, you can't stop it. Who were these people who perpetrated the Holocaust? It wasn't Hitler alone. It was your neighbor, the friend that you've grown up with, your teachers, your scholars, your athletes. It was the most famous people in your culture, the philosophers, the poets, the writers. Very few people did anything about it. Otherwise, six million Jews and five million others wouldn't have been killed. It's very important to tell the story of the very few people who risked everything to help, but those stories have got to be kept in context. A lot of good people went bad during the Holocaust. Of the people who planned the Final Solution, more than half were Ph.D.s. When they were asked to come up with the Final Solution, they just did it. They didn't ask if it was right or wrong. There was no moral compass. And you have to have a moral compass somehow. Think about those people, Germany's best and brightest, and then contrast them with the simple Danish fishermen, who in the middle of it all risked their lives to save people. Under cover of darkness, they helped the Jews get out in their boats. Then there was the whole French village of Le Chambon that saved 5,000 Jewish children.

The Holocaust was a big bureaucratic plan. This was not a few people. We have in the museum a boxcar that took the Jews to the camps. Now think about boxcars. Think about what it takes to make that happen. Somebody had to come up with a master plan, which railway tracks to use. Someone had to design and others had to build the boxcars. It wasn't Hitler who did that. Someone had to make sure the boxcars got to their pick-up places on time. Who made sure the victims got on them? Who made sure the boxcar got to its destination? Who made sure the people were pushed out? Who cleaned the boxcars? Who made sure they got back to pick up more victims? Thousands of boxcars. Hitler and two SS people didn't do it.

Do you know who did it? Engineers, regular engineers. Just as doctors and scientists developed the killing methods, and lawyers created the laws to take away Jews' rights legally. Regular people.

And think about the ovens. How did they get ovens? They had RFPs—requests for proposals—just like we write today. Different corporations sent in proposals: My oven is better than yours. I can guarantee that our oven can burn 500 people an hour and last for twenty-five years. The German equivalent of Westinghouse or General Electric made the ovens.

It took millions of people, perpetrators and bystanders, to mount the Holocaust. After Kristallnacht, the night when the Nazis destroyed and looted Jewish synagogues and business establishments in Germany, they told people not to do business with Jews anymore. Well, they had a problem on their hands—the insurance industry. The insurance industry said, "Wait a minute. If we don't pay the Jews for all this destroyed property, people are going to stop buying insurance. But if we pay, we'll have to pay out a fortune." So they made a deal with the German government, which ordered them not to pay. When I went to the insurance industry here in the United States and said, "You've got to give to the museum," I told them that story. And they did give. When we went to the labor unions, we said, "Look, Hitler and the Nazis did just what the Communists were doing in China. They were destroying the labor movement." The Nazis didn't want people to be able to unite. Within six months, Hitler destroyed the whole labor union movement. And because of that, the unions gave $3 million to the museum, lots of different unions.

In 1987 I was at Auschwitz. That's where I saw the bone fragments at a crematorium that James Ingo Freed [the architect of the museum] would see. I thought about my daughters, my wife, my parents—where I came from—that's where I made a vow to do *something*. I had heard about the museum plan in 1985, but I didn't think much about it. I thought it was just another project. But there in 1987, at the crematorium, I made the vow. I didn't know what I was going to do or how, but I was going to do something in memory of my grandparents and the rest of the people who had perished. Whatever it took, I was going to do my part to make sure that the world never forgets and hopefully it never happens again. Neither you nor I nor anybody in the world can ever bring back my family or the millions of others who perished. Nobody can do that. But we can make sure the world never forgets.

When each of my daughters, Talia and Ariella, was born, I thought deeply about the Holocaust. I agonized over how I would explain what happened to their family in World War II. You want your children to be positive, to look to the world as an open place with unlimited potential. How are you going to express to them that people destroyed their people just because they were Jewish?

If we can teach the world about the dangers of anti-Semitism, bigotry, racism, and prejudice, maybe we can prevent this from ever happening again to my children or somebody else's children. If we can truly educate this country and the world to the dangers, maybe we can prevent the Holocaust from happening to others.

Then, Educate

First you have to remember, then you have to educate. That museum is not just an edifice. That museum is reaching out to schools all over America.

I would not have sacrificed five years of my life and so much time away from my family for just a building. The main objective in that museum is education. It's the refutation to the Holocaust deniers and those people of the world who say that the Holocaust is a myth, perpetrated on Christians by Jews.

It's incredible that the Jewish people are still here. Before the war, there were 17.5 million. After the war, there were only 11.5 million, and there were no poorer people than the Holocaust survivors. These people had been basically teenagers when they were put into camps, and in their early twenties when they came out, hardly more than skeletons, people who didn't have the benefit of a complete education, with no parents to guide them and no hope. They had nothing. Everything had been taken away from them. If you were from eastern Europe and you found yourself in a refugee camp, you couldn't go back home because the Communists had taken over. What were you going to do? If you went to Israel, you found yourself in a war for independence. If you were lucky and got into the United States, you came into a new culture where not only did you know no one, but you didn't even know the language. You would think that these people would have high murder rates, high crime rates, but they didn't. Of course they're not without problems, but as a group, look what they've accomplished. They have contributed to society in many fields of endeavor. Over $30 million for the museum was raised by Holocaust survivors. There are eighteen survivors who each gave $1 million or more.

Leadership

One thing I learned about leadership through all this—it's doing the right thing while trying to do things right. You've got to have personal credibility. You've got to have integrity. You've got to be honest. You should be forward-looking. You need to have character—doing what you say you are going to do even after the emotion wears off. That's hard. You've got to be an inspiration, and you've got to love change. Leaders of organizations must understand the concept of a "conscious use of self"—how you're perceived, how you're coming off to the people around you. I don't believe in quality time: people need you when they need you. Relationships are important.

Leaders take the first step. They help define the vision—maybe that's what Max De Pree means when he says, "The responsibility of the leadership is to define reality." It's too tough today—the day-to-day demands of leadership are so hard, the rejection. "Was my decision right? Was it a mistake?" You have to allow for mistakes; that's why there are erasers on pencils. There are always obstacles. Some people use obstacles as stepping-stones. Everybody knows the story about Thomas Edison. He didn't *fail* to invent the lightbulb 10,000 times; he just learned how *not* to invent the lightbulb. People don't remember the out you made early in the game when you homer in the ninth inning.

But the day-to-day demands of leadership are too tough when you haven't internalized the answer to the question "What's in it for me?" The future is not about exploiting people—it's got to be about servant leadership and helping them.

Slave Labor Camps in China

I want to tell you about my friend Harry Wu. I see these guys setting up an exhibition of photographs taken in China. And the buildings in their photographs look like those in Auschwitz. So I get into a conversation with these guys: "What are you doing?" I ask. "We are trying to help people, show what's happening in the *laogai,* the system of slave labor camps in China, which could have up to ten million people in them right now! And few people care." Think about it. The Chinese government has these slave labor camps. Ten million people! These people are making products—all kinds of products. Many of these people are political prisoners. It is against the law in the United States to sell a product made by slave labor, but that law is not always enforced.

Harry Wu was in the Chinese slave labor camps for nineteen years. He is a normal person, like you or me. What did he do? At the time Mao was telling people to comply, Harry criticized the Soviet invasion of Hungary, and he was put in prison for nineteen years. Harry tells stories of how they use persuasion. You know how they use persuasion? Strip you naked and tie you to a pole and let the mosquitoes feed on your blood.

Harry was finally released. He went back to China a couple of years ago, taking tremendous risks to secretly document slave labor practices. He's devoting his life to educating the world about the Chinese *laogai.* They call him a troublemaker, and he recently wrote a book about his experiences. Harry Wu is one man standing up against big China. He lives in the

United States with his wife, and he could live a nice, comfortable life, but he says he can't forget the people he left behind in those camps.

Obstacles

Dream Stealers

You talk about DreamMakers. Let me tell you about people I call "dream stealers." You've got to be ready to face massive rejection, especially if you're bringing about change. We are in what I call a psychological jet lag. It's easy to talk about change, and it's easy to talk about rejection, but it's hard to take either. To succeed you must persist. Calvin Coolidge said, "Nothing in the world can take the place of persistence. . . . Persistence and determination alone are omnipotent."

Most people never dream, and many of those few who do let the dream stealers influence them and quit. A dream stealer is someone who says it can't be done, or it shouldn't be done. Some dream stealers are well-intentioned people who don't want you to fail—they feel sorry for you because they think, "Oh, God. It's not going to work out—it's going to ruin his family."

When I started with the Holocaust Museum, many people gave me reasons why it was going to fail: "Nobody wants to remember the Holocaust." "Why build it here? It happened in Europe." In the Jewish community, some said it would draw money away from other needs. There was an article by a well-known journalist and author named Judith Miller in the *New York Times Sunday Magazine* criticizing the Holocaust Memorial. Henry Kissinger was quoted in that article saying that putting it on the National Mall could cause anti-Semitism. People were also saying that there were already too many of these memorials; why do we need another one?

Complex and Competing Issues

Today, after it's all over, people talk about how easy it must have been. It was by far the most difficult thing I've ever done. It was very difficult for all the people involved because of the politics, the presidential issues, the massive amounts of money that had to be raised quickly, the design—the initial design was rejected by the National Capital Planning Commission, the commission that must approve anything built on the National Mall. After this rejection, the leaders had to recruit a new architect. He went to Auschwitz for ideas, and had the same experience I had there. He was at the same crematorium and saw the bone fragments I saw in the soil. His name is James Ingo Freed, a partner of I. M. Pei, and his design made architectural history.

It was very difficult trying to raise money for the museum, hard work. A New York museum led by Elie Wiesel, founding chairman of the commission that led to the United States Holocaust Memorial Museum, had had to lay off almost everybody on staff due to lack of financial support. (The New York museum found alternative sources of funding and opened a scaled-down version in September 1997.) I didn't want that to happen to us. And then a great thing happened. The gates opened in the Soviet Union, and Jews could get out. The Jewish community focused on Operation Exodus, a life-saving campaign to raise money to get the Jews out of the U.S.S.R. "This is our chance," they thought, "we can get them out. Who knows when the door can swing shut?" And people were asking, "Why are you raising money to build a Holocaust Museum now? We're raising money to save lives. How can you go to people and ask them for this money when we need every penny to save lives?" What a problem.

However, I said to them, "If we didn't know about the Holocaust, we wouldn't know why it's so important to get Jews out of the Soviet Union. We have to do both!" Holocaust Museum leaders gave generously to Operation Exodus. Mr. Meyerhoff gave a seven-figure gift. Bill Lowenberg, the museum's vice chair, led the Operation Exodus effort in San Francisco. At this point, we had to shift gears and mount other campaigns, a survivor campaign, a corporate campaign, and a trade union campaign. Gerry Greenwald, now the CEO of UAL, heard Sandy Brock, the wife of former Secretary of Labor Bill Brock, read a poem about the shoes of somebody's little girl.

I heard her read that poem, too. The first thing I thought about was that there are several hundred thousand pairs of shoes at the Majdanek Camp. Somebody's innocent little child was murdered for nothing except for being Jewish. I imagined my daughters in those shoes, and I said to myself, "I'm doing the right thing with this museum."

Anyway, Gerry Greenwald reacted to the poem about the shoes and persuaded Chrysler Corporation, where he was at that time an executive, to donate $1 million. He became the Campaign to Remember's corporate chairman. He in turn recruited people like Bob Galvin at Motorola and Ed

Woolard of DuPont and other corporate leaders. We had many other fund-raising campaigns. It was important that support for a Holocaust Museum be broad-based and not be perceived as coming only from Jews. If there are any people who don't need a museum, it's the Holocaust survivors and the Jews. They know the story.

Lessons We Learned

DreamMakers express vision and values. "One thing I learned about leadership through all this—it's doing the right thing while trying to do things right. You've got to have personal credibility. You've got to have integrity. You've got to be honest. You should be forward-looking. You need to have character—doing what you say you are going to do even after the emotion wears off. That's hard. You've got to be an inspiration, and you've got to love change."

DreamMakers engage others in their vision. "It's easier to take day-to-day rejection when you have a vision. If you can see your vision, and can get other people to see it and internalize it, not only in terms of today but in terms of what it will mean for this country and the world and, more important, for them, their families, and their future families, they will persist through the roughest times."

DreamMakers make their dreams a reality. "The campaign raised nearly $200 million—including eighty gifts of $1 million or more, and one thousand of $50,000 or more—from nearly 300,000 contributors from all walks of life. . . . People of all ages, from every conceivable race, religion, industry, and occupation, supported the United States Holocaust Memorial Museum Campaign to Remember."

DreamMakers focus on education and continual learning. "First you have to remember, then you have to educate. That museum is not just an edifice. . . . The main objective in that museum is education."

DreamMakers learn from their mistakes. "You have to allow for mistakes; that's why there are erasers on pencils. . . . Everybody knows the story about

Thomas Edison. He didn't *fail* to invent the lightbulb 10,000 times; he just learned how *not* to invent the lightbulb."

DreamMakers trust feelings, emotions, and intuition. "I'm saying to myself, 'This is it. I really want to do this. And I'm going to do it, and it doesn't matter what it takes. No obstacle will stop me.' I have always believed that if you truly know *why* you are doing something, you will figure out *how* to do it."

DreamMakers are both passionate and compassionate. "When the firm hired to find candidates for the Holocaust Museum job asked why I thought I could do the job, I said, 'It's destiny. I've worked in top fund-raising campaigns, I was born in a displaced persons camp. For me, the campaign is the right place, at the right time, right now.' I know that's a bold, overused statement, but I was sincere. They didn't ask me anything else after that."

DreamMakers follow a moral compass. "All the parents in the neighborhood got a letter asking them to sign a petition to keep our school segregated. All the other parents signed the petition, threatening not to send their kids to school, but my parents refused to sign. It was because of the Holocaust and what they'd gone through. They said, 'We didn't go through all that and survive to discriminate against somebody else.' "

DreamMakers demonstrate responsibility toward a larger community. "I remember saying to my girlfriend, when we were raising the money to go over to Israel, 'Six months from now we'll be back to our normal lives.' But that never happened. Everything changed. Israel opened up a new world for me. From then on, I wanted to get involved."

DreamMakers are committed to making the world a better place. "In 1987 I was at Auschwitz. That's where I saw the . . . bone fragments at a crematorium. . . . I thought about my daughters, my wife, my parents—where I came from—that's where I made a vow to do *something*. . . . I didn't know what I was going to do or how, but I was going to do something in memory of my grandparents and the rest of the people who had perished. Whatever it took, I was going to do my part to make sure that the world never forgets and hopefully it never happens again."

MICHAEL LANE, *executive vice president of Sandler & Travis Trade Advisory Services, Inc., concentrates his efforts on all aspects of international trade and customs matters including informed compliance, international trade agreements, and the international trading system. Prior to joining the firm, he served for thirty years at the U.S. Customs Service, where he was deputy commissioner for nine years. Previously, he was deputy assistant secretary, Operations, Department of the Treasury, where he provided oversight to the U.S. Secret Service, the Bureau of Alcohol, Tobacco, and Firearms, and the U.S. Customs Service. Lane has received both the Meritorious and Distinguished Presidential Rank awards, the highest recognition that can be given to a civil servant.*

CUSTOMER SERVICE FOR THE TWENTY-FIRST CENTURY

Michael Lane, U.S. Customs Service

On August 28, 1996, I arrived at the United States Customs Service headquarters in Washington, D.C., to interview Michael Lane, deputy commissioner. My visit brought back memories of the two and a half years I had worked in the Clinton administration reinventing government. We had worked with the U.S. Customs Service as part of our mandate to help agencies create a government that works better and costs less.

The agency launched its journey to create the "Customs Service for the 21st Century" in the fall of 1993 with the vision "to become the most facilitative Customs Service in the world. To achieve compliance with Customs and other agencies' laws at the border at a rate approaching 100 percent by the end of the century. To form partnerships with customers in industry and government to meet our compliance, enforcement, and facilitation goals. And to become the nation's supplier of international trade information."

The first time I met Michael Lane, he was just beginning to put in place a study team to learn the latest and most successful management, quality, and organizational change philosophies and practices. Their mission was to develop a conceptual framework to guide the organization on its journey.

Most agencies move only slowly and painfully toward change. The Customs Service—an organization of 25,000 people that had not gone through a major reorganization in thirty years, had been prohibited by law from any form of reorganization for the past ten years, and was still governed by laws dating back to the first acts of Congress—made deeper, quicker, and more comprehensive changes in its culture and organization than I have seen any company or organization accomplish anywhere. The agency's leaders understood and communicated the compelling reasons for change to all employees, Congress, and other stakeholders. They created and shared a clear vision and clear values, and then they redesigned and aligned their organization's processes, structures, systems, and culture.

The results were astounding. By 1996 the Customs Service had begun to focus on serving its customers (mind you, the notion of passengers, carriers, importers, and the public as customers was not in the culture prior to 1993). The agency had moved to organizing around its work. The management created a more inclusive and participative approach to leading people: They engaged and trained all 20,000 employees in the change process. They empowered their employees to make decisions. They instituted a proactive approach to anticipating and dealing with trade issues. They also significantly increased the use of information technology to support their organization. They drastically reduced the time it takes for passengers and cargo to go through our borders. When I go through Customs today, I truly feel welcomed home and safe.

Michael appears to me as a gentle soul—tough on issues, yet soft on people. I have no doubt that his ability to share and build vision and values with and through others contributes significantly to the Customs Service's reputation as a "can do" organization.

Defining Moments

The Earliest Years

Michael Lane: I was adopted when I was a baby. I was born in 1942, and my father had gone off to war. I was the youngest of four children, and my mother was living in Philadelphia. She didn't really have the money to take care of all of us, and my father never came back. He didn't die in the war; he just never came back to us. My mother's sister, at one time or another, helped my mother with all the kids. My aunt and uncle had no children of their own, and they decided to keep me. Eventually, when I was in the sixth grade, they adopted me. My brother and sisters were with my mother, who never remarried, and I was with my aunt and uncle, whom I always knew as my mother and father. My mother and her sister were always very, very close, and as a child, not understanding this relationship or how it could happen, I was always perplexed by it—maybe even frightened by it. I don't know. Maybe mine was a little bit like the Madeline Albright situation—don't ask too many questions.

What greater sacrifice could two people make? They were really remarkable people in that sense, although poor and not well educated. So today I feel like I had two mothers.

I guess my adoptive mother's relationship with me probably had as big an impact on my life as anything. I essentially grew up as an only child and was revered by my adoptive mother. She made me think that whatever I was doing was always exactly the right thing to be doing. That was not always or even mostly true, but that kind of love gave me strength.

People were always very nice to me. When I was a kid I went to Catholic schools, and the priests were always very good to me, trying to recruit me to be in the priesthood. But I really wasn't thinking about the priesthood. They would take me in the summertime up to the seminary or the prep school to show me all these things, and I always believed in the sentiments of religion. I was thought of as a very devout kid, but there's something—it wasn't more about God, it was about humankind and humanity.

About 1962 I was in the Navy in Norfolk, Virginia. I was eighteen years old or something, walking by a television, and I heard that Ernest Hemingway had just died. Somebody read a poem by John Donne, which I didn't know at the time, and it stunned me. At that time in my life, I'd probably read about five books. I went to the library to try to find this passage by John Donne, an English minister. It's from this passage that Hemingway got one of his most famous titles: "No man is an island, entire of itself; every man is part of the continent, a part of the main; if a clod be washed away by the sea, Europe is the less, as well as if a promontory were, as well as if a manor of thy friends or of thy own were; any man's death diminishes me, because I am involved in mankind; and therefore never send to know for whom the bell tolls; it tolls for thee."

The last part really hit me. I'm involved in humankind, I'm a part of this. If you suffer, I suffer. If you excel, I excel. Things that reflect that sentiment always draw me. If you think about it in the workplace, it really gets you to where people that are concerned about management and organization are concerned about the whole organization and everyone in it.

My first job out of the Navy was working at a place called the Medical Systems Development Laboratory, filled with doctors, engineers, scientists, mathematicians, and me. I wasn't any good at this. I was terrible at it. And about every six months I'd go in to quit. And they'd give me a raise. So I would stay. They made such a fuss about it, and then, maybe six months later, I'd come in and say, "Look, I can't" and I'd get another raise.

Finally I said, "Look, I am leaving. This is not a ploy. I don't want a raise. I can't do this. I know I can't compete here and I'm not doing a good job. I'm not meant for this. And I appreciate how everybody's been kind to me." My boss, a mathematician, said, "Okay, I agree. You're really not as good at the technical parts, but you have something that nobody else here has." I was in my early twenties at the time, and she said, "That's why we want to keep you here." She said, "You really make a great contribution to this organization." I guess even then I was able to help people, to think about the goals of the organization and the purpose of it.

The doctor who headed this company took me out to lunch and asked me questions about management and organization. I was really fascinated and intrigued by these topics at the time, and I wanted to apply those things I'd read about to my own workplace, even though I was a young employee and these people were scientists and engineers and doctors who didn't think that way. I wasn't a particularly aggressive person, but I would try to find ways to help the organization go in the direction that it needed to go in.

And when I think about Customs, I think about how do we serve the nation, how do we serve the administration, how do we serve Treasury, and if there's a national goal, how do we fit into it? Can we contribute? And if our mission doesn't quite fit into it, but we have the capacity to do so, shouldn't we do it?

Coming to the Customs Service

Coming to Customs was probably one of the biggest events of my life. I have been in Customs twenty-six years, but I left it twice for other jobs and once for a sabbatical.

I was very unhappy at my job in 1976. Customs was doing some things that I was upset about. I knew I needed to get away. My boss, one of the deputy commissioners, talked to me about a sabbatical, and I went to USC's graduate program in public administration. I'd dropped out of college my freshman year and I would go back periodically, but I never finished. I never thought of myself as a good student. I didn't really like school that much, and I didn't like college at all. But at USC I was reading books about government and management, and then writing papers, and going to class—that was possibly the best year of my life. I was reading all the books the first week of class. In fact, I would do my papers in about the first three weeks, I'd be so excited about them. Everybody would say, "That guy—what's he trying to do to the rest of us?" I was so energized by the experience—reading about management theory and public administration.

Then I went to the Bureau of Alcohol, Tobacco and Firearms from 1979 to 1982, and we tried to reinvent ATF. Then they started to abolish ATF, and I got to come back here, which was wonderful.

By 1986 I was in a new job at Customs. I was going on vacation, and while driving to the airport, I said to my wife, "You know, I've been in that job nine months, and I've finally got it. I don't feel like I've achieved everything, but I've got it all set up to make that whole office run properly. I know how to do this job now, and when I come back, I'm really going to make it happen."

I got to my vacation place, and the commissioner of Customs called me and said, "The assistant secretary of Treasury is demanding that you be his deputy assistant secretary. He's going to call you. I wanted you to know it."

So Frank Keating called me (he's now governor of Oklahoma), and I took that job. I didn't even know him that well at the time, but I grew to really love Frank. He's just a wonderful person. I've had other mentors. The deputies here in Customs, and the commissioners, too, did some very nice things for me, but Frank was somebody that I worked in partnership with. You know it's a wonderful thing when you work day and night with somebody, and you're so attuned to the same objectives and goals that you don't think about any kind of hierarchical relationship or things like that. When you get to work with somebody like that, maybe it's really the best sort of mentoring—you didn't know it was happening.

I thought we did some good things at Treasury, and as a result, when the deputy commissioner job was vacated here at Customs, Frank saw to it that I got that job, where I've been for almost ten years under different commissioners.

Reinventing the U.S. Customs Service

I always thought Customs was a good agency. They were doing a good job. But the Clinton administration came in and said, "Look, is this good? Is this a good thing or is it a bad thing?" And we opened ourselves up. Customs has been run by laws that dated back to the eighteenth century. Finally, the Modernization Act, which George Weise, the Commissioner, made happen, and Sam Banks was instrumental in, let us change some practices that were just outmoded and out-of-date—making merchants declare the number of guns on a cargo ship, cannons, and things like this. Congress finally gave us the chance to do something about all that, and gave the public an opportunity to be a part of it. We did all those focus groups, which I'd never even heard about until we started doing them. Customs used to be a closed society—look at the building, it's like a fortress—but we did open up.

At first, I didn't want to mess with the organization too much because it took the focus off what we're doing, the actual substance of our work. But over time, George Weise and I talked about this, and I said, "Well, George, if you want me to look at the organization, I want to look at everything. I want to look at what we're doing, the direction that we're going, and everything." And he was entirely agreeable to that.

I was going to do this part-time, but I realized I couldn't accomplish anything if I did it that way. So I said that I wanted six months to really work on it, day and night. And that I wanted to handpick a team that would really represent all of Customs. I was able to handpick some of them, and people I trusted recommended other ones, and we got twenty people who really had the opportunity to look at the organization in a nonthreatening mode.

The Federal Quality Institute was a milestone, exposing me to reengineering, quality, and process management. When the institute brought those people so willing to share their experiences—from Ford, AT&T, Corning, and places that we would never have gotten to, other government agencies that we wouldn't have reached out to—that was an awakening for me. Part of *The Wellsprings of Knowledge* deals with how organizations work and most of the time don't work, particularly agencies around two-hundred years old. We think we know how to do a lot of this stuff, because we're government and we have authority over companies and can put people in jail, put them out of business, fine them. But you can learn from them, and they're quite willing to share. The days with those people were really wonderful. And then Brookings, to another extent, did the same thing. That really made me think,

"Yeah, I can make this thing happen. This organization can make this happen." I think we brought in more outside ideas and expertise in those six months than in any previous period in our two hundred years.

I learned a lot from the book *The Knowledge-Creating Company*. That book helped put us on the path of really trying to make this organization everything it could be. We spent six months trying to define what we needed to be; we got the whole place reorganized. Shortly after that, one person started to redesign our whole commercial system, one of the biggest systems in government and the world, handling almost $1 trillion worth of goods every year and collecting almost $25 billion in revenue. We needed a complete redesign. Chuck Winwood put together a whole way of looking at all our processes from end to end.

We had a rough period where people who weren't involved in the plans for change—the enforcement people—were upset about the organization. We had a seminar with people from Brookings, Rand, and Harvard, people who used to be assistant secretaries of the various departments and scholars, and we went through our entire plan. At the end of the seminar, one of them—a Harvard professor named Malcolm Sparrow—came over to me and said, "You know, you've really missed the boat here on your enforcement programs. You're just going in the wrong direction, and you're going to alienate probably a third of your workforce. I'm writing a book about this. I'll send you a copy." I was depressed about this, but I got his book, *Imposing Duties*, and realized he was right.

During the beginning of the implementation I would hear absolutely ugly talk, almost vicious talk, about how bad a job we were doing and how terrible this was going to be for Customs. But I listened, and I realized these critics were making the same point Sparrow had made.

So I really studied his book and had some other people read it. We redefined enforcement, accounting for those people who weren't going to be involved with process management, and how you had to deal with deliberate violators and free riders on the system. Then we put together ad hoc groups of the alienated people in Customs, and came up with a new approach to enforcement. I had spent a lot of my time in Customs worrying about the mechanics, the trade problems, particularly with Japan, trade fraud, money laundering, and all kinds of things having to do with people sending things to outlaw governments like Iraq, Iran—illegal trade out of the United States. I'd been trying for a couple of decades to get systems set up to deal with all that.

Over the past year, we've been able to make a breakthrough in tying together and building on the ideas about enforcement. I asked Malcolm Sparrow who was the best guy to help us keep moving. He said I should look up Herman Goldstein, a law professor at the University of Wisconsin. Police departments have the Herman Goldstein Prize. This very nice man was just wonderfully supportive and helpful.

I thought the process side was going well, I was happy with that, but I knew that the enforcement side wasn't changing. I couldn't figure out how to do it. And I couldn't inspire people. One day Bob Mitchell said, "You want to think about getting Pete Robustelli in here, because he knows Customs now better and he knows process management." So I asked Pete if he would try to come in, spend some time with me, and teach what we decided to call "Strategic Problem Solving" in this agency. I was told he would have credibility with people on both sides because there were two camps, one against the other, a tremendous amount of alienation. Pete agreed to do it. And we developed a course and curriculum, which I helped with—I gave them an hour or so, and we filmed the discussion.

Now we're using that with every class. We trained the trainers, and we've got experts out there now—we've trained something like 1,500 or 2,000 people. People are beginning to change. They're understanding process management, they're understanding problem solving, they're becoming open to the idea of doing analysis and threat assessments. It's tremendous! Malcolm Sparrow has been a good and tough critic. He's given me some ways to measure what we're doing, ways of beginning to make us a learning- and knowledge-based organization. And now that everybody's had their say and we've really overhauled the process management, it's going just great. We married up our process management with the technology, which had been a traditional strength of this agency. The technology people were on all the teams that looked at reengineering, redesigning, and process mapping, so that technology could be the enabler for changes that needed to be made.

There's going to be a huge, long-term payoff. It's a tremendous investment, and it's taken time, but people can see the genius of this. We've got everybody now tied together: import specialists, inspectors, agents, computer people, auditors—all tied together in the definition of this process. Some of the solutions they've come up with have been magnificent. Our systems are going to be the systems of the next century.

We developed a tremendous partnership—everybody being able to see the whole system and help define the whole system, and working toward a common goal, gives meaning to the common goal and to the work. That process is going on here.

What About Me?

I finally did a presentation called "What About Me?" for all the regional commissioners and the assistant commissioners. We went through the new mission statement, the strategic intent. We discussed values. Then I explained the process and looked at strategic problem solving.

And I said, "Now we'll go back to the fundamental question. That's why we're here today. *What about me?* That's what we've got to figure out. That's Customs—the kind of agency we've decided to be, the way we're going to act, the things that we're going to do, our goal, our contribution to the nation, our method to achieve it. What about me? Do you see yourself in there? Does every employee see himself or herself in there? And if they do, they're in the right spot. If they're not sure, then it's our obligation to find a way to help them get on board with it, to understand and achieve our common goals. And if they still don't, well, they're probably in the wrong place. And that goes for all of us.

Working Together

We're all flawed, terribly flawed. So we have to work together. The important question we have to ask is, "How can we meld ourselves together and become more than the sum of our parts?" This team thing is on the right track. Good groups have always known this secret. I said to my successor, "If you're going to make personnel changes here after I leave, the burden isn't on the individual to be the ideal person, because nobody is. You guys know how flawed I am, and Customs has survived it. We all have weaknesses. The key is to work around our weaknesses and build on our strengths." Working in partnership, teams and alliances—internal teams, external partnerships with other agencies and alliances—combining that with our technology. One day—it'll be long after I've gone—learning all this and getting it to work will make Customs an organization that people look to and say, "Those people have learned what they need to do and they're doing it."

You know, 50 million people a year come in through the airports, 400-and-some million come into the country by air, land, and sea—you're just going to have problems. But now, we provide much more information. And we measure things.

Half the letters that come to our desks are really intended for other agencies. Now that entire process is better. Improvement is happening on the cargo side and on the export side. We're developing allies in other groups, and forums have been established that keep everybody opening up. We've seen major improvements that are really resulting in faster cargo and also simply more speed in getting everybody from their planes to their cars.

Management thinker Peter Drucker says that what makes people feel good about themselves is making contributions to important things in measurable ways. Through process management, we have measurable capabilities that were never there before, and our measures are now industry's measures. We can go to industry with a compliance assessment and a plan to help them get where they want to be.

Now we have companies setting up teams for Customs compliance, and they're setting goals for themselves. People are starting industries out there to help companies get into compliance. It's more of a partnership, rather than an adversarial relationship. If you're doing something bad, we're still going to try to put you in jail or fine you or kick you out of business. But if you're like most companies, you want to pay your taxes and get it right the first time. That's what we're giving people the opportunity to do.

Vision and Values

How Organizations Can Help People: The Broader Context

When I think about all these things going on in eastern Europe and Bosnia, I get upset. Obviously, the various administrations are asking, "What do you do about it?" We had an opportunity to help, to send our people over there. We ended up with fifty or sixty people from Customs over there, and people on the Hill were upset about it. "We didn't fund you for this. You shouldn't be doing that." We took a lot of heat for it, but those people did some wonderful things. Now I see letters, or somebody will stop me and say, "You know, probably the best thing you ever did was help out in eastern Europe. You saved thousands, maybe tens of thousands of lives."

I guess that's what we need to do when we believe what John Donne was talking about. It's context. It's being involved in humankind and thinking about how your organization can help people. People often ask me, "How do you succeed?" And you know what? I never knew. I never had a plan, I never said to myself, "I'm going to do this in five years, I want to be that, I want to be this." Sometimes I think that I'm out of sync with everything and everybody. But when I've had a job, I've always tried to figure out how I can help my part of the organization be more effective at achieving the goals of the larger organization. And so on up the line. And, you know, that's kind of the way I do think about things. I thought about this agency for a long time in those terms, and I think about my own role in it, no matter where I am, as "How do I help them, and what are we trying to achieve?"

Even as a very young person, I would always think that. "Why are we doing what we're doing?" When I was a student, I thought, "How can I make my own decisions, given the context?" Because the teachers never did explain how one subject related to another. They would just say, "Okay, we're having this subject now," and start teaching. But if I couldn't understand why something was important, I'd just say, "The heck with this." So I would sometimes make foolish, ignorant decisions because I couldn't see the context. I always tried to step back and look at the big picture and how what I was doing at the time was connected to everything else. Before I could articulate it, I had this urge to look for the context, and if I didn't see it or couldn't figure it out or didn't ask the right question, or if I did ask the right question but didn't get the right answer, I would make my own decision.

Doing What's Right

At the same time, I've always felt that once you see the connections, you have to do something. I was in Hong Kong for a couple of weeks recently, and I came back on a Saturday morning. I was exhausted from the flight, twenty hours, and I got a message from the commissioner that Treasury wanted me to head up the law enforcement support of all the Treasury officers down at the Olympics in Atlanta. The commissioner knew I wouldn't want to do this, but the question was *would* I do it. I didn't think I was the right person for it.

In the end, I agreed to help out. I thought, "This is our nation, a lot is depending on us. We've got to make this right." And it's very much our responsibility to do it. It is not in our mission statement. But people have to, if they have the capacity, make these kinds of contributions. It was the most wonderful thing—the degree of cooperation between ATF, the IRS, Secret Service, Customs, and even the different parts of the Customs Service. It was an example of the nation, the government, pulling together and supporting a common goal. It's what we're supposed to do. Because it must be done.

I think that working for the government provides people with the opportunity to do the right thing. If you always act in the best interests of the government, in the best interests of the employees, and make the right things happen and act in the right way, you'll never regret it.

I've always been uncomfortable spending time on values statements because I believe it all comes down to a simple thing—doing what's right. The really good people in Customs would frequently say to me, "We don't need a values statement. Just tell the employees to act like George or Walt"—two employees of the highest character. There's a lot to be said for that approach.

Obstacles

I never graduated from college. And for the jobs I'm in, most of the people have college degrees—and what you get through the discipline of education. I didn't do that. So that was an obstacle for me, but the people in management positions here and elsewhere would move me along in spite of that. I guess I compensated for it, but when I did really get exposed to education that was meaningful to me, I was astounded by it—books about organizational management and leadership.

And then there are things that I'm not good at. I don't have good mathematical or scientific skills. I'll read a book on science and it will stun me and astound me, and I'll be thrilled by the wonder of it, but I don't understand it. My ex-wife has an aunt in a nursing home, always a very nice person, and now she has Alzheimer's. My ex-wife and her son would take her places, and she'd say, "I don't know where I am or who these people are, but I'm having a grand time." That's what I feel sometimes about some of these technical concepts that I couldn't fully understand.

I don't really see myself as a person with the skills that I might like to have—with the skills of an engineer or a scientist or even a manager. Mitchell prepared a résumé for me several years ago when I was thinking about leaving, and when I read it I thought, "You really can't do anything!" So I guess you learn to adapt over time and, I've learned to say to myself, "Well, I can overcome those shortcomings."

Help Along the Way

I've had plenty of help in my career. Governor Keating has been a big help to me. Bob Mitchell has worked with me for ten years, this selfless person who always makes me think that I had all the ideas and could do anything. He's that kind of leader that generals talk about, the one who makes the other person think he made it happen. And Robin, who has worked with me for eight years. There's just been a tremendous consistency of support. I've gotten a lot of confidence from working with these people. I know I can always count on them. And I'm not talking about loyalty: I'm talking about partnership. I don't know what made people so good stay with me for so long, but I do know that to the extent I did anything good, it was because of them.

Vision for a Better World

I'm worried about people losing hope. I'm tremendously worried about it. What happens to these people? In the case of all the changes at Customs, at first I didn't answer the "What about me?" question for our employees.

Some time ago, I went to this James Martin seminar. He worked at IBM, a British scholar, one of the first gurus of data processing. He wrote all the early books that were really the intellectual capital of data processing. I read them all but understood maybe only 20 percent of them. This was in the 1970s. He was a physicist and computer scientist, and he talked about systems, but he also talked about current problems in our world and our capacity to deal with them. For every problem that people were fretting about, he offered hope and solutions. And many of his ideas have come to pass.

Technology is freeing us and wealth is still being created. Our environment is cleaner. We're being developed as individuals, as humanitarians, as artists. Fewer and fewer of us are needed to produce all the food, clothing, and other consumer products. Then how do we share the wealth? I'm not talking about Communism; I'm just talking about how you share the fruits of capitalism. The wealth created through technology can help close the gap between the rich and the poor—it isn't doing that now, but it can do that.

What opportunities are we going to give people who are losing hope to employ themselves, and how are we going to share whatever work there is? That's the vision that's missing. You can't hold people accountable for getting jobs where there is no industry or there are no jobs. Everybody can't be an entrepreneur.

All of the politicians and CEOs and people who care—and there are scores of people and organizations that do—somehow all of these people have got to be brought to bear on the problem of how we share this wealth.

Lessons We Learned

DreamMakers express vision and values. "I believe it all comes down to a simple thing—doing what's right. The really good people in Customs would frequently say to me, 'We don't need a values statement. Just tell the employees to act like George or Walt'—two employees of the highest character. There's a lot to be said for that approach."

DreamMakers work with others to build a shared vision. "We developed a tremendous partnership—everybody being able to see the whole system and help define the whole system, and working toward a common goal, gives meaning to the common goal and to the work."

DreamMakers understand that we are all connected and interdependent. "That last part really hit me. I'm involved in humankind. If you suffer, I suffer. If you excel, I excel. Things that reflect that sentiment always draw me. If you think about it in the workplace, it really gets you to where people that are concerned about management and organization are concerned about the whole organization and everyone in it."

DreamMakers value and nurture interpersonal relationships. "You know it's a wonderful thing when you work day and night with somebody, and you're so attuned to the same objectives and goals that you don't think about any kind of hierarchical relationship or things like that. When you get to work with somebody like that, maybe it's really the best sort of mentoring—you didn't know it was happening."

DreamMakers tap into the extraordinary potential in all of us. "I said to my successor, 'If you're going to make personnel changes here after I leave, the burden isn't on the individual to be the ideal person, because nobody is. You guys know how flawed I am, and Customs has survived it. We all have weaknesses. The key is to work around our weaknesses and build on our strengths.'"

DreamMakers focus on education and continual learning. "My boss . . . talked to me about a sabbatical, and I went to USC's graduate program in public administration. I'd dropped out of college my freshman year and I would go back periodically, but I never finished. I never thought of myself as a good student. I didn't really like school that much, and I didn't like college at all. But at USC I was reading books about government and management, and then writing papers, and going to class—that was possibly the best year of my life."

DreamMakers learn from their mistakes. "During the beginning of the implementation I would hear absolutely ugly talk, almost vicious talk, about how bad a job we were doing and how terrible this was going to be for Customs. But I listened, and I realized these critics were making the same point Sparrow had made. So I really studied his book and had some other people read it."

DreamMakers follow a moral compass. "I think that working for the government provides people with the opportunity to do the right thing. If you always act in the best interests of the government, in the best interests of the employees, and make the right things happen and act in the right way, you'll never regret it."

DreamMakers demonstrate responsibility toward a larger community. "I guess that's what we need to do when we believe what John Donne was talking about. It's context. It's being involved in humankind and thinking about how your organization can help people."

JOHN ABBOTT *is president of the 21st Century Learning Initiative. An Englishman currently working in Washington, D.C., Abbott began his career teaching geography for seven years at a highly selective English grammar school (students age eleven to eighteen), during which he led expeditions that allowed groups of his students to live among the nomads in the mountains of Iran. He then became principal of a 400-year-old English comprehensive school (community high school). In 1985 he was named director of Education 2000, a British not-for-profit foundation concerned with creating communities determined to use all their resources, both formal and informal, to support young people learning how to learn.*

LEARNING

John Abbott,

Education 2000

One day I received a call from Rita Cleary, a close friend and the president of Visions of a Better World Foundation. She asked me if I would meet with John Abbott, a man from England who has undertaken the seemingly impossible job of reforming education systems worldwide by challenging our basic assumptions about how people learn. He was leading an initiative called Education 2000, bringing some of the best minds and hearts from around the world together to make sense of learning.

As always, my life was full of commitments, most of which involved nonprofit work that filled my soul but not my bank account. My work was going well; however, I needed to prioritize. So I had recently made a decision to focus my efforts on my most important commitments. My intention was to have a telephone conversation with John Abbott and be done with it. When he phoned me with an invitation to afternoon tea at the Four Seasons Hotel in Georgetown, Washington, D.C., however, my resolve failed miserably. The Four Seasons has a special place in my heart, and for now I was following my heart rather than my head. It is a very good thing I did.

When I met John, my first impression was the stereotype of a mature English schoolmaster. Within minutes, I realized that here was a man committed to radically redefining and redesigning the education process, including the roles of teachers and learners and total community participation. It was amazing how two people—John and I—with totally different backgrounds had such a strong common alertness to a system gone dreadfully wrong. Influenced by my memory of school and most of all by watching my daughter painfully go through a system that doesn't make sense, I wanted to help John Abbott in whatever way I could. And I realized I had discovered another DreamMaker.

John speaks with deep authority about what motivates people to learn: "Emotion drives learning, not intellect." He understands and can articulate the grand complexity of our minds and the need instilled in us through generations of evolution to see patterns in order to learn. And John directs our attention and his own passion, as so many others in this book also do, to the great "connectedness" that speaks to what it means to be human—to the rich and diverse web of life that we all need to sustain us.

Defining Moments

John Abbott: I believe that every child is the end point of the evolution of millions of years. However awkward and uncertain they may look, they are the very best that many generations have produced. John Barrow, the author of *The Artful Universe*, wrote, "We want to explore some of the ways in which our common experience of living in the universe rubs off on us." I believe that the complexities of our minds and bodies are witness to an incredibly long history of subtle adaptation to the nature of the world and its other occupants.

You see, humans are complex beings. Summarizing what a number of biologists and neurologists are saying, this is because the environment in which we have evolved goes deeper than the superficial world of other living creatures. Our complexity springs from the laws and constants of nature that determine the form and fabric of the universe. And here's the key part: The complexity of our minds and bodies is a reflection of the complexity of the total cosmic environment in which we find ourselves and in which the human race has, as it were, grown up. The nature of the universe has imprinted itself upon us in ways that constrain our sensibilities in striking and unexpected ways.

I feel that we are wasting enormous amounts of human potential and that, even when we're not consciously wasting it, we are putting up false ideas of happiness so superficial that they leave people feeling empty and depressed. The easiest way I can describe this is to talk about my own experience. I had this superb early childhood. I grew up in a city on the south coast of England, Portsmouth, capital of the British navy. The house we lived in, which we moved into just after the war [World War II] ended, was surrounded by bomb sites on three-quarters of the perimeter. The city had been devastated by German bombs during the war. My father was a clergyman, which meant basically that we didn't have very much money. We didn't have many toys, but we had a splendidly interesting experience.

The Wood-Carver

My parents had a man who came in on Friday nights to help do odd jobs. Now this man had hands like a surgeon but in fact was no more than a stoker in the navy. He had spent his entire life throwing coal into the boilers of battleships. His career was as simple as that, because as a child he had been apprenticed to a carpenter. And he was one of the last naval apprentices who was a genuine carpenter. But by the time he reached adulthood, they didn't need anyone who could build wooden ships; the only job for him was throwing coal into boilers.

However, his great interest, and the way he expressed his creativity, was wood carving. And he was the most magnificent carver, which is actually a skill possessed by many sailors. You know, they lived long boring lives at sea, and they made model ships in bottles and things like that. Well, this guy came along into my life when I was ten or eleven, and I was fascinated. He would sit me down in a corner and say, "Look at this beautiful thing I've made, and look at that beautiful carving in the church." And I thought, those are marvelous. And he said, "If you want to do that, you've got to learn how to sharpen a chisel; here's how to sharpen a chisel." And so I thought it was important to sharpen a chisel because I saw what I wanted to make. Then he helped me to understand the nature of the wood, the way the grain changes, and the shades that reflect past storms. Thus when I was ten or eleven, I was already looking at an aspect of creativity with the eye of a professional.

He was only one of scores of people that I encountered as a young child who were truly artisans. The secret was that they were utterly fascinated with the detail of getting everything not only right, but beautiful. After that, I went away to boarding school, a traditional upper-middle-class thing to do. And I was severed from my home at the age of thirteen, which I think was all wrong, actually.

A Proper English Education

This was one of the great English private schools, where the whole principle was that you had to be toughened up to become a leader. It was all part of the imperialistic rich tradition. Nobody thought we'd ever go into business. But if we didn't go into the Foreign Office or if we didn't go into the army or the navy, we'd become a lawyer, or we might become a minister, or we might become a university professor, but for sure we were going to be the leaders of the world. The idea was that at thirteen you were taken away from your family and broken into a new way of life. I almost survived that.

The one subject that I could not pass was Latin. I had passed all the other subjects I needed to get to university, to get to Oxford, but in those days you had to have Latin as well. I know exactly why I didn't pass Latin. I was taught by a very boring teacher, and so bored himself that he spent all the time telling us how he won the war single-handedly driving his tank in the African desert. I failed Latin the first time, I failed it the second time, and I was coming up to what would be the third and final time, and, as sure as eggs are eggs, I would have failed that exam, too. Then the school carpenter, a man so menial he wasn't even allowed into the teachers' room, took me to one side and said, "Congratulations, you've been chosen to represent the United Kingdom as a schoolboy wood-carver at an international exhibition." And I was excited beyond all measure. I thought, "There's one thing I can do better than anybody else. I am up with the real professionals."

But within a couple of hours I suddenly realized that my whole world was going to come crashing about me because the school would take no notice of such an achievement. It wasn't a rugby result, it wasn't a debating result, it wasn't one of the conventional things that you did. It didn't figure. But to me, it figured so much that I actually said, "Right, if I have to pass Latin in six weeks' time, what is standing in my way? My teacher is standing in my way. I will only pass Latin if I take responsibility myself for learning Latin." So that afternoon I told my teacher that because I had to pass in six weeks' time, I wouldn't be coming to any more of his lessons. I'd teach myself. If that seems an extraordinary story now, in 1958, when it actually happened, it was truly bizarre because that was me—just a youngster, by myself, taking on the entire faculty.

I can remember them now looking through the glass door leading to the library, wondering what I was doing. And I felt they were willing me to fail, because my success would condemn them. But I did succeed; I passed the exam. I think I forgot everything I ever learned in about six months. But I still carve wood. A great deal of what I believe in is encompassed in that story. That Barrow quote I mentioned and a thousand other quotes are actually saying that learning is the thing the human race is good at when it understands what it is trying to achieve.

The Apprenticeship Model of Learning

The model of learning in apprenticeship was very simple. And it's been there, I think, since the beginning of time. The older person says to the younger person, "I'm building a ship, I'm building a cathedral, I'm building this house, I'm planting these crops so that we don't starve in six months' time." And the child at a very young age sees why these people are doing what they're doing. Then there was the whole principle of what we call basic skills. Because adults in that sort of society were so busy, they had to invest economically in the skills a young person developed. First they gave them skills fundamental to making a living in particular circumstances. The more they were able to practice those skills, the more the teacher removed support from the child and said, "All right, you can now do that, so I won't support you while you're doing that anymore. I'll only support you as you come on to the next level of skill." And so on to the next level of skill. It's the whole concept of what the psychologists now call fading: If you don't know what you're doing, then your first resource is to talk to the person who knows more about it, or perhaps to talk to the other person who's learning at the same time.

The race was on to demonstrate that by the end of your apprenticeship you were actually better than the person who had taught you. Hence the definition of the term *masterpiece*. You only completed your apprenticeship when you were able to complete your masterpiece. Now, in that sort of holistic approach, learning and working were completely interconnected—so was living. Learning, working, and living were completely and utterly interconnected. If you didn't learn as you worked, you wouldn't produce something better than somebody else produced. Nobody would buy it, and you wouldn't live. What is coming out of evolutionary psychology and neurology and similar fields now is that this model of learning is deeply ingrained in the human species.

In the Mountains of Iran

I saw that in real time years ago, when as a teacher in England I used to take my senior high school students to live with the nomads in the mountains of Iran every summer, as they migrated up and down the mountainside. We were actually watching so-called primitive people live in the way they had lived since the time of Abraham, Moses, and possibly half a million years before. And what fifteen- and sixteen-year-old Iranian boys and girls did in comparison to fifteen- and sixteen-year-old educated English children—working, playing together—the contrast was quite enormous. Of course the Iranians were far better adapted to living in that particular environment, yes. The English were far better adapted to dealing with abstract skills, yes. But the Iranians—and they wouldn't like to be called Iranian; they still thought of themselves as Bakhtiaris, Kurdistanis, or Armenians—they saw themselves as an integral part of the tribe, with real jobs to do. They had a sense of purpose and direction quite absent in most of the English boys.

That was proved one night when one of the tribal chieftains said to me, "We feel very honored that you come and live with us every summer. And we like the young people you bring with you, but we have a basic question. How is it that these young men are so selfish that they leave their families and don't support them? Presumably their families are having to work harder if their children are not there with them." To the so-called primitive tribespeople, there was the sense that learning and growing up were integral lessons about being a community, an attitude largely missing among these boys from the sophisticated West.

Patterns and Complexity

All that comes together in what we now understand about the extraordinary complexity that exists in the way in which the brain handles information. We've been going through a rapid transformation of ideas in the last ten or fifteen years. Up to fifteen years ago, we considered the brain as a super-computer. Certain parts of the brain did certain things. Educators got a hold of this notion and thought that if we divided knowledge into ten or twelve subjects and taught each subject, we would provide children with everything that they know, apart from how to make sense across the various little bits. Now we're understanding from neurology that the brain doesn't put history into one side of the brain and the future into another side. It doesn't put color into one place and movement into another. It's all gloriously mixed up and interconnected. And the access point to that interconnection is more often an emotional drive than an intellectual one.

As an English family, we've been swapping our house in England with friends in America for the last eight or nine years. So our children got used to spending most of our summer holidays in the United States, in particular in Virginia, and to visiting endless historic sites and visitors' centers, which I have to say you Americans do very well.

We also got used to listening to Garrison Keillor telling his glorious stories on the radio. We got them on tape and were playing one in England late one night coming back from Derbyshire, and I thought the children were asleep in the car. Garrison Keillor was describing his one-room schoolhouse out in Minnesota and saying that at one end there was a portrait of George Washington, and at the other Abraham Lincoln, both smiling at the students like two long-lost friends. A little seven-year-old voice in the back of the car said, "Daddy, that can't be true. They weren't alive at the same time." I nearly stopped the car. I said, "How on earth do you know that?" They had never studied American history. Tom said, "Because when we went to Mount Vernon, they said it was sad that George Washington wouldn't live till the nineteenth century. And I know," he said, "from what I read in that book about Abraham Lincoln, that he wasn't born until eighteen hundred and something or other."

I thought that was pretty amazing and told our son to go back to sleep. A couple of years later, we were telling that story in America, and sitting at the table was a professor of education, who said, "I wish our elementary schools taught history as well as that." And my wife, quick as a flash, said, "It's not quite as simple as that. Tom, who's your best teacher at school? Who do you enjoy most?" And he said, "That's easy—my math teacher. She always teaches us to think about things in terms of patterns or connections." And that's why Tom had got so deeply ingrained in his mind the sequence of history, the sequence of pattern. It had nothing to do with a history lesson.

It had nothing to do with informal learning. What it had something to do with was pattern creation.

The Web of Life

Everything that I am saying is about the fact that we do children a grave disservice if we think about learning as memorizing facts in a classroom. Do you know that across the Western world no child between the ages of five and eighteen spends more than 20 percent of his or her waking hours in a classroom? The vast majority of time is spent outside the classroom, beyond the school. The contrast between the world that I was fortunate enough to grow up in and the world now is stark. In that world of a bombed-out city, with people busy rebuilding and starting a life again, and because of this tradition of learning from your elders, every older person had time to spare for me when I was walking down the street or playing with my friends. And although nobody ever said it in this sort of language, the community believed the children belonged to the community.

Not only did I have the experience of the artisan teaching me how to carve wood, but I also walked along the seafront with an admiral who had once surveyed the China seas; his widow later gave me his surveying instruments. Now, there was the web of life. There was a web of life, too, with the tribal people in Iran. Such connections matter enormously. Their absence impoverishes our lives.

I went to university in Ireland, one of the last real old-world universities, and for years afterward I had a farmhouse in the west of Ireland, among people who still understand the web of life. By and large they still haven't succumbed to turning the television set on at all hours of the day and night. And so of an evening, rather than going into the local town seven or eight miles away, people would gather at one or another person's farmhouse. All ages would sit down together for what they called a *ceilidh*. Every age group sat around the fire; there were lots of cups of tea and glorious cakes and all the rest of it, and the old people told stories and the young people played their musical instruments. And the young children, if they wanted to dance, they danced, and if the old people wanted to dance, they danced. Nor was this contrived. It all has to do with that business of what we learn from each other and how we learn collaboratively. Emotion drives learning, not intellect.

Education 2000

After a dozen years of being a high school principal, I lost faith in the school's ability to take on all the issues that the rest of the world thought we should be taking on. And this expectation seemed to me totally and utterly stupid. Well-meaning people were just being stupid or lazy. I thought if I could set up a nonprofit organization, and if I could persuade some of the great and the good in England to become my trustees, I could start getting them to become interested in these ideas and to pay me for the work I wanted to be doing.

So I went into the heartland of England and said, "There are some big issues here you had better start taking ownership for." I had a very simple idea: Take one community, one town, or a section of a town—say, fifty or sixty or seventy thousand people—and observe what would happen if all of those people started thinking about what education and learning are all about. I also asked people to provide every child with a word processor, so that instead of writing out essays freehand, they could draft and redraft. I said that would cause a revolution.

My trustees thought this was a splendid idea, and they raised enough money to ensure that there were computers in all the high schools at the time. Everybody could start using word processors. And I spent day after day with other people, getting groups of communities to come together to think about these issues and, in particular, to think about how much better off children would be if they could learn to think about writing as a constructive exercise.

Then I said something fundamental to the whole idea, and going right through to what I'm doing now. I said, "I don't think this country is ever going to be much richer than it is at the moment. Therefore, while somebody may give you money for these computers, they're never going to give enough money for every school in the country to have them. Take this as an experiment to see what you're going to do differently, so that when the new money runs out, you can rebudget some of the money that was there beforehand." That became a very nasty problem. People were very happy to accept new money and have lots of discussions. But they didn't like saying how this would change things.

I said that the justification for putting all this money into computers was that as the child takes control of his or her own writing, that child is no longer tied to paper and pencil. He or she is consciously starting to think more about how the brain works. And if you take all that I was saying about cognitive apprenticeship, I'm utterly convinced that children, properly supported when they are very young, can actually begin to take an objective view of themselves as learners. And they'd say, "I know how to do that, just let me get on with it. When I have a problem I'll come back to you."

The challenge is to support the elementary school teacher with many more resources. If the elementary schools can produce children who really understand how to think for themselves, the children will then take responsibility. That changes the nature of the high school beyond all recognition. Rather than having the largest class size when children are young and the smallest when they're in the last year of high school, it should be the other way around. And you'll be able to fund this on an ongoing basis by turning it the other way around. You'll be saying to children that the older they get, the more responsibility they have to take and the less instruction they will get—but the support will still be there. It's a weaning process.

Now, as soon as I started saying these things in England, I came up against another vested interest that I didn't begin to understand. Everybody said, "You don't know what you're talking about. It doesn't work like that. It's never worked like that. Children need good, caring teachers around all the time, for as many years as possible." And I asked what happens when that kind of support is not there. "Well, it's part of growing up; they grow up the minute they leave school." And I said that children should be growing up all the time. I then ran into the most horrendous problems from the British government, which was then under strong conservative control, and which said the only thing running the schools was the teachers. Therefore, they started reinforcing the status quo.

So I then found myself getting more and more onto the international circuit, the lectures. And I got invited many times to America to talk about what I was doing, and I was increasingly saying, "Well, that's what I started to do, but I can't go any further, because nobody understands what I'm talking about."

A Systems View

I found that other speakers in the United States were actually far more thoughtful about the nature of learning. And I kept asking, "Why can't children understand the nature of learning rather than just leaving it as a secret the teacher has?" I found—as I started listening to Peter Senge and others like him—that this isn't just a question of teachers knowing what to do differently; it's a whole system that comes into play here.

And then I realized that I didn't understand how systems work. So that started a three-year process, which led in December of 1995 to my coming to the United States. I'm convinced now not only that these problems are universal, but that they have to be understood over and above politics. And, unfortunately, if they become the property of any one country, then they will automatically become the stuff of party politics. All these things are interconnected. Intellectually, I've never tried to synthesize conclusions; they go across such an enormous range of issues. But actually everything we are understanding out of the new science is about the nature of humankind: It is that the issues that truly concern me are all interconnected, highly dependent one with the next—and therefore the quicker we learn to see how all these things do come together across the board, the better.

Vision and Values

Creation of a World Not Fit for Children to Grow Up in

We come to being who we are because we take what our inheritance has given us in terms of the evolved structure of the brain, and we shape it in ways that either go with that structure or go against it. What I'm doing at the moment is drawing a whole team of people together to get our minds around the fact that we seem to have got into a spiral of activity, including economic activity, which is producing enormous materialistic gains for very many people and has opened up opportunities of a kind which we have never before dreamt of. And don't let's minimize it. Everything is a result of so many of these gains.

But they come at a cost difficult to quantify but of enormous significance. I can put it in quite dramatic terms and say that the cost is the creation of a world not fit for children to grow up in. The ecologists are talking about the desperate need to create a sustainable community at an ecological level. I'm saying that as long as we talk about learning as being a matter of school reform, then we're in danger of continuing to create a nonsustainable human race. The human race learns through experience, not through instruction. You need both, but the emphasis should be learning through experience rather than through instruction.

I believe that most of the children who do well in school have discovered a sense of vision and purpose outside school and then see the artificially contrived learning situations in school as a useful means to an end. And therefore they do well. To have a society in which the implied ethic that children get outside school is "Do as I say, not as I do" means that the child is totally lost. There is nothing that you can do in terms of teaching values and ethics that compares with *experiencing* the development of values and ethics.

The desire to respond quickly to the opportunities created in the industrial society led to the creation of a view of learning that is overly paternalistic and too much based on accepting that there was so much social change that the normal structures couldn't handle it. And therefore the schools said to parents, "You don't understand looking after children. Give the children to us, and we'll do it." Literally, that was being said. You see it in the English aristocracy at the moment: "Since we don't know how to bring up our own children, we send them off to some prestigious school."

What we have now is an education system that reflects the fact that our way of living does not connect with the human species in its deepest understanding—that is to say, we're moving into a crisis of enormous proportions. We've created wisdom about technology and economics and all the rest of it, but we don't understand what it actually means to have human satisfaction. The children, as it were, are blowing an evolutionary whistle and are saying, "This just is not sustainable." If your form of Saturday evening entertainment is a trip to the shopping mall, you are then continuously subjected to thinking that happiness is all to do with buying things. I give speeches under the title "Who Needs One More CD?" There is an out-of-stepness here, which I don't think schools can possibly solve by themselves.

I wrote something for the British prime minister recently, the theme of which was that an incorrect understanding of learning is the essential reason we have a dependent society. With a dependent society, we've got a disaster on our hands because people don't feel that they are part of the process. If we want to change that feeling, then I think we have to understand some of the more basic things about the nature of human existence—that people are collaborative, problem-solving creatures.

The crisis we're facing at the moment is in the lack of a sense of individual purpose for those lost generations. I don't believe in a lost generation, but many people have lost a sense of purpose. Matthew Fox, in *The Reinvention of Work: A New Vision of Livelihood for Our Times,* offers a chilling statement. He says, "An unemployed adult is a unique species. Every animal, every child, in its own way has a job to do." Humans and work are interconnected: "By their works you shall know them," or whatever the exact quotation says. An unemployed person is broken off from that chain of being. As long as our society associates status with the job that you do, what is the message? What is the purpose for those people who are outside the system?

This is chilling and terrifying because the individual brain is always trying to find purpose. If the individual is excluded from the common purpose, then it will create a focus on the outside. The synthesis of the problems in education and the larger problems in society as a whole has been made in such a compelling way that there is a serious group of people saying we've just got to face this as a total issue. We can't just do the community bit or the unemployment bit, this, that, or the other. We must reinvent human society.

Respect

It's amazing how often I go back to the Old Testament: "What is man, that thou art mindful of him?" People deep down don't understand that each child is totally and utterly unique and is at the leading edge of evolution's reinventing itself. When our ancestors looked up at the stars and tried to work out what it all meant, they were trying to work out what *they* were all about, not the stars. If you deny people the chance to work out what *they* are all about, what a bleak world we will have created.

The Old Testament says, "Love the Lord thy God and thy neighbor as thyself." The web of the ecological universe that we're in—that's us, that's life. And I'm saying, "Love life and love your neighbor as much as you love yourself—everybody matters." All the rest follows from that. I remember how struck I was by Max De Pree's book *Leadership Is an Art,* and his story of the millwright. I think the idea that every person is worthy of respect in his or her own right is utterly and completely intrinsic to what I'm talking about. And I think teenagers understand that. They want to be themselves first and foremost; they want to discover themselves, and they are caring of other people.

Obstacles

People find it far, far harder to synthesize new ideas than most of them actually realize. We are all comfortable in our own understanding. I can't give you chapter and verse, but I sense that there are small groups of people popping up all over the place who have the same sense of interconnectivity. And we all lumber under the same difficulties. The issues are quite complicated to explain to people who are not initiated into them. You cannot handle this like piecemeal change. We all know that if we don't get it right, it's going to get worse. We want to start as quickly as possible. And if only we could help each other by making sure that some of the people that stand in our way are just better informed!

The reason I focus on children is partly where I come from. But I suppose it's more than that. Within twelve months, I think I shall be spending more of my time giving lectures and running seminars for seventeen- and eighteen-year-olds than for almost anybody else. I think they're the ones who intuitively grasp what all this is about. We can't afford to be cynical; we've got to get this right. To the cynic I say, "You're a disgrace. You're a disgrace to your ancestors." To the hopeless, I say, "We're with you, and we won't let it rest."

And to the children: "We'll do our damnedest to make sure the world's not quite such a mess to pass on to you as it would otherwise be. But you're going to have to be pretty tough." I believe children change the world. Children change the world because our thoughts probably started with very powerful thinking when we were young. They're not afraid to ask the impossible questions. I think the older we get, the more we tend to say, "You can't possibly handle that." Or, "That's not my responsibility." In this regard, things would be better if we all stayed children inside.

E. F. Schumacher's book *Small Is Beautiful* has the interesting subtitle "Economics as if People Mattered." Which is nice, of course, and he actually says, "We're not blind! We're men and women with eyes and brains. We don't have to be driven hither and thither by the blind workings of the market, or history, or progress, or any other abstraction." The feeling here in Washington is as if the only thing that matters is an open market. And it is such a sacred god that we all have to fall down and willingly be sacrificed in front of it. There's another biblical statement that's relevant here: "Is work made for man or man for work?" The answer is that work is made for people, period.

Help Along the Way

I have had precious allies along the way. At the closest level, I have always had two or three trustees who, in a highly intuitive way, have said, "Yes, you are—you must be—right. We know you're fighting against enormous odds." There've always been just enough people like that. At a different level, I get enormous support from audiences that I talk to about these issues, who very quickly let me know that what I'm talking about matters to them and that, by God, they need to hear it as much as possible.

Then, of course, there was the wood-carver.

Vision for a Better World

My vision is very simple. It's a vision of young people with smiles on their faces, genuinely feeling that they can shape the future, which will be good for them and good for everybody else around them. It's about human potential on a very, very large scale. It's confident, healthy people feeling that they really understand themselves, and because they know about themselves, they want to be useful to other people. In a real sense, you can't respect other people unless you first respect yourself.

Lessons We Learned

DreamMakers engage others in their vision. "I spend day after day with other people, getting groups of communities to come together to think about these issues and, in particular, to think about how much better off children would be if they could learn to think about writing as a constructive exercise."

DreamMakers understand that we are all connected and interdependent. "Humans and work are interconnected. . . . An unemployed person is broken off from that chain of being, from interconnectivity. As long as our society associates status with the job that you do, what is the message? What is the purpose for those people who are outside the system?"

DreamMakers support diversity and honor the integrity and contributions of all people. "The idea that every person is worthy of respect in his or her own right is utterly and completely intrinsic to what I'm talking about. And I think teenagers understand that. They want to be themselves first and foremost; they want to discover themselves, and they are caring of other people."

DreamMakers question and challenge the status quo. "That changes the nature of the high school beyond all recognition. Rather than having the largest class size when children are young and the smallest when they're in the last year of high school, it should be the other way around. . . . You'll be saying to children that the older they get, the more responsibility they have to take and the less instruction they will get."

DreamMakers focus on education and continual learning. "In that sort of holistic approach, learning and working were completely interconnected—so was living. Learning, working, and living were completely and utterly interconnected. If you didn't learn as you worked, you wouldn't produce something better than somebody else produced. Nobody would buy it, and you wouldn't live. What is coming out of evolutionary psychology and neurology and similar fields now is that this model of learning is deeply ingrained in the human species."

DreamMakers trust feelings, emotions, and intuition. "Now we're understanding from neurology that the brain doesn't put history into one side of the brain and the future into another side. It doesn't put color into one place and movement into another. It's all gloriously mixed up and interconnected. And the access point to that interconnection is more often an emotional drive than an intellectual one."

DreamMakers demonstrate responsibility toward a larger community. "I wrote something for the British prime minister recently, the theme of which was that an incorrect understanding of learning is the essential reason we have a dependent society. With a dependent society, we've got a disaster on our hands because people don't feel that they are part of the process. If we want to change that feeling, then I think we have to understand some of the more basic things about the nature of human existence—that people are collaborative, problem-solving creatures."

DreamMakers are committed to making the world a better place. "The ecologists are talking about the desperate need to create a sustainable community at an ecological level. I'm saying that as long as we talk about learning as being a matter of school reform, then we're in danger of continuing to create a nonsustainable human race. The human race learns through experience, not through instruction. You need both, but the emphasis should be learning through experience rather than through instruction."

RITA CLEARY *is a social entrepreneur whose background encompasses over twenty years of experience in organizational and community development. She is a cofounder and partner of The Learning Circle, a company that partners with leading organizations and communities to create programs that develop organizational competencies to accomplish extraordinary results. She is founder and chairperson of the Visions of a Better World Foundation. In cooperation with other national, professional, and grass roots organizations, the foundation seeks to build bridges across sectors and cultures to generate collaborative learning within and across communities for the common purpose of creating a better world.*

COLLABORATION

13

Rita Cleary,

Visions of a Better World

Foundation

I met Rita Cleary ten years ago at Peter Senge's Organizational Learning Research Center, and she quickly became a friend and precious ally. During my stint in Washington, D.C., she was always cheering me on. Rita called me often, coached me wisely, and extended her heart to me when I needed encouragement and love.

Rita is president of Visions of a Better World Foundation. She is deeply committed to doing all she can to bring love and compassion to our world. She has woven together a network of people from all over the world who are creating miracles in their own communities, and she has created a vehicle for these communities to learn from and support one another.

Rita is also the founder and president of the Learning Circle, which has a mission to advance the principles of a learning organization throughout businesses and communities.

Most important, Rita lives her vision and values. She carries love, compassion, and hope to everyone she meets. Of all the reasons I have to value and respect her as a friend and colleague, the most important is that Rita was one of the people who believed in me at a time when I questioned whether I was good enough and strong enough to pursue my own personal vision. As I'm sure you've noticed by now, DreamMakers always believe they can accomplish their vision—and they have others who believe in them. DreamMaking is a process of believing and being believed in.

Defining Moments

Rita Cleary: I have been on a personal journey to discover all that I can know about myself, and how to make sense of and relate to the interdependence of humanity, the Earth, and spirit. And so it was a matter of curiosity, trying to understand how the whole of things worked, that put me on a path of discovery. I always had a sense of wonder and wanted to understand more deeply why things were working the way they did. In some ways, I sort of felt like a scientist, only without having the "official" title. But maybe, at some level, we're all scientists. I had this thirst for learning. I wanted to understand how the whole of the system that we live in works together. I never thought about how to do this. I just began and then wondered how I could contribute what I had learned to bring benefit to and learn from others.

Early Years

There were a couple of defining experiences for me. One was that I was brought up in a family where my mother, who was very sick for a long time, operated on absolute faith to achieve her vision—to stay alive until her children were grown. I used to watch the miracles day after day. She was one of the first patients who ever had open-heart surgery. She was operated on in 1950, and they told us that the probability of her making it through the surgery was less than 50 percent. I was seven, my brother was four, and my older sister was ten. Before undergoing the surgery, she set a goal for herself: that she would live until her children were grown. I watched her perform miracles with that faith.

We were brought up in the Roman Catholic tradition, believing in the power of prayer. That's how I watched my mother hang in there as she went through one incredible trauma after another. And she did it, God love her, with a great sense of humor and a deep conviction that she was going to make it.

It was mainly from her example that I conjured up the courage to learn about how she was living her vision. My mother was very intuitive, and I watched her go into silence and ask for strength and direction. I watched her put her intuitive knowing into practice by using it to guide her through difficult times and obstacles. She trusted her intuition implicitly. I learned to trust my own by watching her. I thought everyone lived by their intuition. It wasn't until very much later in life that I learned intuition was not something that most people had in the forefront of their minds and actions.

My mother waited until my brother was about to turn twenty-one before she began to have conversations concerning who was to take care of what after she was gone. Then she decided, "Okay, now it's time—I have reached my goal." And she let herself go. I watched that mystery, the power of faith in action, throughout my first twenty-three years of life. I learned about spirit. I learned that the power of positive thought and faith in God could really perform miracles.

I began reading a lot about psychology and parapsychology, trying to understand more and more. I met very special people along the way who guided me in developing and using the leadership skills of intuition, compassion, faith, and courage that I had learned from my mother. I learned to apply these skills in my profession. As I become clear in my destination, in my aims for how I want to be in the world and what I want to accomplish, I can bring that vision to the groups of people I'm working with.

A Heart Closed Down

I think it was 1979 when I attended a National Training Labs program, a human interaction lab. For the first time in my life I experienced a guided meditation—or, perhaps I should say, a guided visualization. That's when I began to recognize a whole spiritual dimension beyond the traditional religions that I had been exploring and learning about. After I attended that program, I began to study Chinese philosophy, and then, to my amazement, an invitation came across my desk to go to China as a guest of the Chinese Association for Science and Technology.

The experience of being in China for a month, traveling with nine other vice presidents of corporations whom I had never met before, was what I would consider a transformational point in my life. I could best describe it by telling you that I experienced childlike joy as I looked into the eyes of the Chinese people. I saw an innocence and love there that reminded me of myself as a child. By this time in my adult life, with all the experiences that I had had, I began to realize that my heart had closed. When I met the eyes of the Chinese people, it was as if they had given me a key that magically started to unlock the child inside me and unlock my heart. It was a major reawakening for me. On my trip home from China I kept asking, "Why has this happened? What does it mean?" Through my intuition I received an answer: global-scale system change.

I didn't know what those words meant, and, even more important, I didn't know anyone who was involved in doing that type of work. But I did know that it was time to leave my corporate position of seven years to learn what I could about global-scale systems change. At first I thought I could bring together a network of colleagues, which I had established through my ten-year career in human resource management and organizational development, to create methodologies to foster large-scale system change from the micro to macro levels.

However, I learned very quickly that innovative concepts and methodologies take years to develop, and that in order to offer validated models we needed to partner with some leading thinkers who had been researching these perspectives. I began to hook up with some of the leading innovators of methodologies that could be applied from the micro to the macro level. I was introduced to Nancy Post, who had spent fifteen years translating the Chinese medical model into a large-scale system-change model for organizational development. Nancy introduced me to another innovative thinker, Bill Smith. Bill had developed a model of power in organizations, and he and his colleagues were using it to transform Third World countries. I worked with Nancy and Bill, first learning their models and then helping them take their work to the next stage of development. In 1990 I was intuitively guided to the work of Dr. Peter Senge of the Massachusetts Institute of Technology's Organizational Learning Research Center. Since that time I have worked closely with him to take his concepts and ideas out to the global community that has expressed interest in his work.

Global Cooperation

One day, shortly after I began working with Dr. Senge, a friend who was a professor at a local university came to my home to visit me. He came with a colleague who was serving as the coordinator for the United Nations' Global Cooperation for a Better World project. They explained that the project was dedicated as a United Nations Peace Messenger initiative and that volunteers from over fifty countries were involved. They asked if I would serve on the Massachusetts Advisory Board for the project. This was my first invitation into what could be defined as a global-scale systems-change project. Without a moment's hesitation, I accepted the offer.

Within a few months, I found myself invited to the United Nations, and I began listening to representatives who had been working with the project. I will never forget listening to a gentleman from Trinidad, Ken Butcher, who was serving as the minister of cultural affairs for the Caribbean. He was talking about how they had used the processes defined in this project to transform Trinidad. There was also a woman from Greece, Drossoula Elliot, the publisher of a well-known magazine in Greece. She was taking the concepts from this global cooperation project and applying them to the work of scientists from around the world. I started traveling annually to India, to meet with people from the other countries who were working on the project, and began to learn more and more about applying the concept of shared visioning to organizations and community development.

The research project was framed in such a way that three activities were going on at the same time—one for leaders of countries, leaders of major organizations; a second for grassroots people; and a third for what I would call middle-level managers or professionals. Each person or group was asked to think about their vision of a better world. People were originally asked to think about their current reality and then to think about their vision, and to think about the values that would need to be put in place to support their vision. All of this was done through the art of conversation. And then individuals or groups, depending on who was participating in the conversation, were asked to donate their visions and three promised action steps to a global vision bank for the project. It was just extraordinary to review the visions and action steps that were being submitted to the vision bank.

There were a couple of rules, which at first we thought were quite simple but that turned out to be a challenge to implement. First, no money could change hands—everything needed to be given in a spirit of cooperation. If you needed to get printing done, you would have to go to a printer and get that person to offer it in cooperation with the project. You couldn't take money; people could only *give* whatever resources and skills they had. Second, all conversations needed to be framed positively. There was no dwelling on the past. The question wasn't "How can we make things better?" but "What is it that we want to create?"

The project eventually grew to include 129 participating countries, and when the vision bank closed, a lot of work was done by the coordinators to organize the visions that had been sent in. Eventually a book was created, called *Visions of a Better World*, that summarized the highlights of the project. That book was launched at a global dialogue held at the United Nations in September of 1993. About sixty people attended the first phase of that dialogue. It was a great conversation, led by none other than Michele Hunt. Then there was an evening celebration that I think had about three hundred to five hundred people in attendance from at least a hundred different countries.

During the UN dialogue, someone asked whether or not the coordinating organization, the Brahma Kumaris World Spiritual Organization, planned to continue the work of the project. The Brahma Kumaris responded by saying no, they had decided that they were not going to continue it. They had other projects they planned to do. The people who were attending the dialogue at the United Nations said that, based on their experience, they felt it extremely important that this work continue, and the way to continue was to do it themselves. It was therefore decided that each country represented at that dialogue would take up its own countrywide initiative to continue the work.

Visions of a Better World Foundation

I committed to making something happen here in the United States. I very consciously tried to bring together a group that would represent a diversity of all sectors, ages, and genders. People on our initial council included Andy Campbell, who was working on the reinvention of government with Vice President Gore; Cathy Pratt, who worked with the Discovery Channel; Lester Heath, CEO of a privately held corporation; Joan Vitello, who was president of the Critical Care Nurses Association, with 80,000 members; and Gene Carter, president of the Association for Supervision and Curriculum Development in Washington, D.C., with some 250,000 teachers in its network. Peter Senge of MIT's Organizational Learning Research Center and Kathryn Johnson of the Healthcare Forum, along with many others, agreed to serve on our advisory council. As we began our conversations, we decided to create a nonprofit foundation and began a dialogue among ourselves to determine who we were and what it was that we would be doing to continue the project.

Since the foundation's inception we have put into practice the concepts of a self-organizing learning organization. We took on a number of different initiatives as we were continuing to sort out our purpose—what we knew we wanted to do, why we wanted to do it, our values, and how we wanted to work together. We decided that the best way to do that was to create some real practice fields. We decided to create a book titled *Women of Spirit* that would present some outstanding women with leadership skills. We would create that book and send it to the United Nations' Fourth World Conference on Women, held in Beijing, and give it out free of charge to the women who had the courage to attend. As a follow-up, we planned an initiative in Oxford, in the United Kingdom, where we brought together a group of thirty women from fifteen countries to begin a conversation about women in leadership and spirit. We followed that in 1996 by hosting a major gathering in collaboration with Simmons College, one of the leading women's schools in Boston. Six women, who ranged in age from seventy to eighty-nine, were honored guests. The conference was called Women of Wisdom. It was a real celebration around the contributions of these women, and an opportunity to have direct learning experience with them, which inspired all of the people who attended the gathering.

Another major program that we've undertaken is the Planting the Seeds for a Better World conference, spearheaded by Joan Vitello and Susan Dupre, who took it upon themselves to create a gathering of people interested in learning more about how we were working together as a foundation. Their hope was to ignite the spirit of community leaders and inspire them to begin initiatives in their local areas. A series of conversations is now under way in cities across America, including Washington, D.C., where representatives held their own Planting the Seeds for a Greater Washington conference at the World Bank.

Vision and Values

The vision for the foundation is to ignite the spirit of all people to conceive and make real their aspirations for a better world. The three guiding values of the foundation are positivity, or remaining positive in all situations; compassion, or love, respect, and caring for all; and humility, or the consciousness of being a trustee in service. A fourth value that I would add, which is of utmost importance to the people of the world, has also guided our initiative: learning and staying open so that we can together, collectively, learn how to do that which we have dreamed of for the well-being of all people.

Obstacles

The greatest obstacle on my journey has everything to do with me; it has nothing to do with the world outside myself. As much as I've studied, as much as I know, and as much as I can feel the probability of a shift in the level of consciousness for all people, I sometimes fall back into old patterns of fear, doubt, and negativity. Only through a personal commitment to check myself on a moment-to-moment, day-to-day basis can I keep that from happening.

To young people, I would say, "My heart goes out to you." My heart goes out to you because I know how hard it was for me way back when, and I know that my difficulty isn't a fraction of what the youth of our world are facing today. We're all looking for love, and it's hard to keep the heart open. It's easier to use your brain and to settle for the old ways, but my message is—no matter what—keep the balance, keep your heart open to the possibility. Only you know your dream. Keep the hope, and find a way. Never underestimate the power of commitment. Never underestimate the power of your linkage with spirit. Never underestimate that which can be achieved.

Vision for a Better World

I have come to realize that America's fundamental truths—that all people are created equal, that they are endowed by their Creator with certain inalienable rights, that among these are life, liberty and the pursuit of happiness"— were meant for all people in all parts of the world. Many citizens are making the choice not to accept the fear and despair in society. They are reaching out to reconnect with spirit and with one another. These architects of change are starting to work together and learn from each other at local, national, and international levels in an effort to inspire others to become involved in the creation of a better world. Many now understand that "we the people" are the people of the world, not just of one nation. It is time for each of us to go deep within our hearts and ask ourselves, "What are the unique gifts and visions I have for the world? How can I share these gifts and visions as a trustee in service to humanity and the world?"

Lessons We Learned

DreamMakers express vision and values. "The vision for the foundation is to ignite the spirit of all people to conceive and make real their aspirations for a better world. The three guiding values of the foundation are positivity, . . . compassion . . . and humility."

DreamMakers engage others in their vision. "As I become clear in my destination, in my aims for how I want to be in the world and what I want to accomplish, I can bring that vision to the groups of people I'm working with."

DreamMakers work with others to build a shared vision. "The research project was framed in such a way that three activities were going on at the same time—one for leaders of countries, leaders of major organizations; a second for grassroots people; and a third for what I would call middle-level managers or professionals. Each person or group was asked to think about their vision of a better world."

DreamMakers focus on education and continual learning. "Of utmost importance to people of the world . . . [is] learning and staying open so that we can together, collectively, learn how to do that which we have dreamt of for the well-being of all people."

DreamMakers demonstrate responsibility toward a larger community. "I started traveling annually to India, to meet with people from the other countries who were working on the project, and began to learn more and more about applying the concept of shared visioning to organizations and community development."

DreamMakers are committed to making the world a better place. "The people who were attending the dialogue at the United Nations said that, based on their experience, they felt it extremely important that this work continue, and the way to continue was to do it themselves. It was therefore decided that each country represented at that dialogue would take up in its own countrywide initiative to continue the work. I committed to making something happen here in the United States."

MICHELE HUNT *is a leadership change catalyst and founder of Vision & Values, a leadership consulting firm based in Washington, D.C. Appointed by President Clinton to serve as director of the Federal Quality Institute, she was formerly on the top management team at Herman Miller, Inc., as corporate vice president for people and quality. She is a member of the Society of Fellows at the Aspen Institute and serves on the board of directors of the ServiceMaster Company, the Foundation for Enterprise Development, and the Society for Organizational Learning chaired by Peter Senge.*

A PERSONAL
REFLECTION

14

Michele Hunt,

Vision & Values

I have been a student of DreamMakers all my life. I was blessed with having the two most remarkable people in the world for parents. I must have circled around this planet, negotiating with God, saying, "I don't want to come through until those two wonderful people come together." They taught me to love and believe in myself, which gave me the seeds to my personal vision. They taught me to live with my head and my heart, to care about everyone and everything. They helped me believe that anything is possible if we dream deeply enough and commit ourselves to those dreams. They set me on my journey to participate in a vision to create a better world. Through their example, I came to understand what is possible.

Defining Moments

An Exciting and Challenging Childhood

My parents worked for the U.S. Air Force to help desegregate military bases in the 1950s and mid-1960s in Arizona, Alaska, and Kentucky. Then, from 1964 through 1967, stationed in the Panama Canal Zone, they worked to build the morale and spirit of young soldiers en route to Vietnam. I have always felt a great sense of pride in what these two beautiful, gifted, and courageous African Americans were able to do. They believed in the impossible, and they seemed to have no fear. They used love, hope, and optimism combined as their compass. They were repeatedly told that their dreams and ideas were unrealistic, and yet they moved ahead, creating those very dreams seemingly with ease and grace.

I never saw my parents submit to fear or defeat, even in the face of public humiliation. During the days the Air Force was still segregated, my father, in an attempt to enlighten people, gave a speech on brotherhood in the White section of the mess hall—or should I say, on top of the Whites' table. He was not arrogant; he made no threats. He simply needed to speak his truth. Needless to say, people weren't ready to hear it. He was jailed for five days.

I remember the first time Dad told my two brothers and me about this event. We were very young—about six, seven, and eight—but old enough to understand we were being told something very, very important, something we needed to learn from. As he told the story, he cried (and still does every time he recounts it), but his unrelenting message to us was and still is today "But don't you *ever* hate. Love is the answer, and you pity those who don't understand the truth." Yes, there were and are always tears—but never defeat.

There were tears especially when injustice touched home and their children. I was born in 1949 and so was traveling with my parents and brothers as they moved from one military base to another. My early years of school and development were in places that were not very hospitable to African Americans. The elementary school environment in the South during the 1950s provided a particularly tough testing ground for the child I was. It was common for us to be the only Black kids in our grades. Very early my parents' teachings and model behavior helped me navigate through tough times.

I experienced things then that I would do anything to shield my own child from. Of course, I was often called "nigger." I can recall living in Kentucky, my brothers and I playing outside like all of the other children. But the kids would lock their arms and sing, "Tick-tock, the game is locked, no niggers can play." I recall feeling very confused by this. Of course, my family also experienced all of the other intended and unintended humiliations Black Americans in the South had to endure: separate drinking fountains, and the inability to use public restrooms or sit at a café counter to eat.

But there was a very significant and special day in my life, when I was in the fifth grade, that really became an important "defining moment" for me. The entire class was planning the fifth-grade play in the gymnasium, which felt to me at the time equal in size to Yankee Stadium. I had chosen a seat way up high in the bleachers so that I could see. I was so excited about the whole thing.

I don't remember the name of the play, but I do remember my assigned role. The teacher, standing down on the gymnasium floor, found me in the group—the only African American in the fifth grade—and gave me my part.

"Michele, this is your role." Then she began to imitate a person picking cotton while she sang, "Cotton needs a pickin' so bad, cotton needs a pickin' so bad, oh Lordie, help me pick some cotton." And then she pointed to me and said, "Now, come on down here and try your role."

I got up and began to go down those bleachers. It seemed like my feet were immersed in concrete, and it seemed like a very long way down. But by the time I got down to the gym floor where the teacher was standing, excitedly and naively asking me to play this role, with probably no bad intentions but great ignorance about how it might affect a young child, something new had happened to me. The concrete on my feet had melted away, and I felt light as a feather. In the process of going down those steps, I took on the personal responsibility to *not* play that role. I walked down, smiled at the teacher, and walked out of that gym. I continued to walk out of the school and on to home.

I did not panic. I don't remember crying. I only remember sitting on the steps of my house, looking at the dandelions filling the big field in front of our assigned military housing. It was a beautiful sight, and the day was one of the best days of my life.

I sat there until my parents came home from work. I didn't run to them in fear, hurt, or anxiety. I actually went to them in pride, because I had taken responsibility for making a decision that was nurturing, just, and healthy for me. And it had been their gift of the power of vision and values that had guided me.

You see, my father, every morning when we got up, would take me into the bathroom, have me look at myself in the mirror, and have me say seven times, "I'm healthy, I'm happy, I'm beautiful, I'm intelligent, and I'm wise." I would look at him and to say to myself, Of course!, and you are crazy. It wasn't until years later that I understood what he was doing. My father understood the power of imaging and vision early in his life and mine. It had been my self-image that would not allow me to play that assigned role.

And my mother holds deeply the value of personal responsibility. When I would come home and complain about injustices, she would listen patiently and lovingly and say, "Uh-huh. Yes, darling, uh-huh," and her response was always, "Okay, what are you going to do about it?" And she would always advise me that "people treat things like you do, sweetheart," and ask me "How are you treating this?"

My parents' view of life and their way of life have touched all three of their children. Much of what I, the youngest, have learned has come from my brothers, both DreamMakers in their own right.

The elder of my two brothers, Teddy, contributed twenty-five years to directing a community college program for students with special needs and challenges. His choice of this work did not surprise me. Growing up, Teddy, who was very popular because of his effervescent personality and remarkable sense of humor, always befriended and defended people who were excluded or less fortunate. He would always dance with the girls the other guys ignored at a party, always come to the defense of the boys who were small and frail and who were often picked on by the bigger boys. Not only did he look out for those who were excluded, but he genuinely valued their friendship. Teddy has the gift of being able to see the best in people, and a mission to create safe, fun spaces in which people can be themselves. Children, the best and toughest judges of people's sincerity, love Teddy and his wife, Jan. Although Teddy and Jan do not have "birth" children, they are godparents to eight, and their life is full of joy.

Bruce, the middle child, developed early on a sense of independence based on what he believed was right and just, and he relentlessly followed his heart and blazed his own path. Even when his friends would encourage him to "leave the sissy sister home," he never abandoned me when we were young; I hold a mental image of Bruce taking my hand and kindly taking me along with him despite the boys' ridicule and taunting. Independent of public opinion and having an insatiable desire to chart his own course, Bruce could not accept working for a traditional organization—or for anyone, for that matter. This led him and his wife, Debbie, to create the Detroit Windsor Dance Academy and Company. Since 1984, over 3,000 young people have discovered dance and the beauty of the arts at their academy. These young people, from a range of socioeconomic levels, have gained self-esteem and self-discipline and benefited from being part of a caring, compassionate community.

These lessons, these values, this great, great love to be given and received, this sense of self-worth, this vision my parents shared with us and others, that love is the answer—these are the things that sustained me and led me down a path to find and share the stories of DreamMakers with the world.

The Prison System and Seeing "Systems" at Work

After graduating from college and beginning as the first of two female probation officers to handle adult male felons on probation, I thought the way to make a difference was to influence people's lives, person by person. And I still believe that this is one of the most powerful ways to make a difference. However, in my impatience, I quickly realized that even if you offer hope, skills, and new perspectives to people, if they are locked in negative and oppressive systems, it's difficult for them to change, grow, and contribute. So my pursuit of management positions or other positions of authority was catalyzed or, rather, motivated by my desire to be in a position to change systems and structures that put people in boxes, limit people's potential, demean people, and are unnatural for living beings.

I learned my lessons about trying to change systems from the outside early. While I was still a probation officer in Detroit Recorders Court, in the early 1970s, I was appalled by the abusive power that the Detroit Police Department Stress Unit was wielding over Detroit citizens. In particular, on one occasion I received a call from a man I had on probation, who had been arrested at about 2:00 A.M. Generally, I made it a point to go to the precinct and interview the guys on probation when they were arrested, to make sure I got the information while it was fresh in everyone's minds. But I was tired, and the young man was locked up in the First Precinct, which was directly across the street from my office, so I made the decision to visit him later that morning.

When I got there, I was told he was in the Detroit Receiving Hospital. I was quite certain that he had been physically secure and unharmed when I talked to him at 2:00 A.M. I was outraged and, in my own way, decided to do something about it. While on my lunch hour, a colleague and I developed and circulated a petition against the abusive power in the law enforcement ranks. As you can imagine, a twenty-one-year-old Black female who was a pioneer in the courts doing something like this drew a great deal of attention. Within twenty-four hours, I was paged to come to the chambers of the judges and was promptly fired.

They fired me based on something called the Hatch Act, which prevented state employees from engaging in political affairs. But I was smart enough to know that my actions were nonpolitical and, rather, community-oriented, and therefore decided to fight. There was very little fighting that I had to do once the judges realized that they did not have the legal basis to fire me. Within two days, I was back to work. I knew then that if I had been in the spotlight before, as a pioneering female supervising men on probation, I would truly be in the spotlight now, given my recent actions.

But my father and mother always taught me to take a lemon and make it into lemonade. I realized that the system was going to be focusing on any errors and warts, but at that level of focus they could also see my skills and accomplishments. Three years later, I was promoted to supervise female offenders at a halfway house and received an outstanding commendation signed by all thirteen judges.

In my ongoing quest to change systems that are oppressive and inhumane, I went on to spend nine years in the Michigan Department of Corrections, my last two and a half years working as the first female treatment director and deputy warden in a male prison. As treatment director I supervised programs for rehabilitation, such as the prison's school system, psychological services, recreation, religious services, and medical services.

We put in place a responsibility model for the inmates, which basically said that the more responsible behavior an inmate demonstrated, the more opportunity that individual would have to participate in the design of the programs and systems that affected him. The result was wonderful. In partnership and collaboration, the inmates, community volunteers, treatment staff, and custody teams created viable and exciting programs, including a tutorial program that had every single inmate paired with a community volunteer tutor. We also had a live, creative prison theater, an arts program, and a recreation program that included golf clinics, cross-country skiing clinics, and classes on sculpting—all funded and staffed by community volunteers. Now here we had people who for the most part had not been raised in an environment that was supportive, optimistic, and healthy, that was lacking in adequate education and often missing strong family guidance. And yet these people were able to use their gifts to create extraordinary programs.

The World of Business

After nine years in the Michigan Department of Corrections, I made the decision to give the private sector a try. This was a very difficult decision because, having gone to college during the late 1960s and early 1970s, I believed that the private sector corporations only made money over the backs of people. So I was very careful and deliberate in my research as to what organization I wanted to join, and I found this extraordinary place called Herman Miller, Inc., right in my backyard—one of those predictable miracles that Carl Jung and Joseph Jaworski talk about.

Herman Miller is an office furniture company headquartered in Zeeland, Michigan, with an international reputation for quality and design.

The De Pree family, which led the company for its first seventy years, had the insight and foresight to value diversity, to seek new and different ideas, and to lead with values and vision. On about my eighth interview, I was taken on a plant tour. You could have eaten off the floor of this particular factory. There were fresh flowers in every break area, and the employees had large, friendly smiles on their faces, and you felt the energy in their work. I was convinced that this was a model plant, specially maintained to impress customers, potential employees, and other visitors. At one point, however, I ducked into an auditorium where a meeting had just ended and observed a member of the housekeeping staff at work. She was not only putting the chairs back into place in theater style, she was meticulously and carefully ensuring that the legs of the chairs were perfectly aligned! I watched her attention to detail and her incredible display of ownership, and I wondered what kind of environment engendered this kind of behavior. By the way, over time I found many Herman Miller work sites of equal quality.

Herman Miller was constantly in pursuit of achieving its vision within the boundaries of its shared values. This wasn't always easy because, as diversity expanded, values sometimes clashed. We had to pursue the core values that transcended different lifestyles, ethnic groups, and religions. Since most of the decisions were guided by vision and values, we also had to allow time and space for dialogue, debate, and reflection prior to making those decisions.

Values and Diversity

I experienced the power of this kind of environment in a very personal way. When I was thirty-two years old and had already been at Herman Miller a couple of years, I discovered I had five fibroid tumors in my uterus. I was advised by my doctor to have a hysterectomy. On my visit to the doctor for my final consultation before surgery, my doctor informed me that I was pregnant and would surely die if I went through with the pregnancy. Without even asking me what I wanted to do, he was on the phone scheduling me for an abortion. Before he hung up, I got up and left. On my drive home, I went inside myself—much as I had many years ago in that gymnasium during the fifth grade—and experienced an amazing calmness. I listened to my heart and was assured that everything would work out. I pictured bringing my baby home and what life would be like.

During this very difficult pregnancy, I heard about a new job reporting directly to Max De Pree, who was by then the CEO and chairman of the board for Herman Miller. The position was heading up Corporate Relations, responsible for shareholder relations, government relations, and community and media relations nationwide. It was the opportunity I had been waiting for, and I applied. On the day I was to come in to interview, though, I went to the doctor for a standard checkup and was told that I had further complications and must be checked into the hospital immediately. When I got to my room in the hospital, I called Max De Pree and told him of my situation and offered to withdraw from the competition. Max asked me two questions. He said, "First, are you in labor?" I said, "No." Then he asked, "Are you in pain?" I said, "No." Then he said, "Let's interview." So I interviewed over the phone and won the job while on maternity leave, still facing two months of pregnancy and three months of maternity leave.

Now, Max comes from a community that strongly believes in traditional family values, yet he respected my decision to pursue a job while on maternity leave, knowing I would have a young infant and a job that would require travel. I know that it was difficult for Max to hold these tensions, just as it was for me. However, by doing so, he was able to create a win-win situation. I won, and Herman Miller won too. Dr. Derrick Lenters of Holland, Michigan, had the courage to partner with me when all other doctors I had contacted refused. Against all odds, this partnership, fueled by vision and commitment, enabled Nicole to find her way into this world. Nicole has brought me great joy and love and has been my greatest teacher. Given how I see my daughter today, it turned out that she won as well.

Of course, this is a two-way street. Max De Pree had accepted my decision and commitment to both job and baby; I now had to accept full responsibility for that decision. Within several weeks of starting my new job, Max asked me to go to Washington to help defeat a federal bill—Retail Dealer Agreement Act. This bill granted a hundred-mile exclusivity right to Herman Miller–independent dealers, which would have prevented us from having more than one dealer in major cities and would have crippled our distribution capability.

With great opportunities come great challenges. I went into Max's office and asked, "Are you serious? You want me to actually go to Washington and kill this bill?" Max said, "I hired you because I have high expectations of you and have confidence in your abilities. I'll give you the resources and the time. However, right now you're wasting time in this conversation. You need to focus on killing that bill."

Two years later, through galvanizing the support of multiple constituencies, including the union, we were able to defeat this bill. My success was due in large measure, I believe, to Max's high expectations and ultimate belief in my capabilities.

A Learning Organization

By the time I joined the leadership team at Herman Miller as a vice president, my colleagues and I were on a quest to learn how to be the reference point for excellence—how to become a true learning organization, and how to uphold our core values in all situations.

One of the most memorable experiences for me was time spent with corporate officers and directors at the Aspen Institute in Maryland. During these sessions we would read diverse extracts from Plato, Carol Gilligan, Paula Underwood, Parker Palmer, John Gardner, and others. We used these readings as a framework to engage in dialogue around diversity, quality, and change. One of our readings was the letter written by Martin Luther King Jr. from jail to the Birmingham clergy. I can recall a compelling moment at the end of one of the sessions. One of the officers shared with the group his feeling that the King letter had been written for him. He said that he clearly saw that now he had a responsibility to go home to his family and friends and share the letter and undo the biased education and misinformation he had given his children about people of color.

Although many of us are no longer at Herman Miller, we remain touched by the ideas of a powerful vision, deep values that honor diversity and individual identity, and personal empowerment through participation, and we are carrying what we learned there into our new work situations and environments.

Reinventing Government

I left Herman Miller in 1993 when I was invited by President Bill Clinton to serve my country in the Reinventing Government initiative led by Vice President Al Gore. It was truly very difficult to leave Herman Miller, but it was time to move on and tackle more of those systems I knew needed changing.

I entered a world I had no idea existed. When I graduated from college in 1974 the federal government was the most desirable place to work. People were proud to go there to serve their country. In 1993 I walked into a world that had grown rigid and outdated, lacking any sense of spirit. I was director of the Federal Quality Institute, working with the cabinet agency leadership teams in seeding the transformation process by bringing to them the state of the art in private sector management, leadership, and organizational practices, ideas, and tools.

I recall in one of my early days meeting with a team of people who had called me in to give them an overview of how corporate America was going through its renewal and transformation. It was apparent to me that they truly did not want me there. Someone had told them to invite me to a meeting. Now, I'm the kind of person who doesn't necessarily like to be where I'm not wanted, so I had every intention of simply giving them a quick overview of the reinvention strategies and getting out of there. But I looked at this team of people, and they were all pretty much my age—Baby Boomers who had graduated from college in the late 1960s and early 1970s. I asked them, "What brought you to the federal government?" Their pilot lights lit up and roared. They gave me story after story of what was going on in our country at the time they joined, and how they came here to make a difference, to participate in rebuilding our cities after the riots of the 1960s. When their energy subsided, I asked another question: "How do you want to spend the second half of your life?" Then they began to discuss how they might bring the spirit and vitality, mission, and vision and values back into their work.

Somehow along the way, most of the spirit that these people had originally brought to their work had been suffocated. In the federal government, rules, regulations, procedures, and what I'll call "ethical regulations"—that is, legal considerations—have replaced vision, values, spirit, and mission. Ethics and the ethical oversight processes have become ways to ensure that the status quo remains, which results in many creative, intelligent people being unable to contribute their gifts. I came to believe that my fifteen-year-old daughter has more freedom and is treated with more dignity than federal workers.

I'm sure that no one intentionally designed this system to dampen the spirit, creativity, and imagination of millions of people—people who came to government with the intention of serving their country, believing in deep, bold visions for our country, and guided by a value of service. But I saw many defeated, frustrated people who had lost their vision and ability to dream. Many even became terrible cynics.

Still, despite the obstacles, there are success stories, and people do remarkable things; Michael Lane of the U.S. Customs Service is just one example. I have always been able to find examples of individuals—DreamMakers—who are able to rise above the playing field, to hold on to their visions and values, and make a difference.

Going Independent

In June of 1995, I launched my own business, called Vision & Values. I was concerned about getting caught by the very system I was trying to change and losing some of my own spirit. I took the great leap—"the great fall into the abyss," as Meg Wheatley describes it in *Leadership and the New Science.* Anyone who has decided to establish his or her own business from scratch knows exactly what I am talking about. But it was time for me to pursue my dreams. I decided that at forty-six it was time to take what I had learned from the people, challenges, and opportunities in my life and put them to work for my personal vision and contribute in a more meaningful way, unconstrained by the structures of organizations.

Vision & Values

The mission of Vision & Values is to partner with leadership teams in their journey to create organizations that accomplish extraordinary results by unleashing the collective gifts and energy of their people and stakeholders. I serve as a partner and a catalyst in the transformation and renewal of people and organizations as they move to new levels of performance and participation. My fundamental beliefs are that the answers lie within an organization, and that we need to find ways to tap in to the genius of people.

My work has focused on the power of shared mission, vision, and values and creating environments that enable people to contribute their diverse gifts and ideas toward accomplishing the organization's goals. At its very core, my work seeks to liberate people from restrictive, obsolete structures, processes, systems, roles, and thinking, and in so doing empower them to participate in the redesign of their organizations in harmony and alignment with their vision and values.

Obstacles

Because of the way I was raised and what I have discovered about the power of vision and values, I don't often think in terms of obstacles. But I must admit that there are moments—many, many moments—when I feel weary, defeated, and abandoned, when I lose confidence. Like Rita Cleary, I believe the only real obstacles are those that come from within myself, and I need to be constantly, vigilantly aware of them. When I allow fear, anger, jealousy, and bitterness into my heart and mind, I am sapped of energy, and the daily problems of life—the minutiae—sweep me away, pull my attention away from what I and we know we have the capacity to become. It is in those moments that I draw the most strength from the DreamMakers I have known, including my parents, and the newest DreamMaker in this family, my daughter, Nicole. Like Joyce and Juliet in Aruba, and Janet and Gary Smith, like members of high-performance teams, organizations, and communities, we pick each other up when one or the other is down.

Most of the time, fortunately, my eyes are on the future, and it is one of great hope and promise for all peoples of the world.

Vision for a Better World

I believe, like many people in this book, that now is the most exciting time in the history of humankind to be alive. Because so many barriers are breaking down, we have the opportunity and responsibility to recreate our world in a way that leverages what we have learned from history's mistakes, tragedies, and successes.

I love the butterfly story. It serves as a great metaphor for me during these times. Just before a caterpillar goes through its transformation into a butterfly, it is in a cocoon that is dark and deteriorating. Things must look very bad to the caterpillar—messy, ugly, even life-threatening. Soon, however, a butterfly emerges, but only when the caterpillar has learned to release itself from what it was so that it can become what it needs to be next.

For humankind to let go, however, we must call on all that makes us human—dream of a new world together and have the courage to let go of the old world. We have the advantage of being able to *choose* our next stage of being in this world—and we must choose well, and wisely, and with great respect for the dignity of all of life. People around the world are using the power of vision and values to create better lives, organizations, and communities. My hope is that everyone will find the DreamMaker within herself or himself and put it to work in this most remarkable, unprecedented time of change. Together, we can create the world we want for ourselves and our children and the children to come. It is not only our right but our responsibility.

FURTHER READING

Bennis, Warren. *Why Leaders Can't Lead: The Unconscious Conspiracy Continues.* San Francisco: Jossey-Bass, 1990.

De Pree, Max. *Leading Without Power: Finding Hope in Serving Community.* San Francisco: Jossey-Bass, 1997.

Dow, Roger J., and Cook, Susan P. *Turned On: Eight Vital Insights to Energize Your People, Customers, and Profits.* New York: HarperBusiness, 1996.

Drucker, Peter F. *Post-Capitalist Society.* New York: HarperBusiness, 1994.

Handy, Charles. *The Age of Paradox.* New York: McGraw-Hill, 1995.

Hesselbein, Frances, Goldsmith, Marshall, and Beckhard, Richard, editors. *The Leader of the Future: New Visions, Strategies, and Practices for the Next Era.* San Francisco: Jossey-Bass, 1996.

Jaworski, Joseph. *Synchronicity: The Inner Path of Leadership.* San Francisco: Berrett-Koehler, 1996.

Kidder, Rushworth M. *Shared Values for a Troubled World: Conversations with Men and Women of Conscience.* San Francisco: Jossey-Bass, 1994.

Land, George, and Jarman, Beth. *Breakpoint and Beyond: Mastering the Future Today.* New York: HarperBusiness, 1992.

Parker, Marjorie. *Creating Shared Vision.* (To order: Marjorie Parker, Norwegian Center for Leadership Development, P.O. Box 77, Holmenkollen 0324, Oslo, Norway. Tel: 47 22 49 69 05. Fax: 47 22 49 69 34. E-mail: Marjorie@online.no.)

Pollard, C. William. *The Soul of the Firm.* New York: HarperCollins, 1996.

Rosen, Robert H., and Brown, Paul B. *Leading People: Transforming Business from the Inside Out.* New York: Viking, 1996.

Senge, Peter M. *The Fifth Discipline: The Art and Practice of the Learning Organization.* New York: Currency/Doubleday, 1990.

Wheatley, Margaret J. *Leadership and the New Science: Learning About Organization from an Orderly Universe.* San Francisco: Berrett-Koehler, 1992

Wheatley, Margaret J., and Kellner-Rogers, Myron. *A Simpler Way.* San Francisco: Berrett-Koehler, 1996.